WHERE DO WE GO FROM HERE?

HOW TOMORROW'S PROPHECIES
FORESHADOW TODAY'S PROBLEMS

DR. DAVID JEREMIAH

W PUBLISHING GROUP

AN IMPRINT OF THOMAS NELSON

Published in Nashville, Tennessee, by W Publishing, an imprint of Thomas Nelson.

Published in association with Yates & Yates, www.yates2.com.

Thomas Nelson titles may be purchased in bulk for educational, business, fund-raising, or sales promotional use. For information, please email SpecialMarkets@ThomasNelson.com.

ISBN 978-0-7852-2421-1 (eBook)
ISBN 978-0-7852-6457-6 (IE)

Library of Congress Control Number: 2021942695

ISBN 978-0-7852-2419-8

Printed in the United States of America
21 22 23 24 25 LSC 10 9 8 7 6 5 4 3

Contents

Introduction

While writing this introduction, I'm watching the grim recovery efforts in Surfside, Florida, where the Champlain Towers South condominium collapsed in the dead of night, one floor pancaking onto the next, burying scores of people under tons of concrete. Most were sleeping in their beds, unaware of the suddenness of the coming catastrophe.

There had been signs, including warnings of water seeping beneath critical parts of the structure and weakening its integrity. But the alarm sounded too late.

Three thousand miles away, residents of San Francisco's lavish Millennium Tower absorbed the news with apprehension. Their fifty-eight-story skyscraper with its dazzling views and luxury amenities has sunk eighteen inches into the soft downtown soil on which it was built. It's tilting, and some view Surfside as a warning to the new Millennium.

I'm concerned about the new millennium too—our trembling twenty-first century. I'm burdened for the underpinnings of our culture, our eroding foundations and structural cracks. Like you, I've studied the signs of the times and believe we're approaching a global cataclysm—one predicted in our Scriptures and unfolding before our eyes.

All this came to me in a sort of rush months ago as my wife, Donna, and I were having breakfast. We made the mistake of watching the morning news. Every story was more distressing than the one before. We sat there viewing the burning cities, backbiting politicians, runaway infections, heated elections, social upheaval, racial tensions, skyrocketing crime, shouting pundits, deafening lies, eroding sands, and cracking foundations.

I looked over at Donna and said, "You and I are watching the dismantling of America."

This book was born in that moment.

I began to look at these crises and controversies in a new way. I realized they are not isolated movements, philosophies, or events. They are as interconnected as a spider's web. COVID-19 seemed like an arbitrary crisis as it unfolded, but it didn't occur in a vacuum, and the world's response revealed our souls. Add to that emerging globalism. We're only one existential crisis from a one-world government.

And what about our worldwide economy, hanging by a strand?

Think of the degradation of our culture. It seems as if every member is a lover of self, a lover of money, a lover of pleasure—and eager to cancel anyone who disagrees with them. This translates to extreme persecution for the church in much of the world and to eroding religious liberty at home. Across our country, an unprecedented spiritual famine is causing an epidemic of emaciated hearts. In the process, many professed Christians are abandoning the faith. This has created a vacuum for the rising tide of socialism to flood into our land.

Simultaneously, events in the Middle East are turning Jerusalem into the powder keg of history. Again! Throw a pandemic in the midst, and there you have it—a world in chaos.

I've told you all that to say this: I refuse to be discouraged, and so should you!

This is no time to retreat. It's time to live by conviction. When Moses sent the twelve spies into the promised land to reconnoiter the territory, ten of the spies were overwhelmed with fear and despair. They were daunted by the giants they saw. But two of the spies, Joshua and Caleb, said, in effect, "Let us go forward! We can take the land!"

Years later in recalling the event, Caleb told Joshua, "I was forty years old when Moses the servant of the LORD sent me from Kadesh Barnea to explore the land. And I brought him back a report *according to my convictions*" (Josh. 14:7 NIV, emphasis added).

Well, in this book I've explored the territory of our times, and I am bringing back a report according to my convictions. This is not bravado. I'm speaking as honestly and as humbly as I can when I tell you we cannot be still, we cannot be silent, and we cannot live by lies. We must live by our biblical convictions. We can no longer ignore the warnings or sleep in beds of ignorance. I believe we're approaching the consummation of the ages.

For as long as I've had a Bible, I've studied scriptural prophecy. I've preached and written about the last days from the beginning of my ministry. Perhaps you've read some of my previous books regarding the Bible's message on the end of the world and the return of Christ. I love writing about biblical prophecy because it's God's transfusion of hope to our hearts.

But I've never written a prophecy book like this one. In the pages that follow, I'm going to deal with ten prophetic issues as current as the morning news. In each chapter, I'll tell you where we are, what it means, and where we go from here. We'll thread our way through problems that Jesus predicted—precursors of the tribulation—and we'll learn how to do the next right thing.

The Lord told us about this epoch in advance, and it's a privilege to be His agents on the crest of history. We are not helpless, and our world is not hopeless. Even as the world collapses, the Lord is building His church. We can say something, do something, pray something, preach something, and live by the convictions of Christ.

Aleksandr Solzhenitsyn wrote in *The Gulag Archipelago,* "In keeping silent about evil, in burying it so deep within us that no sign of it appears on the surface, we are implanting it, and it will rise up a thousandfold in the future."[1]

God's people are more than conquerors. We have a way forward. I urge you to study the marching orders at the end of every chapter in this book. Put into practice the things I'm going to recommend. Set your mind fully on the hope you have in Christ, and be ready to pay any price, challenge any foe, and confront any lie for the sake of the gospel.

At any moment, Jesus Christ will descend from heaven for His people. We haven't long to wait. But until then, we need to understand what the age requires—and we need to do what the Lord commands.

In one of the strangest stories in the Bible, the Lord grabbed the ancient prophet Ezekiel by the hair of his head, transported him in a vision from Babylon to Jerusalem, and dropped him into a scene of unimaginable evil (Ezek. 8:3). Ezekiel saw the depravity and decay of his own country, a country which he deeply loved. His nation was disintegrating. But God gave him a work to do. He commissioned him to be a watchman on the walls.

God may not grab your hair, but I pray He will grab your heart. I pray He will show you afresh the triumph of the gospel and call you as His watchman to sound the alarm and to proclaim the truth.

Remember what God later told Ezekiel, "I searched for a man among them who would repair the wall and stand in the gap before me on behalf of the land so that I might not destroy it, but I found no one" (22:30 CSB).

I want Him to find at least two!

One you, and one me.

Come, join me in dedicating the rest of your earthly life to living by biblical convictions, exalting in the triumph of the gospel, and doing all you can to repair the structures of society and to stand in the gap before the Lord on behalf of the land. Don't be fearful, and don't let the times overwhelm you. This world will not end in rubble, but in His return! Our risen and exalted Lord Jesus Christ, our enthroned Savior—He knows the way forward.

He will show us where to go from here.

A deadly virus is quietly spreading throughout our nation. It is far more lethal than COVID-19, and most Americans are totally unaware of the threat that it poses to our freedom and way of life. This disease is called socialism and, until recently, it had been considered public enemy number one by Americans. That is no longer the case. A 2020 poll showed that 40 percent of Americans had a favorable view of socialism, and that number goes to 61 percent when the polling is for those between the ages of eighteen and twenty-four.

From the erosion of free speech and free exercise of religion to the looming threat of a one-world government that allows for no opposition, socialism is a pernicious force that the followers of Christ must be ready to face head on. Our freedom, and perhaps our very lives, depend on it.

Chapter 1

A Cultural Prophecy— Socialism

"But as the days of Noah were, so also will the coming of the Son of Man be."

MATTHEW 24:37

Under the cover of darkness, a middle-aged man inched out the window of his seventh-story apartment, then silently repelled seventy-five feet to the ground. A pair of bolt cutters snipped off his ankle monitor, and the man jumped into a waiting car. This was no movie. After fifteen years of imprisonment on bogus charges, Iván Simonovis was escaping Venezuela.

Simonovis had once been a Venezuelan hero. As a key member of an important SWAT team, he ended a seven-hour hostage situation, all of it captured on national television. That propelled him to celebrity status. After being appointed safety officer for Caracas, he dedicated himself to fighting crime and removing the corruption that had defined the capital's police force for years.

Things changed when Simonovis ran afoul of Hugo Chávez, Venezuela's Marxist president and emerging dictator. Chávez viewed thedecorated safety officer as a potential rival and accused him of crimes against humanity. The charges were false, and the trial was a sham. In the blink of an eye, Iván was behind bars with no hope for reprieve. For stretches of time, he was allowed to see sunlight for only ten minutes a day.

In 2014, Iván was moved to house arrest to seek treatment for nineteen chronic health conditions, many of them caused by his imprisonment. Knowing this was his only chance, he arranged his daring escape. After speeding off in a car, he spent three weeks evading security in a cat-and-mouse pursuit. A fourteen-hour ride in a small fishing boat got him to a Caribbean island, from which he flew to the United States.[1]

Iván could recall when Venezuela was the wealthiest nation in South America. The per capita income of its citizens was greater than those of China and Japan, almost rivaling the income of US citizens. The people of Iván's generation enjoyed religious liberty, political freedom, personal dignity, and economic opportunity.[2]

But when oil prices crashed in the 1980s, and then again in the 1990s, the Venezuelan economy experienced a dip. That dip became a dive in 1998 when the Venezuelan people elected Chávez as their president. Once in power Chávez relentlessly implemented the socialist playbook formulated by the Soviet Union, Cuba, China, and other nations. His first task was to rewrite the Venezuelan constitution, guaranteeing citizens the so-called free rights of government-provided health care, college education, and social justice. When the Supreme Court ruled against Chávez on several important issues, he responded by stacking the court with twelve new justices, all loyal to him.

Socialism totally engulfed the country when Chávez was reelected in 2006. Fully in control of the courts and the legislature, he moved quickly to nationalize the media, removing voices of dissent. Then he authorized government agencies to seize privately owned wealth and property from Venezuela's citizens—all in the name of "fairness" and "equality." Chávez took control of the nation's oil industry, expelling foreign investors and influence. He nationalized power companies, farms, mines, banks, and grocery stores. His final step was to eliminate term limits for elected officials, setting himself up to rule for the rest of his life in the style of Russia's Stalin and Cuba's Castro.[3]

Not even Chávez could evade the last enemy. He died from cancer in 2013. But his hand-picked successor, Nicolás Maduro, continued to implement Chávez's agenda—even going further in some areas to force a Marxist agenda on the Venezuelan people. Today Venezuela is descending into anarchy, and record numbers of Venezuelan migrants are fleeing northward, trying to reach the border into the United States.

Socialism, Prophecy, and You

Right now, you might be wondering what all of this has to do with you. If Venezuela has proven that socialism is a bad idea, why should anyone care?

You should care because socialist visions and policies are invading the United States. You'll hear them discussed under four different names: socialism, communism, Marxism, and cultural Marxism. From my studies, it seems many people consider these terms nearly synonymous. As you read the rest of this chapter, these four titles will show up, but they all refer to the same invasive ideology, one that seems to deceive people with unusual ease.

Consider this: Hugo Chávez had plenty of cheerleaders in the United States during his rise, including Hollywood stars like Sean Penn, Michael Moore, Oliver Stone, and Danny Glover. Socialism seems to hold an almost hypnotic power over many thinkers, and it's spilling into the common culture. A 2020 poll showed that 40 percent of Americans had a favorable view of socialism. That was up from 36 percent in 2019. Even more frightening, 47 percent of Millennials and 49 percent of Generation Z viewed socialism favorably.[4] Indeed, one 2019 poll in AXIOS found that 61 percent of Americans between the ages of 18 and 24 have a positive reaction to socialism.[5]

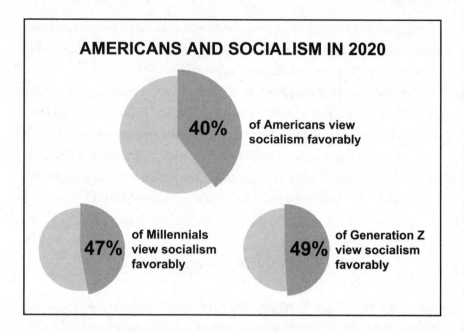

AMERICANS AND SOCIALISM IN 2020

40% of Americans view socialism favorably

47% of Millennials view socialism favorably

49% of Generation Z view socialism favorably

And then there is this: In 2020, Bernie Sanders nearly won the Democratic Party's nomination for president of the United States. This is the same senator from Vermont who declared, "I am a socialist and everyone knows it."[6]

In addition to Sanders, recent elections have seen record numbers of socialist candidates win roles as representatives both in state legislatures and in Congress. Notable among them is Alexandria Ocasio-Cortez. In 2018, she became the youngest congresswoman in history.

Ocasio-Cortez is an avowed member of the Democratic Socialists of America, the largest socialist organization in the United States. Given her young age and massive following, many believe she'll run for president of the United States one day. That's a sobering thought given her stated goals of ending capitalism and implementing the same socialist agenda that failed so spectacularly in Venezuela.

I've come to the conviction that this ideology represents a real and present danger to the freedom and prosperity that has defined America and other Western nations for centuries. As I've researched this book, one verse keeps coming to mind: 2 Timothy 3:1. Here it is in the Amplified

Bible: "But understand this, that in the last days dangerous times [of great stress and trouble] will come [difficult days that will be hard to bear]."

Jesus said it like this, "But as the days of Noah were, so also will the coming of the Son of Man be. For as in the days before the flood, they were eating and drinking, marrying and giving in marriage, until the day that Noah entered the ark, and did not know until the flood came and took them all away, so also will the coming of the Son of Man be" (Matt. 24:37–39).

What were those "days of Noah" like? Genesis 6:5 describes them this way: "Then the LORD saw that the wickedness of man was great in the earth, and that every intent of the thoughts of his heart was only evil continually."

The people of Noah's day ignored and ridiculed his warnings. Noah built and preached for 120 years, and not one single individual outside his immediate family believed him. The people were so indifferent that they didn't understand what was happening until it was too late.

The heedlessness of the people in Noah's day will be duplicated in the last days of our world's history. It will be a day much like ours, a day when ideologies like socialism can sneak in without much attention.

Ask anyone under communism and they'll probably agree: socialism is an invasive weed planted by Karl Marx. Despite its catastrophic failures, it keeps spreading over the earth like kudzu. Will this be the dominant political philosophy on earth when the tribulation begins? Yes, that seems likely. Socialism is tailor-made for the Antichrist's appearance. It creates global conditions that bring great stress and trouble, difficult days that will be hard to bear. And it demands a one-world system of government, which Scripture says will be established before the end of history.

Revelation 13 describes the Antichrist as a beast having vast power and authority. "The whole world marveled . . . and gave allegiance to the beast . . . And he was given authority to rule over every tribe and people and language and nation. And all the people who belong to this world worshiped the beast" (Rev. 13:3, 7–8 NLT).

This beast, or Antichrist, will be empowered by Satan, "who deceives the whole world" (12:9), and aided by the false prophet, who "deceives those who dwell on the earth" (13:14). The Lord warned us against this kind of deception: "Beware lest anyone cheat you through philosophy and empty deceit, according to the tradition of men, according to the basic principles of the world, and not according to Christ" (Col. 2:8).

What Is Socialism?

How, then, should we view socialism today? How should we define it? Listen to the definition offered by the World Socialist Party of the United States: "The establishment of a system of society based on the common ownership and democratic control of the means and instruments for producing and distributing wealth by and in the interest of society as a whole. . . . We call this common ownership, but other terms we regard as synonymous are communism and socialism."[7]

Socialists believe the world's means of production—including infrastructure, farms, factories, energy, natural resources, medicines, and more—should be under the control of "the people." In other words, society as a whole should own the raw materials and the systems that produce wealth. In a free market system, these materials are usually controlled by companies or individuals, but in socialist countries they are owned by "the people."

Of course, there's no way to make decisions based on such a loose concept as "the people." So under socialism, the *government* becomes the sole authority and controller of the means of production. Unfortunately, governments are controlled by specific people—often the kinds of people who seek out power. And those people are entirely corruptible by greed, selfishness, lust, vindictiveness, violence, and the overwhelming desire for authority. As more power flows to the government, the handful at the top become dictatorial.

While I was writing this chapter, a news network ran a story about a Chinese woman named Xi Van Fleet. She had survived the brutal communist regime of dictator Mao Zedong. In an impassioned speech to a Virginia school board, she elaborated on the similarities between what happened in China during the Chinese Cultural Revolution and what is happening in the United States right now. She said, "They use the same ideology, and same methodology, even the same vocabulary. And with the same goal. The ideology is cultural Marxism. And we were divided into groups as the oppressor and oppressed. . . . And the take out methodology is also very similar. It's cancel culture. We basically canceled the whole Chinese civilization pre-communism."[8]

In his book *We Will Not Be Silenced*, Erwin Lutzer helped us understand the kind of Marxism we're seeing.

Today we face what is known as *cultural* Marxism. It is not being imposed on people on the war battlefields; instead, it's a form of Marxism that wins the hearts and minds of people incrementally by the gradual transformation of the culture. Bombarded with exaggerated and illusionary promises, people accept it because they want to; they welcome it because they are convinced of its "benefits." It promises "hope and change," income equality, racial harmony and justice based on secular values rather than Judeo-Christian morality. It is known for professing inclusion rather than exclusion and promoting sexual freedom rather than what they view as the restrictive sexual ethics of the Bible. It is not stifled by allegedly narrow religious traditions but espouses progressive ideas that are deemed worthy of an enlightened future.[9]

The Roots of Socialism

To understand socialism, we must first understand Karl Marx. When you understand who he was and what he believed, you'll be able to trace much that's happening back to him.

If you study the life of Karl Marx, you'll learn he wasn't just a hater of God; he was a cheerleader for the devil. His family thought him possessed by a demon. A biographer described him like this: "He had the devil's view of the world, and the devil's malignity. Sometimes, he seemed to know that he was accomplishing works of evil."[10]

On one occasion, Marx's own son sent him a letter and addressed it "My dear devil."[11] Marx's partner, Friedrich Engels, declared that ten thousand devils had Marx by the hair.[12]

In 2020, Paul Kengor wrote a book titled *The Devil and Karl Marx: Communism's Long March of Death, Deception, and Infiltration.* Frankly, it was difficult to read, so dark was its subject. According to Kengor, Marx was a tyrant, a racist, and a misogynistic radical who hated God and wanted to see the world burn.

In his 1837 poem "The Pale Maiden," Marx composed these self-descriptive words:

> Thus Heaven I've forfeited,
> I know it full well.
> My soul, once true to God,
> Is chosen for Hell.[13]

Four years later, in 1841, he wrote these lines, which are even more damning:

> Look now, my blood-dark sword shall stab
> Unerringly within thy soul. . . .
> The hellish vapors rise and fill the brain
> Till I go mad and my heart is utterly changed.
> See the sword—the Prince of Darkness sold it to me.
> For he beats the time and gives the signs.
> Ever more boldly I play the dance of death.[14]

In 1849, one year after publishing his crowning work, *The Communist Manifesto*, Marx was evicted by his landlord who was fed up with his filthiness. "Karl drank too much, smoked too much, never exercised, and suffered from warts and boils due to lack of washing. He stunk . . . As for the family apartment, everything [was] broken down, busted, spilled, smashed, falling apart—from toys and chairs and dishes and cups to tables . . . and on and on."[15]

Karl Marx fathered an illegitimate child by his maid, Helene Demuth. He blamed the child on Engels, who thought it was a great joke. Since Marx never had a job, he mooched off everyone—his parents, Engels, and anyone else that he could find. His wife, Jenny, was so miserable in their marriage she wanted to die, a wish she pondered daily. His daughters, Jenny and Laura, fulfilled their mother's wish. Jenny poisoned herself when she was just forty-three. And in a death pact with her husband, Laura also committed suicide when she was sixty-six.

Marx died in despair on March 14, 1883. Just before his death, he wrote to his friend Engels, "How pointless and empty is life, but how desirable!"[16] He was buried in Highgate Cemetery, considered the center of satanism in London.

I wonder how many who are championing socialism and Marxism are aware of the poisonous roots of this doctrine. Their founder was a hideous person; and what he was, socialism became! This is a spiritual battle of truth versus lies. It brings to mind Ephesians 6:12: "For we do not wrestle against flesh and blood, but against principalities, against powers, against the rulers of the darkness of this age, against spiritual hosts of wickedness in the heavenly places."

As many have noted, Karl Marx is ruling the world from his grave. Here are some of the characteristics of his hellish ideology.

Marxism Is Anti-God

Karl Marx hated Christianity, which he saw as a source of oppression. To him, religion was "the opium of the people." For communism to succeed, loyalty to the church had to be replaced by loyalty to the state. On one occasion, he described the church as "medieval mildew" which must be scraped away.[17]

Other socialist leaders have followed the same path, including Joseph

Stalin, Fidel Castro, Pol Pot, and beyond. Each of these men saw organized religion as an enemy—a competitor that needed to be controlled or eliminated. As one scholar noted, "Religion was the enemy, a rival to Marxist mind control, and it had to be vanquished regardless of costs and difficulties."[18] In the Soviet Union, one of their favorite slogans was, "Let us drive out the capitalists from earth and God from heaven."

Another historian noted: "[In Russia] as early as the spring of 1918, an open campaign of terror was launched against all religions, and particularly against the Russian Orthodox church. [It was a] policy of terror . . . felt by every religious faith."[19] In the following years, countless Orthodox bishops and priests were murdered, and those who survived were denied their civil rights and subjected to economic oppression.

Despite what many claim to believe or propose, Marxism is not compatible with the free expression of religion.

Marxism Is Totalitarian

There's another general fact about Marxism we should grasp. It quickly becomes totalitarian. The term *totalitarianism* was first used by supporters of fascist dictator Benito Mussolini, who summed it up this way: "Everything within the state, nothing outside the state, nothing against the state."[20]

Rod Dreher adds,

> According to Hannah Arendt, the foremost scholar of totalitarianism, a totalitarian society is one in which an ideology seeks to displace all prior traditions and institutions, with the goal of bringing all aspects of society under control of that ideology. A totalitarian state is one that aspires to nothing less than defining and controlling reality. Truth is whatever the rulers decide it is. As Arendt has written, wherever totalitarianism has ruled, "[I]t has begun to destroy the essence of man."
>
> Today's totalitarianism demands allegiance to a set of progressive beliefs, many of which are incompatible with logic—and certainly with Christianity. Compliance is forced less by the state than by elites

who form public opinion, and by private corporations that, thanks to technology, control our lives far more than we would like to admit.[21]

Marxism Is Divisive

Marxism thrives on division. In historic Marxism the division was promoted between classes of people: the oppressors against the oppressed; the bosses against the workers. Men like Hugo Chávez went out of their way to ensure that the poor hated the wealthy.

In today's cultural Marxism, the exploited divide is often racial, sexual, and/or gender-related. I believe that's one of the reasons we've lost some of the progress we've made on race relations. Whatever it is or however far it might be removed from actual racism, whenever a socialist or Marxist can't figure out how to respond to an issue, they always—and I mean every time—call it racist.

This is tragic for many reasons. It's very hurtful to be branded a racist if one has done or said nothing that would lead a rational person to make such an accusation. Once racism has been pinned on a person, it's almost impossible to get rid of it, no matter what you do. But there's another seldom-discussed sadness with playing the race card: if everything is racist, nothing is racist. All of us know there are still racial issues that need to be dealt with in America and around the world, but the true issues get lost in the avalanche of unwarranted accusations.

Marxism Is Deadly

In 1999, *The Black Book of Communism* attempted to calculate a Marxist-Leninist death toll for the twentieth century. It revealed the most colossal case of political carnage in history:

- Latin America: 150,000 deaths
- Eastern Europe: 1 million deaths
- Vietnam: 1 million deaths
- Africa: 1.7 million deaths
- Cambodia: 2 million deaths

- North Korea: 2 million deaths
- USSR: 20 million deaths
- China: 65 million deaths

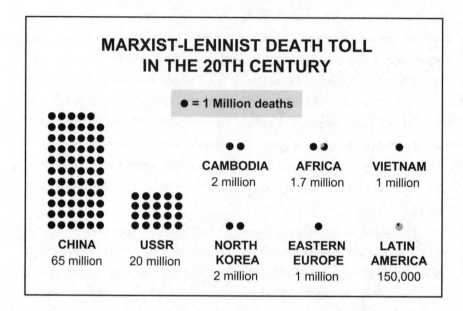

The butchers who led this assault on humanity included Joseph Stalin in Russia, Mao Zedong in China, Kim Il-sung and Kim Jong-il in North Korea, Fidel Castro in Cuba, Nicolae Ceausescu in Romania, and others.

The death count that resulted from Marxism between 1917 and 1979 would "equate to a rate of multiple thousands dead per day over the course of a century. Even Adolph Hitler got nowhere close to that. In fact, neither did the two deadliest wars in history, World War I and II, which need to be combined and doubled to get near Communism's butcher bill."[22]

Aleksandr Solzhenitsyn was fooled by none of it. He taught that "socialism of any type and shade leads to a total destruction of the human spirit and to a leveling of mankind into death."[23]

What Does This Mean?

I'm afraid this new political trajectory in our nation is more than just a trend. It is a seismic shift toward a Marxist agenda. We are harvesting the weeds from Karl Marx's toxic garden. If you look closely, you can draw the connections.

The Destruction of Monuments

It's become common in recent years to see news headlines or live video of protest groups surrounding, defacing, and eventually removing statues and other historical monuments they consider to be offensive. These incidents began with controversial monuments of Civil War participants, but they have expanded to include key men and women from history—even figures such as George Washington and Abraham Lincoln.

When we witness these events, we're not simply seeing a bunch of rowdy young people tearing down statues. Instead, these are part of a concerted effort to attack and ultimately erase the past.

As Milan Kundera wrote during the rise of communism, some people rewrite or erase the past. In that way, the masses forget who they are and can be drawn into a new future. He said, "The first step in liquidating a people is to erase its memory. Destroy its books, its culture, its history. Then have someone write new books, manufacture a new culture, invent a new history. Before long the nation will begin to forget what it is and what is was."[24]

Totalitarians are determined to wipe out everything that is not in their particular interests. Remember Mussolini's definition of totalitarianism: "Everything within the state, nothing outside the state, nothing against the state."

On the contrary, it's interesting to discover that the word *remember* is found 164 times in the Old Testament. Socialism wants you to forget; Christianity wants you to remember. "Remember the former things of old," God said through the prophet Isaiah, "I am God, and there is none like Me" (46:9).

13

Yes, remember all that God has done for us. On the basis of past mercies, we can build a future of grace. We can say with the psalmist, "For You, O God, have . . . given me the heritage of those who fear Your name" (Ps. 61:5).

Biblical heroes built monuments to remind future generations of God's goodness and guidance. For example, when Israel entered the promised land they went through the parted waters of the Jordan River, a story told in four verses in Joshua 3:14–17. But the entire fourth chapter of Joshua describes what happened next. Twelve strong men from the tribes of Israel erected a monument on the western side of the river. Joshua said, "When your children ask their fathers in time to come, saying, 'What are these stones?' then you shall let your children know, saying, 'Israel crossed over this Jordan on dry land'" (4:21–22).

Psalm 77:11 says, "Surely I will remember Your wonders of old."

The Bible itself is largely a history book, telling the stories of flawed heroes who, through faith, conquered kingdoms, worked righteousness, obtained promises, and became valiant in battle (Heb. 11). But revisionist historians are scrubbing our children's textbooks of all that is biblical or Christian, and they are rewriting our history to suit their own secular and socialist agendas.

Cancel Culture

Don't think it's just statues and histories that are being torn down. It's also anyone who doesn't kneel at the altar of prevailing political passions. You are canceled. Elsewhere in this book you'll find an entire chapter on this subject, but for now I want to point out that this, too, is a child of totalitarianism. In cultural Marxism, there can be no room for tolerance or dissenting opinions.

While working on this chapter, I found it frustrating to watch the news because I felt I was drowning in illustrations. For example, I watched a school board in New Jersey cancel the titles of the holidays on its scholastic calendar. It will no longer be Christmas or Thanksgiving or Martin Luther King Jr. Day. From now on, these will all be referred to as student holidays. But here's the kicker: When one of the parents in the back of the room tried to raise an objection, the chairman of the school board slammed his fist on the table and said, "This is not a debate."

Case closed. Discussion over. Opinion canceled. The attempt by that board of education to eliminate the holidays was later overturned, but perhaps not for long.

Dreher wrote, "Today in our societies, dissenters . . . find their businesses, careers, and reputations destroyed. They are pushed out of the public square, stigmatized, canceled, and demonized as racists, sexists, homophobes, and the like. And they are afraid to resist, because they are confident that no one will join them or defend them."[25]

Before the First Amendment is ushered out the door, let me remind you of what it says:

> Congress shall make no law respecting an establishment of religion, or prohibiting the free exercise thereof; or abridging the freedom of speech, or of the press; or the right of the people peaceably to assemble, and to petition the Government for a redress of grievances.

The Dismantling of the Nuclear Family

Marxism reaches its cold fingers into your very home. Marxists want to raise your children and determine your income. Families based on Judeo-Christian values bred inequality, Marx thought. As Lutzer put it, Marx believed Christian homes "feed on greed and systemic oppression. Such families had to be dismantled if the Marxist vision of equality was to be realized. . . . In Marxism, the family is perceived as a unit in which wives are suppressed by their husbands and children are suppressed by their parents. These clusters of oppression have to be broken up; mothers have to leave their homes and join the workforce."[26]

God created the family to be the glue in human society. For example, when God desired to create humanity itself and establish people within the ecosystem of our world, He did not reach down and fashion a full-blown society. He did not create cities or nations with laws and roads and structures.

No, He created a family. He began with Adam and Eve, and He told them to "be fruitful and multiply" (Gen. 1:28).

Similarly, when God desired to reveal Himself more intimately to a human civilization that was staggering under the influence of sin, He did not accomplish that mission by fashioning a philosophical system. He did not thunder from heaven in great speeches with powerful rhetoric.

Instead, He spoke through a family. He told Abraham, "Sarah your wife shall bear you a son, and you shall call his name Isaac; I will establish My covenant with him for an everlasting covenant, and with his descendants after him" (17:19).

And when God chose to take on human flesh in order to fulfill His promises and provide salvation for all people, He did not join a kingdom or seek to win an election. He did not attempt to connect Himself with an existing power system.

Instead, He joined a family. The angel told Mary, "And behold, you will conceive in your womb and bring forth a Son, and shall call His name JESUS" (Luke 1:31).

Socialists know that as long as the family remains strong, socialism cannot flourish. So, there's an ongoing attempt to subjugate the home to the government.

The Redistribution of Wealth

This ideology also teaches that all human assets should be claimed by the government and redistributed to the masses by a more equitable formula. This would supposedly rid the world of poverty. But somehow it has never worked out that way. It doesn't take a scholar to see that wherever this principle has been implemented, the poor have gotten poorer and the few elitists who have been assigned to redistribute the wealth have themselves become filthy rich. Equality cannot be engineered.

Economist Iain Murray said, "The central issues with income inequality, is that the people who seem to be the most concerned with it never really ask the question, how are the poor actually doing? Because when you asked that question and look at the data that answers it, you will see that the poor do the best in economically free societies and do the worst in societies where they are controlled in one way or another, whether it be by socialist, or fascist or authoritarian regimes."[27]

Jude Dougherty, dean emeritus at Catholic University, understood the impossibility of universal equality when he wrote that people "differ in strength, intelligence, ambition, courage, perseverance and all else that makes for success. There is no method to make people both free and equal."[28]

Defunding the Police

Socialists are especially keen on keeping the reins of law enforcement in their tight fists. In America, their first step is to villainize the police, then to defund them. That's why some cities have slashed their police budgets. And surprise! Each of these cities has seen a dramatic uptick in violent crimes in the months that followed. In Minneapolis, murders rose by a mind-numbing 46 percent. In Portland, Oregon, murders more than tripled. And the Los Angeles Police Department reported a 38 percent increase in murders.[29]

Police officers are retiring early, and the recruiting of new police officers is at an all-time low. Unless something changes, our once beautiful cities will become wastelands where gangs rule the streets while politicians go to and from work in their limousines accompanied by their expensive security personnel.

There's a remarkable verse in the Bible about police and law enforcement officials. The apostle Paul called them "God's minister to you for good" (Rom. 13:4). Like all other humans, police officers are fallible, but without them our society would not be viable. The Lord views them as His ministers to maintain order on earth.

Whatever you do, don't miss the socialist's motivation for vilifying local authorities. No matter how loudly they deny it, they are simply trying to let the local government fail so that they can federalize our cities and states, moving control for all that happens to Washington.

Where Do We Go from Here?

If we stopped the chapter at this point, we'd all be pretty grim. But darkness cannot withstand light, and Marxism is no match for the Master. Our Lord Jesus Christ "has gone into heaven and is at the right hand of God, angels and authorities and powers having been made subject to Him" (1 Peter 3:22).

So let's formulate a biblical strategy for exalting Christ in a world where socialism is once again on the rise.

Review What the Bible Says

First, we have to grasp what the Lord has to say about issues related to Marxist thought. Dr. Albert Mohler gave us a well-considered summary:

> The Bible reveals several important economic principles. Scripture affirms the dignity of work (Ephesians 4:28) and the fact that those who refuse to work should not eat (2 Thessalonians 3:10). The Bible clearly affirms private property (Exodus 22:7) and condemns theft (Exodus 20:15) and covetousness (Exodus 20:17). Saving (Proverbs 13:22), thrift (Proverbs 21:20), land ownership (Acts 4:34–37), and investment (Matthew 25:27) are all honored in Scripture, and the Bible teaches that the laborer is worthy of his wages (Luke 10:7). Socialism contradicts or subverts every one of these principles.[30]

It's particularly important to have a firm grasp on the ending of the second chapter of Acts. Someone will likely tell you the Bible teaches socialism here, and that the early church was communist. Here is the passage they are referring to:

> And they continued steadfastly in the apostles' doctrine and fellowship, in the breaking of bread, and in prayers. Then fear came upon every soul, and many wonders and signs were done through the apostles. Now all who believed were together, and had all things in common,

18

and sold their possessions and goods, and divided them among all, as anyone had need. (Acts 2:42–45)

This is a story of personal *sharing*, not public *socialism*. The generosity of the early church would have baffled Karl Marx. In their pentecostal enthusiasm, the early Christians wanted to help the poor and to share with one another. No one asked them to do it. No one applied any pressure. Their own internal hearts of kindness compelled them to give to those in need.

This was friends sharing with friends, not the government seizing assets from one person, keeping some for itself, and redistributing the rest. Neither the city fathers of Jerusalem nor the imperial court of Rome ended up with as much as a widow's mite.

That was fortunate for those early believers, because generosity was key to the early Christians' survival in the face of persecution. The Jerusalem believers eventually faced extreme oppression and were scattered from the city—yet they remained faithful. People under persecution often have better priorities than the rest of us, and those disciples showed how Jesus is more important than all this world can offer. Our earthly resources are secondary to our heavenly inheritance.

So, Acts 2 is a story of generous hearts, not governmental control. It's also a story of humble dependence on God for all the needs of life. Jesus said, "For after all these things the Gentiles seek. For your heavenly Father knows that you need all these things. But seek first the kingdom of God and His righteousness, and all these things shall be added to you" (Matt. 6:32–33).

Refuse to Live by Lies

We must also remain true to the truth. Proverbs 29:12 says, "If a ruler pays attention to lies, all his servants become wicked."

After his expulsion from Russia for writing his famous work, *The Gulag Archipelago*, Aleksandr Solzhenitsyn published a final message to the Russian people: "Live Not by Lies." In this essay, he challenged his fellow Russians not to yield to government pressure. Here is some of what he wrote:

> Let us admit it: we have not matured enough to march into the squares and shout the truth out loud or to express aloud what we think. It is not necessary. It's dangerous. But let us refuse to say what we do not think.
>
> Our path is not that of giving conscious support to lies about anything at all. And once we realise where the perimeters of falsehood are (everyone sees them in his own way), our path is to walk away from this gangrenous boundary. If we did not paste together the dead bones and scales of ideology, if we did not sew together rotting rags, we would be astonished how quickly the lies would be rendered helpless and would subside.[31]

Later in the essay, Solzhenitsyn offered a list of what citizens must not do if they are to be faithful to the truth. They must *not*:

- Say, write, affirm, or distribute anything that distorts the truth.
- Go to a demonstration or participate in a collective action unless he truly believes in the cause.
- Take part in a meeting in which the discussion is forced and no one can speak the truth.
- Vote for a candidate or proposal he considers to be dubious or unworthy.
- Support journalism that distorts or hides the underlying facts.[32]

Christians, too, have been called to refuse falsehood—even to accept or listen to what is false.

"Lying lips are an abomination to the LORD," wrote Solomon (Prov. 12:22). "He who works deceit shall not dwell within my house," echoed the psalmist. "He who tells lies shall not continue in my presence" (Ps. 101:7).

So much of what we hear in our culture today has no connection to common sense, and it often feels easier just to ignore the falsehoods and mistruths. But ignoring them allows those falsehoods to continue. Even to thrive!

Instead, let us refuse to live by lies.

Resolve to Follow Christ and Not Just Admire Him

Jesus said, "If you were of the world, the world would love its own. Yet because you are not of the world, but I chose you out of the world, therefore the world hates you" (John 15:19).

Now, let me ask you something. If we are not of this world but chosen out of the world, shouldn't everything about us be under the King's control? Shouldn't we yield all we are and all we have to the King of kings and Lord of lords? If so, it is God—not government—that orders our lives. To persevere in an increasingly socialist culture, you're going to have to decide whether to be a Christ-follower or merely a Christ-admirer.

Søren Kierkegaard wrote something similar: "The admirer never makes any sacrifices. He always plays it safe. Though in words, phrases, songs, he is inexhaustible about how he praises Christ, he renounces nothing, will not reconstruct his life, and will not let his life express what he supposedly admires. Not so for the follower. No, no. The follower aspires with all his strength to be what he admires."[33]

This is what Jesus was talking about when He explained the cost of discipleship: "If anyone comes to Me and does not hate his father and mother, wife and children, brothers and sisters, yes, and his own life also, he cannot be My disciple. . . . So likewise, whoever of you does not forsake all that he has cannot be My disciple" (Luke 14:26, 33).

There's no getting around this, nor do we want to. This method of discipleship has brought untold blessings to endless generations of Christians for the last two thousand years. Now it's our turn to put these words into practice.

Rethink Small Groups

Today's evolving political culture also compels us to upgrade all the small group ministries in our churches. As many of us learned during the COVID crisis, small groups are vital in rough times. Going back to the second chapter of Acts, let's remember the form established for us by the early church: "So continuing daily with one accord in the temple, and breaking bread from house to house, they ate their food with gladness and simplicity of heart, praising God" (vv. 46–47).

At our church in San Diego, over three thousand people are part of small groups, and they lightened the stress of many hearts during the lockdown. I expect that number to grow as we look back over our shoulders and look forward into the future. Technology can help. Zoom small groups played a big part in holding our congregation together during the fourteen months we were apart. Furthermore, the government has more difficulty tracking small groups than large crowds.

One person wrote, "What the experience of the church under communism, and a discerning read of the signs of the times today, tells us is that all Christians of every church should start forming these cells—not simply to deepen its members spiritual lives, but to train them in active resistance."[34]

Small groups are not retreats from the rest of the world. They are gatherings that help us care for one another, study the instructions of Scripture, cope with the world, and advance with the gospel. They are biblical in nature, and they will prepare us to resist the socialist thought army that is surely coming after us.

Resist Any Way You Can

And speaking of resistance, let's remember Peter's words in Acts 5:29: "We ought to obey God rather than men." Hopefully, we'll be able to continue as law-abiding citizens of our various nations, but anytime the government tries to force us to violate our biblical beliefs, we have a responsibility to speak up. You might be surprised to learn how receptive some of our leaders are to a calm, but assertive, word on behalf of our religious liberty.

For example, Elizabeth Turner worked hard on her valedictorian speech for Hillsdale High School in Hillsdale, Michigan. She intentionally highlighted her faith in Jesus. In the draft of her speech she said, "For me, my future hope is found in my relationship with Christ. By trusting in him and choosing to live a life dedicated to bringing His kingdom glory, I can be confident that I am living a life with purpose and meaning. My identity is found by what God says and who I want to become is laid out in Scripture."

That didn't go over well with school officials. Her principal told her, "You are representing the school in the speech, not using the podium as your public forum. . . . We need to be mindful about the inclusion of religious aspects. These are your strong beliefs, but they are not appropriate for a speech in a school public setting. I know this will frustrate you, but we have to be mindful of it."[35]

This didn't just frustrate Elizabeth; it frustrated my friend Robert Morgan when he read about it. Picking up the phone, he called the school and spoke with someone in the principal's office. Rob was gentle and soft-spoken, but he questioned the school's decision. "This is an infringement on the student's civil rights," he said. "It's an erosion of our freedom of speech and worship." He was directed to the office of the Hillsdale Superintendent of Schools, where he left a message on the answering machine. Then he posted a link to the story on his social media sites.

"I had just gone to the grocery store to get a banana for lunch," Rob said, "when my cell phone rang. To my total surprise, Superintendent Shawn Vondra was on the line. He wanted me to know Hillsdale High School will certainly allow Elizabeth and all their valedictorians to express their genuine faith without censorship. Superintendent Vondra's call was so warm it almost felt we'd been friends for years."

Rob told me it wasn't his phone call that made all this happen. It was the outpouring of support from Christians all over the country. One of these supporters was Mat Staver at Liberty Counsel. He sent a legal complaint to Hillsdale High School, alleging that federal law had been broken when they tried to censor a student's speech for a school event.

Everyone's voice played a part, and this is an example of the power of our voices speaking up.

Remember Venezuela

Today, Venezuela is a social and economic wasteland, with 96 percent of citizens living below the poverty line. Most people earn less than a US dollar a day. Poor economic management brought about inflation rates of more than ten million percent, which is why a roll of toilet paper cost 2.6 million bolivars (the Venezuelan currency) in 2018.[36] And the lack of investment in commodities means the nation is barren of essential medicines and medical services. As a result, an estimated 5.5 million refugees have fled Venezuela in recent years—a number that represents more than a sixth of the nation's total population from 2014.[37]

In short, a country once defined by freedom and opportunity is now oppressed, barren, and hopeless. That is the fruit of a Marxist revolution.

No form of government on earth is perfect. Every political philosophy is defective, including democracy and the free market system. But some ideas are worse than others. Marxism is among the worst ideas ever conceived. Just ask its oppressed multitudes and its countless casualties. We should be aware of its history, herald its dangers, and oppose its spread.

The best news of all is this: When Jesus returns, "the government will be upon His shoulder. . . . Of the increase of His government and peace there will be no end, upon the throne of David and over His kingdom, to order it and establish it with judgment and justice from that time forward, even forever" (Isa. 9:6–7).

Our Lord will "judge between the nations, and rebuke many people; they shall beat their swords into plowshares, and their spears into pruning hooks; nation shall not lift up sword against nation, neither shall they learn war anymore" (2:4).

Socialism, Marxism, and all the other ugly "isms" of history will be . . . well, they will *be* history. And our Lord Jesus Christ will reign forever and ever. When the twelve spies explored the promised land, only two of them brought back a faithful report—Joshua and Caleb. It was Caleb who later said: "And I brought [Moses] back a report according to my convictions" (Josh. 14:7 NIV).

It's time for us all to live by convictions, not by convenience. And remember, the battle is the Lord's, and the truth cannot be intimidated.

The world is getting smaller every year. We can be almost anywhere on the planet within twenty-four hours. We know more—and more quickly—about the news in far-flung countries than we do about what's happening in our own neighborhoods.

Though there are many benefits to being so interconnected, there are also dangers. The "global" empires in the past—Babylon, Persia, Greece, Rome—might have had efficient infrastructure and ease of doing business, but it often came at the cost of personal and religious freedom. Not to mention the old adage that the bigger they are, the harder they fall. And when an empire falls, you can bet there is plenty of collateral damage.

In our modern day, calls to increased globalization seem to go along with talk of a single government, currency, and culture. But whose? And to what end? Should we be worried? What does the Bible have to say about all of this?

Chapter 2

An International Prophecy—Globalism

All the world marveled and followed the beast.

REVELATION 13:3

A story recently spread over the Internet saying the United Nations was quietly working on shadowy plans to create a "new world order" and a one-world government. Among items under discussion: a global currency, a central bank, the end of national sovereignty, mandatory vaccines, universal basic income, microchipping of citizens, and the end of fossil fuels. Many of these goals could be achieved by 2030, said the report, which was titled U.N. Agenda 21/2030.

The United Nations quickly disavowed the report, and the media debunked it.

But why did this story spread so quickly? Because every element of it seemed plausible! When we look around at the world today, it's easy to believe governments and influential people behind the scenes—the powers behind the power—could be laying just those types of plans. In fact, sometimes it's easy to feel such things are on the horizon—that they are inevitable.

This is especially true in light of a global emergency like the COVID-19 pandemic, which nearly crushed the world's economy. Imagine what would have happened had the mortality rate of the pandemic been exponentially higher. Such an existential global crisis would certainly call for a unified global response.

If and when that happens, there's no going back. We will have officially jumped headfirst into the waters of globalization, global governance, and a global economy.

Even at this present moment, we've already got our toes in those waters. In his book *The Ages of Globalization*, Jeffrey D. Sachs wrote about the importance of having a global response to pandemics like COVID-19: "Disease control is not the only area where global cooperation is vital today. The case for global cooperation and institutions extends to many urgent concerns, including the control of human-induced climate change; the conservation of biodiversity; the control and reversal of the massive pollution of the air, soils, and oceans; the proper uses and governance of the internet; the nonproliferation of nuclear weapons; the avoidance of mass forced migrations; and the ever-present challenge of avoiding or ending violent conflicts."[1]

During the coronavirus crisis, former British prime minister Gordon Brown vocally called for "a temporary form of global government" to deal with it.[2]

Professor Arvind Ashta of the Burgundy School of Business in France wrote, "Perhaps, the situation created by COVID-19 might serve to highlight the particular advantages of shifting to a world federal government. This may trigger a change that would not only help mitigate the damage caused by the pandemic, but would also offer a solution to many of the other challenges humanity currently faces."[3]

Each of these statements is a call from serious-minded people toward a greater, more intentional establishment of globalization. But what does that actually mean? What is it that such people want to happen? Let's bring this conversation down to a definition.

Globalization is exactly what it sounds like—the global spread of finance, trade, technology, resources of all sorts, movements of all kinds, information, and people. It's the entire world being bound up in interconnected systems.

Dr. Albert Mohler wrote, "Globalization means that we now understand ourselves as living in an economy and in a community that is irreversibly connected globally. We are able to get on an airplane in virtually any American city and be at any spot on the globe within twenty-four hours. Globalization means that headlines from around the world can arrive as quickly as headlines from across the street. There is a growing awareness of the fact that we are now part of a global civilization that includes, and seems to reach, virtually every inhabitant of the planet."[4]

Jason Fernando wrote for *Investopedia*, "Globalization is a social, cultural, political, and legal phenomenon. . . . Culturally, globalization represents the exchange of ideas, values, and artistic expression among cultures. Globalization also represents a trend toward the development of a single world culture."[5]

Notice that! A single world culture. Perhaps I'm just a Doubting Thomas about this, but I don't relish the thought of a single world culture. What kind of culture would it be? What forces would prevail? And what kind of economic influences would take over? Perhaps most importantly, what would happen to the distinctly different—and distinctly wonderful—cultures that exist today when we travel from region to region around the globe?

Globalization will ultimately involve a single economy with a single currency. Yet even now the economies of the nations are so interconnected it reminds me of a game we used to play called Jenga. Players build a tower using fifty-four blocks, then they take turns removing one block at a time, making it more and more unstable. The game ends when the tower falls.

Over a decade ago, I wrote a book about the dangers of a coming worldwide economic Armageddon. Here's what I said:

> Could we be standing today on the edge of a recession from which no one economy, no one nation, no one union will be able to extricate the world? The Bible predicts that such an era is coming. Fueled by the world's economic convulsions, the only answer will seem to be the unification of the nations under one economic system and one world ruler.
>
> One would expect such a process to begin with the gradual consolidation of wealth and power, both nationally and globally. Today as we witness the merging of banks and the centralization of financial regulations, we cannot help but wonder if the Antichrist is waiting in the wings, ready to make his entrance onto the stage of this desperate world.[6]

I wouldn't change a word now, except to add something. The rise of a handful of powerful billionaires and their Big Tech companies are shaping the way we think about globalization. Big Tech is unifying the world in a way that transcends human government and dominates the world economy.

Author Alexis Wichowski called these massive corporations "net states." She wrote, "We're in a world still dominated by nation-states, but increasingly influenced by the actions of net states. Nation-states continue to own the physical territories within their borders, but net states wield significant power both within and across country space, guiding events that affect us both on an individual and on a global level."[7]

Experts refer to the five FAANG companies: Facebook, Apple, Amazon, Netflix, and Google. But don't forget China's Big Tech behemoths: Baidu, Alibaba, and Tencent.

Amy Webb wrote, "Even the best-intentioned people can

inadvertently cause great harm. Within technology, and especially when it comes to AI, we must continually remember to plan for both intended use and unintended misuse. This is especially important today and for the foreseeable future, as AI intersects with everything: the global economy, the workforce, agriculture, transportation, banking, environmental monitoring, education, the military, and national security."[8]

She warned that the world fifty years from now could look vastly different from the world of today.

I don't think globalization will take that much time. One single catastrophic event could trigger the dominoes leading to a globalized government quicker than we think. Scholars are constantly thinking about this.

Leigh Phillips is a British-Canadian science writer and political journalist who writes broadly on current global affairs. In the *Jacobin* magazine, Phillips wrote an article titled "We Need a World Government— But It Has to Be Democratic."

He said a globalization of our political systems "has been taking shape among figures of the technocratic center for some time now, identifying a need for some form of global governance in the face of worldwide threats. The world is already 'governed' by some 1,000 treaties and agencies that involve varying levels of finance and enforcement. For these centrists, moving toward a world government would not be a revolution so much as the next logical step."[9]

To summarize what I've said thus far, the world has been getting smaller with each passing era, its interconnectedness greater, and its inhabitants more vulnerable to a one-world government, given the right conditions. The events of recent years—including the COVID-19 pandemic—have only accelerated the discussions and increased the trajectory of globalism.

That, to me, is bad news. And yet, as we'll see in the pages to follow, it's all in keeping with the predictions of Scripture.

What Does It Mean?

The more we become aware of this larger push toward globalization, the more we often feel frustrated as average citizens of our individual nations. We feel swept along by forces beyond our control—forces that care little for our consent. At times, the relentless surge can be terrifying.

Yet when we look at all this from the perspective of the Bible, it takes away our fear and frustration. Almighty God has a predetermined plan for the history of His planet and its inhabitants. He's moving toward a day soon when "the earth will be filled with the knowledge of the glory of the LORD, as the waters cover the sea" (Hab. 2:14). The psalmist spoke of a time when the whole earth will "be filled with His glory" (Ps. 72:19). The book of Revelation predicts a time when "the kingdoms of this world" will become "the kingdoms of our Lord and of His Christ" (11:15).

Let's take a look at what we can know for certain about the broader scope of historical events—past, present, and future.

What to Know About the Course of History

What we see in today's trends toward globalization was long ago anticipated in biblical prophecy. The first attempt at globalization occurred in Genesis 11, when a powerful warlord named Nimrod (whose name probably means "rebellion") established the empire of Babylon and built the Tower of Babel.[10]

He was called a "mighty hunter before the LORD" (Gen. 10:9). What was he hunting? People. Power. Glory. Wealth. World domination. As the post-flood population grew, Nimrod became the first global tyrant. The Bible says, "He was the first on earth to be a mighty man" (1 Chron. 1:10 ESV). In other words, Nimrod was the father of all future dictators and the first prototype of the coming Antichrist.

The Jewish historian Josephus described Nimrod as:

A bold man, and of great strength of hand. He persuaded them not to ascribe it to God, as if it were through his means they were happy, but to believe that it was their own courage which procured that happiness. He also gradually changed the government into tyranny, seeing no other way of turning men from the fear of God, but to bring them into a constant dependence on his power.

Old Testament scholar Michael S. Heiser wrote, "Nimrod is cast as the progenitor of the civilizations of Assyria and Babylon (Gen. 10:6–12). . . . Assyria and Babylon are the two civilizations that will later destroy the dream of the earthly kingdom of God in Israel, dismantling, respectively, the northern kingdom (Israel) and southern kingdom (Judah)."[11]

When the Southern Kingdom of Judah was invaded by Babylon in 605 BC, a young Jewish man—a teenager—was swept up and taken to the palace of Babylonian king Nebuchadnezzar.

Like Nimrod, his ancient predecessor, Nebuchadnezzar was the most powerful man on earth in his day—the most powerful despot who had ever lived. He enlarged his empire until it stretched from the Persian Gulf to the Mediterranean Sea. It included parts of present-day Kuwait, Iraq, Syria, Jordan, Israel, Lebanon, and Turkey.

Nebuchadnezzar built the most fabulous capital city the world had seen to that point. Even today, the ruins of Babylon are spread over two thousand acres and represent the largest archaeological site in the Middle East. The metropolis was surrounded by a massive wall that was considered impenetrable. Some portions of these walls still exist among the ruins. They are said to have been 56 miles in length, 320 feet tall, and so broad that a four-horse chariot could be driven along the top.[12]

In the heart of the city, a massive ziggurat reached toward the sky. It was a new version of the Tower of Babel. It arose "in seven stages of gleaming enamel to a height of 650 feet, crowned with a shrine containing a massive table of solid gold."[13]

The whole city was something like a fairy tale, with bridges, boulevards, gateways, and lavish glazed bricks. This was the city of Nebuchadnezzar—and of Daniel.

Nebuchadnezzar was the greatest and richest man who had ever lived, but that didn't keep away the bad dreams. One night, the king summoned his advisors and magicians to his palace, demanding they tell him what he had dreamt and what it meant. If they could do the former, he reasoned, they could do the latter.

When they could do neither, Nebuchadnezzar was enraged and ready to kill every last one of them. But Daniel prayed with his friends, and God gave him supernatural insights. Daniel sent word up the ranks that he could reveal and interpret the dream, and soon he was standing before the trembling king.

"No wise man, enchanter, magician or diviner can explain to the king the mystery he has asked about," said Daniel without fear, "but there is a God in heaven who reveals mysteries. He has shown King Nebuchadnezzar what will happen in days to come" (Dan. 2:27–28 NIV).

What follows is the Bible's most foundational sketch of the future of our planet. It introduces us to the total sweep of prophetic world history and gives us a prophetic understanding of globalization. The rest of the book of Daniel and the subsequent book of Revelation (along with many other passages in the Bible) fill in the details. But the framework is fixed forever in Daniel 2.

In his dream, Nebuchadnezzar saw a massive statue. Its head was pure gold. Its chest and arms were made of silver. It was bronze from its stomach to its thighs, and the legs were iron. The feet and toes were partly iron and partly clay. Then Nebuchadnezzar saw a rock quarried by an invisible hand. This rock flew through the air and struck the statue, which toppled and broke into a million tiny bits that were swept away by the wind like chaff. The rock began to grow and soon became a mountain so large it covered the entire earth.

The interpretation is given in the last part of Daniel 2.

- The head of gold represented the empire of Babylon.
- The chest of silver, with its two arms, represented the next great world empire—Medo-Persia.

- The stomach and thighs of bronze depicted the next stage in world history, the Greek Empire of Alexander the Great.
- The legs of iron were predictions of the Roman Empire.
- The feet and toes are a final world empire that will arise in the last days.
- The rock is the One who will come to demolish history at its zenith and establish a truly global kingdom, marked by righteousness and peace.

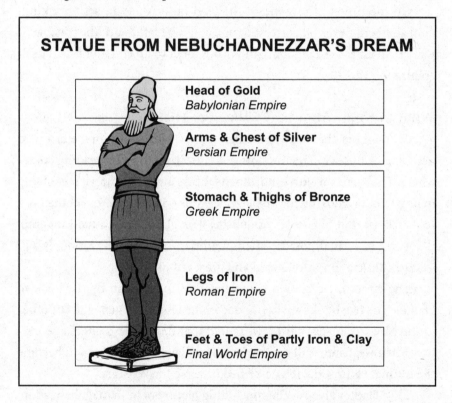

STATUE FROM NEBUCHADNEZZAR'S DREAM

Head of Gold
Babylonian Empire

Arms & Chest of Silver
Persian Empire

Stomach & Thighs of Bronze
Greek Empire

Legs of Iron
Roman Empire

Feet & Toes of Partly Iron & Clay
Final World Empire

In the days of Nimrod, God broke up the globalization of his empire by confusing the languages. Later in the same area—Babylon—Nebuchadnezzar brought the then-known world under his power. Persia did the same, and Alexander did the same. Then came Rome. Under all these governments, there was a sort of globalization, though without holiness and fear of God.

After the fall of Rome, no single nation or empire has dominated the world.

But don't forget the feet and toes. According to Daniel, there will be one more attempt at a one-world government in the future. It will be something of a revival of the Roman Empire made up of a confederation of ten kings or kingdoms, dominated by a Nimrod-type dictator. But it won't last long, for God will bring it to an end with the second coming of Jesus Christ.

"In the time of those kings, the God of heaven will set up a kingdom that will never be destroyed, nor will it be left to another people. It will crush all those kingdoms and bring them to an end, but it will itself endure forever" (2:44 NIV).

What to Know About the Climax of History

Throughout the book of Daniel, we're told there's a predetermined outcome to history. The unfolding events around us are leading somewhere. The earth isn't lurching into the future any more than it's wobbling in its orbit. It is moving toward a rendezvous with the decrees of the Lord Jesus Christ. But before He establishes His global millennial kingdom, there will be a final horrific attempt at man-made globalization. It will lead to a time of unprecedented and great tribulation.

The book of Revelation completes the story begun by the book of Daniel. The two books are twins, one in the Old Testament and the other in the New. In Revelation 13, we're told that during days of great worldwide distress, Satan will raise up a man of lawlessness who will become the ultimate Nimrod. He's described in verse 1 as "a beast."

This chapter gives us the concluding picture of human globalization:

The whole world was filled with wonder and followed the beast. . . .
The beast was given a mouth to utter proud words and blasphemies
and to exercise its authority for forty-two months. It opened its mouth
to blaspheme God, and to slander his name and his dwelling place and
those who live in heaven. It was given power to wage war against God's

holy people and to conquer them. And it was given authority over every tribe, people, language and nation. All inhabitants of the earth will worship the beast—all whose names have not been written in the Lamb's book of life. (Rev. 13:3, 5–8 NIV)

The whole world! Every tribe, people, language, and nation! All inhabitants of the earth! This Antichrist will rebuild the ancient city of Babylon for his world capital (14:8; 18–19) and will be on the verge of uniting the armies of the world in a last great attempt to destroy God's chosen nation of Israel. He will also globalize the economy, forcing everyone to be chipped in some way with his mark—the mysterious 666 of Revelation 13:18. Without this mark, no one will be able to make purchases or engage in commerce. (We will explore these realities more deeply in chapter 4.)

Widespread persecution will spill the blood of thousands upon thousands of believers, and more blood will be spilled in the wars waged in an effort to unify the nations and destroy the Jewish people. Zechariah 12:3 speaks of a day when "all nations of the earth are gathered against [Jerusalem]."

That's when Christ will return—like a rock that strikes the edifice of world history, sends it shattering into the wind, and establishes His own global kingdom instead.

Let me summarize. The world has been dominated by four great globalized empires: Babylon, Persia, Greece, and Rome. Since the days of the Roman Empire, no political entity has dominated the world. But a fifth empire is coming—the revived Roman Empire under the Antichrist. At a moment of worldwide panic, he will push himself to the top of the heap of humanity and establish a one-world government. The world will be in the grip of seven years of tribulation, and near the end of this time of distress the armies of the world will march against the nation of Israel, to destroy it forever.

Can you see how the trend lines of history are moving in this direction?

The Bible says, "For the mystery of lawlessness is already at work;

only He who now restrains will do so until He is taken out of the way. And then the lawless one will be revealed, whom the Lord will consume with the breath of His mouth and destroy with the brightness of His coming" (2 Thess. 2:7–8).

Oh, what a turn of events! This is the moment of Christ's glorious return. This is the climax of human history, when Christ will come again as a Conqueror on a white horse followed by the armies of heaven (Rev. 19:11–16). The Armageddon armies of the Antichrist will be dispersed and annihilated by the spoken words that come like a flaming sword from His lips.

Let me go back to what Zechariah said: "I will gather all the nations to Jerusalem to fight against it. . . . Then the LORD will go out and fight against those nations, as he fights on a day of battle. On that day his feet will stand on the Mount of Olives. . . . The LORD will be king over the whole earth. On that day there will be one LORD, and his name the only name" (Zech. 14:2–4, 9 NIV).

What to Know About the Culmination of History

What then? This is what we often call the millennium, based on the teaching in Revelation 20 that the earthly reign of Christ will last one thousand years. During this time, the Lord will fulfill all the promises He made in Scripture regarding the people of Israel and the ultimate future of earth.

All the world will see globalization at its finest—not under Nimrod, Nebuchadnezzar, Greece, Persia, or Rome. Not under the Antichrist.

Instead, under the Lord Jesus Christ!

What will the world be like during these days? The Lord has filled His Word with information about this thousand-year reign of Christ. It occupies an extraordinary amount of biblical ink. I'll summarize some of it for you.

During the coming global reign of Christ, Jerusalem will be the capital of the earth, and people from all the nations will regularly come to visit, learn, and worship (Isa. 2:2–3). The millennial temple in Jerusalem will be the most beautiful building on earth (Ezek. 40), and it will be filled with the glory of the Lord (43). A deep and mighty river will flow from beneath the temple, turning the desert into a paradise and the Dead Sea into a living lake (Zech. 14:8; Ezek. 47). Fruit trees will grow along both sides of the river, bearing fresh fruit every month (Ezek. 47:12).

The Lord Jesus will be the ultimate international diplomat, negotiating peace treaties between rival nations (Isa. 2:4). He will bring peace to the earth, and wars will cease (2:4). He will occupy the ancient throne of His forefather, David (Luke 1:32–33).

The population of earth will travel to Jerusalem on a regular basis to worship the King and to keep the feasts of Israel (Zech. 14:16). The agriculture of earth will be so improved that the reapers will have a hard time staying ahead of the sowers. The grain and grapes will grow so fast they can hardly be harvested (Amos 9:13). The deserts will become as green as lush mountains (Isa. 35:1–2).

Life expectancy will rival the lifespans of the days before the flood, when people lived to be hundreds of years old (65:20). Nature will be transformed so that wolves and lambs will graze side by side, as will lions and cows (11:7; 65:25).

Songs of praise will ascend from the ends of the earth (24:16), and joy will cover the world (35:10).

Now, this is not eternity. This is not heaven. This is a *prelude* to heaven. Isaiah summed it up when he said: "Nothing will hurt or destroy in all my holy mountain, for as the waters fill the sea, so the earth will be filled with people who know the LORD" (11:9 NLT).

After the thousand-year reign of Christ, earth's history will be over. The old universe will melt away, and God's children will be ushered into the new heavens, the new earth, and the celestial city of New Jerusalem—a topic I cover in more detail in chapter 9.

Where Do We Go from Here?

If the trajectory of history has been moving inch-by-inch toward globalization for millennia, and if the future of our planet is globalized terror under the Antichrist followed by a glorious thousand-year reign of Christ, how should we then live? What sort of people should we be?

In the Bible, there's a single moment of sheer surprise that answers those questions. It's the ascension of Jesus Christ, who rose from the ground and left the globe at the end of His earthly life.

The book of Acts says:

> When they had come together, they asked Him, saying, "Lord, will You at this time restore the kingdom to Israel?" And He said to them, "It is not for you to know times or seasons which the Father has put in His own authority. But you shall receive power when the Holy Spirit has come upon you; and you shall be witnesses to Me in Jerusalem, and in all Judea and Samaria, and to the end of the earth." Now when He had spoken these things, while they watched, He was taken up, and a cloud received Him out of their sight. And while they looked steadfastly toward heaven as He went up, behold, two men stood by them in white apparel, who also said, "Men of Galilee, why do you stand gazing up into heaven? This same Jesus, who was taken up from you into heaven, will so come in like manner as you saw Him go into heaven." (1:6–11)

What a precious promise in that final verse! Jesus will come again "in like manner as you saw Him go into heaven." With that promise in our pockets, here are three concrete ways we can respond today to the good news of tomorrow.

Worship Your Glorified Christ

The first thing I want to do when I read this passage is to worship the glorified Jesus. He came into the world, died for the world, rose from the dead, and left the world. He was caught up into heaven, where He resumed His place at the right hand of the Father. I can't imagine all that was in the heart of His followers as they saw Him ascend, but it must have been a thrilling moment of worship.

One of the disciples who saw Jesus ascend into the clouds was the apostle John. Many years later, he had a vision of Jesus—glorified and magnified. John described in Revelation 1 how he saw "the Son of Man, clothed with a garment down to the feet and girded about the chest with a golden band. His head and His hair were white like wool, as white as snow, and His eyes like a flame of fire" (vv. 13–14).

The same Jesus that walked the dusty roads of Galilee now presides over the affairs of the universe and the annals of history. We're not left alone in a cauldron of confusion. In the midst of a chaotic world, we have a steadfast Savior who is preparing to come again.

Worshiping Him keeps us focused on eternal realities and sane amid the seemingly erratic times in which we live.

Philip Renner is a worship leader in Russia, America, and throughout the world. He was one of the first national Russian-language worship artists, and in his book *Worship Without Limits*, he described how he fell in love with the joy of worshiping Jesus.

When Philip was six, his family moved to the former U.S.S.R. and planted the Moscow Good News Church, which became a thriving congregation in the heart of Moscow. He grew up watching his parents lead worship. Even as a child, Philip was deeply touched by his mother's voice as she led hundreds of people in singing. Sometimes her voice was so loud he covered his ears with his hands, but he knew people were being touched by God.

"Hearing the clapping and testimonies that followed set a fire in my heart to do the same," he wrote.

"As a child, I would often shut the door to my room and pretend to lead people in worship, just like I saw my mother do in the churches we visited. I would pace back and forth in my room, looking at the imaginary crowd and instructing them to lift their hands. How exciting this was for a child with an active imagination! Little did I know then how by pretending to be a worship leader I was actually acting out the dreams in my heart."[14]

Philip's story is unique, but it stirs something within me. I, too, should be caught up in the joy of worshiping my glorified Savior, and my joy should be contagious. Oh, that our children will want to worship our Lord by seeing our example! In uncertain times, we can either worry about the headlines or we can worship Him who is head over all. Just as the disciples gazed into heaven, astounded at their ascended Lord, so we should do the same.

From childhood to old age, a life of praise is a life of peace, for when our eyes are on Jesus Christ, we know it is well with our souls.

Embrace Your Global Mission

But, of course, the disciples didn't stay in that spot gazing into heaven all day. Prompted by two angels, they returned to Jerusalem to prepare for something new—the global mission of the gospel. In a world that is globalizing, we have a mission that is global. As never before in human history, we have an opportunity to take the gospel to every town, every tribe, and every tongue.

Dr. Albert Mohler wrote,

> The church, when it is faithful, always thinks in global terms. The world now thinks of globalization as a great economic, technological, and political fact. The church of the Lord Jesus Christ understands global mission as a command and as a mandate from the Lord. While the world may debate globalization in terms of its economic and sociological effects, the church must see globalization as an unprecedented opportunity. Globalization may be a surprise to sociologists, politicians, and businessmen, but it comes as great promise to followers of the Lord Jesus Christ. The current generation of Christians has unprecedented opportunities to proclaim the name of Jesus in all of the world and to see people of all tribes, tongues, and nations bow the knee to the King.[15]

If you'll look around you, you'll see multitudes of people who are simply bewildered by life and as lost as an airplane over the oceans without navigation. Many of them simply crash. But if we're alert, we can help them begin tracking with the gospel of Christ.

Not long ago, Brenton Winn, then twenty-three, broke into Central Baptist Church in Conway, Arkansas, and smashed everything in sight, including laptop computers and cameras. He scribbled a racial slur on the wall and set the church's family life center on fire. He left the place a mess. It's as though he were in a rage. In fact, he was homeless, high on methamphetamines, and angry with God.

Police identified him from images on the church's surveillance cameras, and he was charged with multiple crimes.

But here's where the story takes an unexpected turn. The church and its pastor, Don Chandler, reached out to the offender. Pastor Chandler talked to the prosecutor and extended forgiveness to the young man. Brenton entered a twelve-month rehab and recovery program, and there he accepted Jesus Christ as his Savior.

Six months later, Brenton was baptized in the same church he had vandalized.

"As I'm starting to understand how God works," he said, "I've realized I didn't pick the church that night. God picked me."

Pastor Chandler added, "You can't preach something for fifty years without practicing it. . . . Had we not shown some grace to him, everything we've talked about and encouraged, would have gone by the wayside. It was simply the right thing to do. This was not a hardened criminal. This was a young man who had made some mistakes. He was on drugs and alcohol when he did what he did. But he was redeemable."[16]

So was Min-ji, a prisoner in a North Korean labor camp. Upon her release, she decided to defect to South Korea via China. While there, she became exposed to the gospel of Christ, but Chinese authorities discovered she was a North Korean defector and sent her to prison. A month into her imprisonment, Min-ji saw two words written by another prisoner in toothpaste on the wall: *Jesus Christ.*

It was her first time to see those two words, and she was deeply moved. Her fellow prisoner shared the gospel with her, and Min-ji was born again. After her release from prison, Min-ji made her way to South Korea where she's being trained by the persecution watchdog organization Voice of the Martyrs. She wants to share Christ with everyone she can.[17]

This is the first time in my life I've heard of the gospel being shared with toothpaste, but the Lord is doing something unusual in our days. Since we live in a globalized world, we've never had more potential in reaching the globe for Christ.

Perhaps you live in a small apartment with only a few things, such as a cell phone or laptop. How can you use those tools to share Christ with someone on the other side of the globe? How can you use social media not to argue and debate, but to love and to care and to share Christ? What can you do in your local church to advance the global reach of the kingdom, and what ministries can you support that will reach the regions beyond? What missionaries can you encourage?

As long as Christ tarries, we must keep going to our cities, states, nations, and to the uttermost parts of the world.

Anticipate Your Glorious Hope

Finally, in addition to worshiping our glorified Christ and embracing our global mission, we should always anticipate our glorious hope.

Going back to the ascension of Christ in Acts 1, Jesus had no sooner disappeared into a bright cloud of glory than two angels appeared. They must have been hurtling down from heaven as Jesus was rocketing up. They said to the disciples, "Men of Galilee, why do you stand gazing up into heaven? This same Jesus, who was taken up from you into heaven, will so come in like manner as you saw Him go into heaven" (Acts 1:11).

From that point, every hero in the New Testament began looking for and longing for the return of Christ.

Paul said, "There is laid up for me the crown of righteousness, which the Lord, the righteous Judge, will give to me on that Day, and not to me only but also to all who have loved His appearing" (2 Tim. 4:8).

Peter said, "But in keeping with his promise we are looking forward to a new heaven and a new earth, where righteousness dwells" (2 Peter 3:13 NIV).

John wrote, "We shall be like Him, for we shall see Him as He is" (1 John 3:2).

William Hepburn Hewitson was a nineteenth-century Scottish missionary to Madeira. One day he was studying the subject of the return of Christ in 2 Thessalonians 2. He became so aware of the truth of our Lord's imminent return that he could hardly contain himself. From that moment, his life was different. He later said his study that day came to him as a sort of "second conversion" and it became an abiding reality that made him constantly long for the Lord's return, waiting for it and watching for it.[18]

We, too, should actively contemplate and anticipate the imminent return of Jesus. This is something we can do even as humanity continues its push toward a destructive version of globalization.

As many scholars have pointed out, this globalization is not the will of God. Instead, He has ordained hundreds of separate nations as a protection against one of the worst results of Adam's fall—humanity's craving for power. Paul explained that God has scattered people and set their boundaries "so that they should seek the Lord, in the hope that they might grope for Him and find Him" (Acts 17:27).

Waiting for Christ's Kingdom

Have you read about the time President Woodrow Wilson was on his hands and knees in a Paris mansion, peering through his spectacles at a huge map on the floor, trying to figure out how to carve up the world? Around him other world leaders were doing the same. They dreamed of a new world order that would hasten globalized peace.

The collapse of Germany meant Europe could be reorganized, and the fall of the Ottoman Empire demanded the redrawing of the borders of the nations of the Middle East. Many of the great dynasties had been wiped away like chalk from a blackboard. The Romanovs were gone; so were the Habsburgs. America had emerged as the greatest nation in history, and Wilson was determined to reconstruct the entire globe. He also dreamed of a League of Nations that could prevent future wars through collective security.

As these rulers studied the map on hands and knees, First Lady Edith Wilson walked in and laughed. "You look like a lot of little boys playing a game," she said.

The president looked up at her over his pince-nez glasses and said, "Alas, it is the most serious game ever undertaken, for on the result of it hangs, in my estimation, the future peace of the world."[19]

Alas is a good word to describe what happened. The League of Nations failed, Woodrow Wilson worked himself into a debilitating stroke, Edith secretly served as shadow president, the end of the First World War sowed the seeds for the second, and we are still fighting endless conflicts over the fracturing of the world that occurred in that Paris mansion.

No, my friend, human-based globalism isn't the answer to our world. It will lead only to the final one-world government of the Antichrist. I don't know how far we are from those tumultuous days. In my opinion, we're only one existential crisis away.

But the Lord still has the whole world in His hands, so we must never fear. Christ will appear just as He ascended, and He will establish a global kingdom to show us how things should have always been. Then He'll usher us through the gates of our eternal home.

In the meantime, let's worship Him every day, speed the gospel on its way to the end of the earth, and look forward to His soon and swift return!

Is COVID-19 a prophetic sign? Is this pandemic an act of judgment against the world like the flood was in Noah's day? While the Bible may not have the answers for which we are looking, the Bible does have answers. These answers will help us understand what is going to happen in the future but more importantly, they explain what is happening to us today.

Like never before, we are on edge. The lockdowns and quarantines seem to have done more damage than the disease. But in the midst of it all, God has been speaking to us through His timeless book. His message of comfort and courage is helping us make sense out of the turmoil. We are standing in the midst of one of life's most defining moments. It will either make us better or make us bitter. The choice is up to us!

Chapter 3

A Biological Prophecy— Pandemic

"There will be . . . pestilences . . . in various places."
MATTHEW 24:7

At the beginning of the COVID-19 crisis, a student at my alma mater, Cedarville University, faced a challenge. Gabe Woodruff, who was enrolled in Cedarville's nursing program, was called up by his US Army Reserves medical unit. He was sent to Detroit to serve COVID patients in that city.

I'm sure you remember the panic of those early-pandemic days. You watched the videos of people dropping unconscious in the streets of Wuhan, China, where the virus originated. You read news reports of hospitals in Italy becoming overrun. You saw constant images of doctors and nurses garbed in Personal Protective Equipment (PPE) to try and establish some form of protection against their own patients.

This was the chaotic climate in which Gabe Woodruff received his call to serve.

Despite the danger and disruption of the deployment, Gabe didn't hesitate to leave his family. He and his wife, Kayla, found direction in the power of Scripture. Gabe said, "One of the things my wife and I would tell each other is if we trust God with our eternal security, why wouldn't we trust him with our present circumstance?"[1]

That sentence perfectly sums up what many of us learned during the worst days of the pandemic. As a pastor, I had to trust God when my church couldn't gather for weeks. As the head of a ministry organization, I had to trust Him with the needs of my coworkers. As a cancer survivor, I had to trust Him with my health. And as a husband, father, and grandfather, I had to trust God with the welfare of my family.

Did you have the same experience? I suppose nearly every human being on earth had to grapple with these issues. How thankful to have a trustworthy God!

And how wonderful to serve the One who knows the future. If you're a follower of Christ, you don't have to live at the mercy of present problems and future fears. Instead, you can evaluate global events in terms of scriptural prophecy, world history, and the biblical agenda leading to the return of Christ.

Remember how quickly this crisis overtook the world. On January 11, 2020, the first COVID-19 death was reported in Wuhan, China. Two months later, on Wednesday, March 11, 2020, the World Health Organization declared COVID-19 a global pandemic after the virus had spread to 114 countries and nearly 120,000 people, killing more than 4,000.

In the opening days of the crisis, Dr. Tedros Adhanom Ghebreyesus, the director-general of the World Health Organization, said at a press conference that he expected "to see the number of cases, the number of deaths, and the number of affected countries climb even higher. WHO has been assessing this outbreak around the clock and we are deeply concerned both by the alarming levels of spread and severity, and by the alarming levels of inaction."[2]

Dr. Ghebreyesus could not have known at that moment how understated his prediction was. Immediately, everything in the world and in our lives began to change, from sanitizing our hands to searching for toilet paper.

On March 12, Ohio became the first state to shut down all K-12 schools. Soon, colleges and universities canceled in-person classes and began teaching courses online.

United States stocks tumbled, with the Dow Jones Industrial Average falling 10 percent—its biggest one-day percentage drop since October 1987.

Broadway theaters went dark, movie theaters emptied, and hospitals filled.

The National Basketball Association, Major League Baseball, and the National Hockey League all suspended their seasons. For the first time since its inception in 1939, college basketball's March Madness tournament was canceled. And for the first time since September 11, and only the fourth time ever, Disneyland closed its gates.

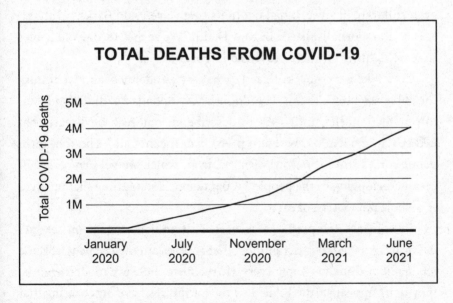

Today, as I am writing these words, the World Health Organization reports more than 183 million confirmed cases of COVID-19 so far around the globe, and nearly 4 million deaths. The Americas were hit hardest, with more than 70 million cases. More than 50 million people in

Europe have been diagnosed with the disease and more than 35 million in Southeast Asia. Four million known cases have been treated in Africa.[3]

The United States of America has been one of the most affected nations on earth, so far as we know—about 33 million confirmed cases, resulting in approximately 600,000 deaths.[4] Many of us know someone who died from this pandemic.

Even as I'm writing this, I'm not sure the worst is over. Today's headlines say: "India's Health Care System in 'Total Collapse' As COVID Surge 'Ravages' Country." In the spring of 2021, that country began experiencing the world's worst outbreak, with more than 400,000 new cases each day. The reports painted a picture of overwhelming tragedy—hospitals short on basic medical supplies, patients dying from oxygen shortages, and families dressed in full protective suits at mass cremations.

"The virus and its second wave is hitting the younger people, and even children, in a way it had not in its first wave," said Barkha Dutt, an author and journalist based in New Delhi. "We've met 18-day-old babies that are fighting for their lives inside ICUs."[5]

Let's take a step back. Exactly what are pandemics, and what does the Bible say about them? The English word *pandemic* didn't show up in our dictionaries until 1853 to describe an outbreak of disease that exceeds an epidemic. The Latin prefix *pan* means "all." The root term *demic* comes from the word *demotic*, from which we get *democracy*. It means "belonging to the people." A pandemic is something that involves the whole population of earth.

By contrast, the prefix *epi* is a Greek term meaning "upon" or "at" or "near." An *epidemic* is an illness that spreads among the people. But a *pandemic* spreads to people everywhere. Since these are modern words, they don't appear in the Bible. But the Scriptures have other terms that describe the same thing. In fact, there are six ancient words in the original Hebrew and Greek texts of the Bible that describe what we would call a pandemic. The Bible uses those words 127 times!

In the New King James Version of the Bible, the word *pestilence*

occurs forty-two times. When I checked this word in my dictionary, it said: "A very contagious or infectious epidemic disease that is
virulent and devastating . . . something that is destructive or pernicious." Another word we see scores of times in the Bible is *plague*.
The dictionary defines it as: "An epidemic disease causing a high rate
of mortality; a disastrous evil or affliction." Additionally, the word
disease often occurs in Scripture, sometimes in ways that suggest
widespread illness.

Not every use of *pestilence*, *plague*, and *disease* in Scripture refers
to a pandemic of spreadable, infectious illness. But many of those references do.[6]

Throughout the Bible, we see repeated examples of God using diseases to accomplish His divine and sovereign purposes.

In Exodus 9, the Lord allowed an infectious skin disease to sweep
over Egypt. It was the fourth plague, and it was epidemic in nature. Every
single Egyptian, young and old, was affected. As the Israelites left Egypt,
the Lord commanded them to follow and obey Him, for, He said, "I will
put none of the diseases on you which I have brought on the Egyptians"
(15:26). On the other hand, God warned His people that disobedience
would bring "wasting disease and fever which shall consume the eyes
and cause sorrow of heart" (Lev. 26:16).

When King David sinned against Israel, the Lord "sent a plague
upon Israel from the morning till the appointed time" (2 Sam. 24:15).
Many people lost their lives in this epidemic.

This isn't to say all illnesses are God-initiated or that He sent COVID-
19 to the earth. We live in a world corrupted by sin, and diseases of all
kinds are one of the consequences of that corruption. Still, the Lord is
not ignorant of what's happening in our world.

The Bible also teaches Satan can send plagues and illnesses. We
know from the biblical story of Job that Satan can afflict humanity with
terrible diseases (Job 2:7). All around us are powerful forces for good
and evil in the unseen world. When global catastrophic events happen,
I often wonder about the extent of demonic activity. We battle enemies

described in the Bible as "principalities . . . powers . . . rulers of the darkness of this age . . . spiritual hosts of wickedness in the heavenly places" (Eph. 6:12).

In the Gospels, the Lord Jesus Christ warned His disciples that "pestilences" will be one of the signs of the last days of human history. These ravaging illnesses will shake the world, seeking to awaken and warn people about the imminence of Christ's return to judge and reign (Matt. 24:7).

In the book of Revelation, the Lord warned a dozen times about terrible pestilence and plagues coming to the nations as part of His judgment of sin, prior to the second coming of Christ. This period is known by Bible scholars as the Great Tribulation (Rev. 7:14), the most devastating period of divine judgment in human history.

A year before the coronavirus hit our world, I wrote a book titled *The Book of Signs*. What I said in that book is as close to predictive prophecy as anything I've ever written. How sobering to read it now after all that has happened!

> It is tempting to believe that modern science has eliminated the fear of plague, but today we may be on the verge of the worst plagues the world has ever known. . . . I am referring to plagues of bacteria that are fast becoming resistant to almost every drug and antibiotic. Even now they are called "nightmare bacteria" and they presently stalk hospitals all over the world. . . .
>
> These new germs contain special genes that allow them to pass their resistance to other germs, spreading disease to "apparently healthy people in the hospital—such as patients, doctors or nurses— who in turn can act as silent carriers of illness, infecting others even if they don't become sick."
>
> In addition to these "super germs," drug resistance in general has been growing, mainly because of the widespread use of antimicrobials and antibiotics in humans and animals. When antibiotics and antimicrobials kill off the weak strains, stronger strains of resistant bacteria

survive and keep growing. Calls for new antibiotic therapies have been issued, but new drug development is becoming rarer. Estimates are that 700,000 to several million deaths result each year from these bacteria. And each year in the United States, at least two million people become infected with bacteria that are resistant to antibiotics, causing at least 23,000 people to die as a result.[7]

What Does This Mean?

My youngest son, Daniel, works for the NFL Network and has become acquainted with many of the football players in the league. Shortly after the COVID-19 pandemic was announced, one of his high-profile friends who watches our *Turning Point* television program came to him and said, "Ask your dad if the coronavirus is in biblical prophecy." I ended up preaching an entire message in answer to that question, and it's had over three million views on YouTube.

Have you asked yourself the same question? Let's face it, the pandemic feels like something we've read about in the Bible. After all, it's the most apocalyptic thing that has ever happened to most of us. Does COVID-19 mean anything set against the larger scale of history? And if so, what?

During the last week of His life, the Lord Jesus left the temple in Jerusalem with His disciples, hiked down the Kidron Valley, and climbed to the top of the Mount of Olives. The city of Jerusalem spread out before them, shimmering in the setting sun. That's when the disciples asked Jesus about the last days, prompting our Lord's most comprehensive teaching on the events related to the end of the world and His glorious return. We call this the Olivet Discourse, and it's recorded in the Gospels of Matthew, Mark, and Luke.

Now as He sat on the Mount of Olives, the disciples came to Him privately, saying, "Tell us, when will these things be? And what will be the sign of Your coming, and of the end of the age?" And Jesus answered and said to them: "Take heed that no one deceives you. For many will come in My name, saying, 'I am the Christ,' and will deceive many. And you will hear of wars and rumors of wars. See that you are not troubled; for all these things must come to pass, but the end is not yet. For nation will rise against nation, and kingdom against kingdom. And there will be famines, pestilences, and earthquakes in various places. All these are the beginning of sorrows." (Matt. 24:3–8)

This passage is so extensive that many have called it the "mini-apocalypse." The broad outline of the prophetic future is given to us here by our Lord. It's His overture to the book of Revelation.

Jesus' disciples asked Him three questions:

1. When will these things be?
2. What will be the sign of Your coming?
3. What will be the sign of the end of the age?

Beginning in Matthew 24:4, Jesus answered those questions. He answered questions two and three in the main body of the chapter, but He didn't answer the first question ("When will these things be?") until verse 36, when He said: "But of that day and hour no one knows, not even the angels of heaven, but My Father only."

That's why I can't tell you the exact time of the second coming. How many people have erred in making misguided predictions about that date! But what I can tell you is this: In answering the disciples' second and third questions, Jesus gave us six key signs pointing to His second coming, or, as He put it in verse 30, "the sign of the Son of Man [appearing] in heaven."

Here are the six things that Jesus said would happen as His second coming began to draw near:

1. Deception by false Christs (vv. 4–5)
2. Disputes and warfare among nations (vv. 6–7)
3. Disease and famine worldwide (vv. 7–8)
4. Deliverance of believers to tribulation (v. 9)
5. Defection of false believers (vv. 10–13)
6. Declaration of the gospel to the whole world (v. 14)

These six signs cover the first three-and-one-half years of the seven-year tribulation period, and they coincide with the prophecies of the book of Revelation. But while these signs will be fulfilled in the seven-year tribulation period, they will not start on a dime. They will build up over time.

I believe we're now seeing early evidence of these signs.

According to Jesus, the generation that sees these signs will also see His second coming: "Now learn this parable from the fig tree: When its branch has already become tender and puts forth leaves, you know that summer is near. So you also, when you see all these things, know that it is near—at the doors! Assuredly, I say to you, this generation will by no means pass away till all these things take place" (Matt. 24:32–34).

If you've followed my teachings over the years, you know I've always believed the Bible predicts the return of Christ for His church, which could occur at any moment now. This event is known as the rapture. Then there will be seven years of global tribulation, the last half of which will be the great tribulation—a unique outpouring of God's wrath as the world hurtles toward Armageddon. When that period concludes, Jesus will return with His church to put an end to global conflicts and pandemics, to judge evil, and to establish His thousand-year kingdom.

So, there are no events predicting the rapture. Without any sign, without any warning, Jesus Christ will return to gather His saints and take them to heaven.

Perhaps you're wondering, *If these six signs are not signs of the rapture—and if after the rapture we're going to be in heaven—why should we be concerned about the signs?* Because future events cast their shadows before them! God's people should be Bible students. Bible students should be interested in prophetic passages. And when we study those prophetic passages, we should learn to spot the signs of the times.

Recently I clipped something from the writings of Mark Hitchcock about this:

> Dr. John Walvoord used to share an apt illustration of how signs of the times relate to the Rapture and the Second Coming. He pointed out how there are all kinds of signs for Christmas. There are lights everywhere, decorations, Christmas trees, music, and even Santa in the mall. But Thanksgiving can sneak up on you. There are no real signs for Thanksgiving. Dr. Walvoord noted that the second coming of Christ is like Christmas. It will be preceded by many very specific signs that Scripture outlines. The Rapture, however, is like Thanksgiving. There are no specific signs for its coming. Yet, if it's fall and you already begin to see the signs of Christmas everywhere, and Thanksgiving has not arrived, then you know that Thanksgiving must be very near. The signs of "Christmas" seem to be appearing all around us today. The coming of Christ to rapture His church could be very near.[8]

Let me circle back once more to the big question on many of our minds: Is COVID-19 a sign of the *rapture*? No. There are no signs of any kind for the rapture. The rapture is a signless, imminent event.

But is this pandemic a sign of the *second coming* of Christ? Possibly. I cannot say with certainty that it is. But neither can I say it is not. It could well be early evidence of number three on Jesus' list of signs—disease and famine worldwide. As I mentioned earlier, some of the tribulation signs could spill over into the final years before the rapture.

Jesus said this "pestilence" would arrive like "birth pains" (Matt. 24:8 NIV). This means it will increase in frequency and intensity in the time leading up to His return. In other words, as the end approaches, we should expect infectious disease outbreaks to occur more frequently, impact more people, and be more deadly.

John MacArthur suggested that "the present afflictions may merely be like Braxton-Hicks contractions—premature labor pains—but they nonetheless signify that the time for hard labor, and then delivery, is inevitable and quickly drawing near."[9]

So, while the coronavirus may not perfectly qualify as a prophetic sign, it is nonetheless a sign. It's hard to see the world so convulsed by an event without looking at it through the lens of Scripture and learning its lessons. Even if COVID-19 is not a sign of the future, it is a sign for today—a reminder of things we too easily forget.

Four lessons have been foremost in my mind.

The Vulnerability of Us All

First, we're all more vulnerable than we like to think.

John C. Lennox, emeritus professor of mathematics at the University of Oxford, wrote, "Many of us had got used to a fairly stable world, where life was reasonably predictable. Now that all appears to be crumbling away: the things we have always counted on have gone and we are exposed as never before to forces way outside our control. People fear for their health, both physical and psychological; for their families and friends, particularly the elderly and infirm; for their social networks, their food supply, their jobs and economic security, and a host of other things."[10]

According to most reports, the elderly and those with an underlying health condition were the most vulnerable to the virus. But as time progressed, we discovered that everyone was vulnerable, including celebrities we sometimes think live in a bubble. Entertainers Tom Hanks, Rita Wilson, Rachel Matthews, and Charlotte Lawrence were some of the first to become infected with the coronavirus.

NBA stars Rudy Gobert, Donovan Mitchell, Kevin Durant, and Marcus Smart, along with the coach of the NFL's New Orleans Saints, Sean Payton, became sick with this disease.

The vice president of Iran, the wife of the Canadian prime minister, and the mayor of Miami got the virus. And as we all watched, so did President Donald Trump.

We've been led to believe that with enough money we can protect ourselves from things like this. No longer. Money can buy you a test, but it cannot buy you invincibility. We're all vulnerable to these super-plagues. No one is safe. No one escapes the possibility of infection.

The Credibility of the Bible

For more than fifty years I have been seriously studying the Bible. I've never failed to be astounded by the events of the tribulation as they unfold in the book of Revelation and elsewhere in Scripture. I've believed them not because I understood how they could happen, but because they were in the Bible. Now, these apocalyptic events seem to be knocking on the door.

The prophet Ezekiel predicted a coming war in which Russia and its coalition armies will try to destroy the nation of Israel. I believe this will happen in the early days of the tribulation. When God intervenes, the evil coalition armies will be destroyed by monumental convulsions of the earth, by military confusion, by multiple calamities like fire and brimstone, and finally by major plagues. The Lord predicts, "I will bring him to judgment with pestilence and bloodshed" (Ezek. 38:22). It will take seven months to bury the bodies (39:12).

Try to imagine it! Unburied bodies everywhere, causing a sickening stench and a malignant plague. According to Ezekiel, God will summon vast flocks of birds to the Middle East to devour the bodies scattered across the land. It will be a "sacrificial meal" for the scavengers (vv. 17–20).

As I saw pictures of the body bags and temporary morgues being utilized to care for the coronavirus victims in New York City, I thought of what Ezekiel said. It's not that the pandemic was fulfilling Ezekiel's prophecies, but perhaps it serves as a faint preview of what's ahead.

In Revelation 9:18, a third of the earth perishes by various plagues caused by demonic forces. In Revelation 11, the two supernatural witnesses have power "to strike the earth with all plagues, as often as they desire" (v. 6). That warning isn't limited to pandemics, but neither does it exclude infectious diseases.

Let's just say I now have a greater understanding of how the tribulation events could take place. When you read those sections of the Bible, read them carefully and prayerfully, and look for emerging trends. The events in Revelation no longer seem implausible. Indeed, they seem to be impending.

The Uncertainty of Life

Contagions also remind us of the uncertainty of life. Did you expect your schedule to be wiped out for an entire year? Were you prepared for your children to be shut out of their classrooms? For your vacation or your wedding to be canceled? For your workload to shift to your kitchen table?

No one expected to stay away from church for weeks or months. How terrible for those who were laid off or whose businesses failed. Few people had their pantries stocked with sanitizers, masks, and toilet paper. Who could have known?

According to the apostle James, we should not be surprised by the unexpected. He wrote this to the scattered Jewish believers: "You do not know what will happen tomorrow. For what is your life? It is even a vapor that appears for a little time and then vanishes away" (James 4:14).

Earlier in this chapter, I mentioned the patriarch Job. Do you remember how he explained the sudden deconstruction of his life? He said:

- "Now my days are swifter than a runner; they flee away, they see no good. They pass by like swift ships, like an eagle swooping on its prey" (Job 9:25–26).
- "Man who is born of woman is of few days and full of trouble. He comes forth like a flower and fades away; he flees like a shadow and does not continue" (14:1–2).

How uncertain and precious are our days! I hope you've used some of this mandated quiet time to reflect on life and give thanks to God for the days and months and years He has given to you.

The Sufficiency of Jesus

The virus also points us to Jesus' sufficiency. As He was preparing to finish His earthly work and return to heaven, He told His disciples: "These things I have spoken to you, that in Me you may have peace. In the world you will have tribulation; but be of good cheer, I have overcome the world" (John 16:33).

That's a familiar verse, but look at it with a fresh pair of eyes. Notice the phrase *in Me*. The Lord's promise to the disciples was the promise of Himself. His peace was to be found in Him!

Jesus didn't say, "In the world you will have tribulation, but I have overcome *tribulation*." No, He said, "In the world you will have tribulation, but I have overcome the *world*." Jesus doesn't just overcome the event. He overcomes the environment in which the event occurs.

That's incredible! Jesus comes to you in the midst of the struggle, when the battle is almost unbearable and the circumstances look impossible. With the voice of absolute certainty and strength, He speaks to you of peace and bestows the encouragement you need. He raises your morale and fills you with strength. He says to you: "My peace I give to you; not as the world gives do I give to you. Let not your heart be troubled, neither let it be afraid" (John 14:27).

Where Do We Go from Here?

I mentioned earlier that actor Tom Hanks and his wife, Rita Wilson, were among the millions of Americans who contracted COVID-19, endured the symptoms of the disease, and then did their best to return to a "normal" way of life. Afterward, Hanks made a point of tweeting about his experience in an effort to lessen the anxiety others might be feeling about the pandemic.

"[It's] going to take a while but if we take care of each other, help where we can, and give up some comforts . . . this, too, shall pass," Hanks posted. "We can figure this out."[11]

That's what we're all doing, isn't it? Trying to take care of ourselves and one another. Trying to move forward. Trying to figure this out.

But what about the possibility that COVID-19 is a sign of the end times? Based on the things we've learned about biblical prophecy and the pandemic, what should we do now? How is the Lord calling us to action?

Let me offer five suggestions on how Christians can continue to live for God during any present or future pandemic.

Prioritize Your Prayer Life

Oh, how this season has driven us to prayer! Don't you suppose the people of earth have prayed more in the last eighteen months than ever before? The more problems, the more prayer. But what kind of prayers have we prayed? Biblical prayers are the best kind, and the prayer of Jehoshaphat in 2 Chronicles 20 has been ringing in my mind. It's highly appropriate for today.

King Jehoshaphat faced an existential crisis when multiple armies headed toward his little nation of Judah. He responded with masterful spiritual leadership. He was determined to trust God and to lead his nation to do the same. He didn't merely trust the Lord in the face of potential military defeat; he was ready to trust God for any disaster looming ahead.

He prayed, "If disaster comes upon us—sword, judgment, pestilence, or famine—we will stand before this temple and in Your presence (for Your name is in this temple), and cry out to You in our affliction, and You will hear and save" (v. 9).

In verses 5–12, the king offered a model prayer. He appealed to God's character, His promises, and His actions in the past. The prayer ended with these superb words: "We have no power against this great multitude that is coming against us; nor do we know what to do, but our eyes are upon You" (v. 12)

A pastor of an international church in China said:

Perhaps you feel powerless against a virus to which you can be exposed even when there are no visible symptoms. Maybe your anxiety rises as specialists still aren't sure all the ways this virus can be transmitted. You might feel discouraged as you watch the infection and death tolls rise. If so, join with Jehoshaphat in declaring that you are helpless, but your hope is fixed on God Almighty.

How many of our prayers should end with a line like this? This is the posture of the Christian. Appeal to God's character, confess your inability, and put your eyes on the Lord.[12]

Sacrificially Serve Others

Despite the hardships of the pandemic, there will never be enough ink to tell the stories of those who, even during this awful time, found ways of serving. Lisa Racine, fifty-eight, worked full time as a project manager for a printing company. But when the virus hit, she adjusted her schedule to take on another job. She started working two or three nights a week at a nursing home. She wanted to serve others, but she especially wanted to serve one person.

Her father was a resident of that nursing home, and she longed to be with him. So she mopped floors, helped in the kitchen, and washed dishes to be near her dad. She violated no regulations, and the nursing home staff knew of the connection. But the job gave her a chance to serve. The first time she entered her dad's room, she was so covered with layers of protective gear he didn't recognize her.

"It's me, Dad!" she said. Those were the best three words in the world to him.[13]

I'll bet you found ways to serve others too. Didn't you find it a great blessing? Don't let that momentum come to an end just because we get back to "normal" life. Moments of danger present opportunities for service, but so do moments that are more mundane.

Also, remember that when the physical needs of this current crisis come to a close, our nation and our world will still have myriad spiritual needs. Which means we will still have opportunities to serve!

During the early days of the pandemic, there were painful food shortages in East County, San Diego, where I live. For several weeks, our church devoted the morning hours of Friday to feeding the hungry. We packed boxes with staples like toilet paper, paper towels, and soap. Into another box went food. As people drove through our parking lot, we placed those two boxes in the trunks of their cars. Before they left the parking lot, we added a gallon of milk and a loaf of bread.

By the time we were finished, we had touched more than 1,800 different families, given out 27,000 boxes of food, and prayed with hundreds of families as they rolled down their windows to say thank you.

We helped a lot of hungry people during those days, but we also met the need of hundreds of our people who had a different kind of hunger: the intense craving to do something that would make things better for the hurting people in our community. Under the leadership of David St. John, one of our pastors, we sacrificially served, and it was an indescribable joy.

As Martin Luther put it, "If you wish to serve Christ and to wait on him, very well, you have your sick neighbor close at hand. Go to him and serve him, and you will surely find Christ in him."[14]

Count Your Blessings

Then what? We get out our calculators and start counting our blessings. The Bible says, "From his abundance we have all received one gracious blessing after another" (John 1:16 NLT).

Paul wrote, "Blessed be the God and Father of our Lord Jesus Christ, who has blessed us with every spiritual blessing in the heavenly places in Christ" (Eph. 1:3).

God has blessed us with every spiritual blessing in the heavenly places in Christ—period! In times like these, our blessings become clearer, richer, and more meaningful. Something happens deep in our hearts when we count those blessings.

When life causes us to slow down, our focus sharpens. The peripheral values that clutter our lives fall away, and we can focus on existential issues and eternal blessings—the ones we overlook when we're too busy. Haven't you noticed how the simple blessings of life are often the best ones?

The Bible says, "In everything give thanks; for this is the will of God in Christ Jesus for you" (1 Thess. 5:18).

Corrie ten Boom, in *The Hiding Place*, relates an incident that taught her always to be thankful. She and her sister, Betsie, had just been transferred to the worst German prison camp they had seen yet: Ravensbruck. On entering the barracks, they found it extremely overcrowded. Worse yet, it was infested with fleas.

On the morning of their arrival, the sisters had been studying 1 Thessalonians—a text that reminded them to rejoice always, pray constantly, and give thanks in all circumstances. Betsie told Corrie to stop and thank the Lord for every detail of their new living quarters. Corrie at first flatly refused to give thanks for the fleas, but Betsie persisted, and Corrie finally succumbed to her pleadings.

Then something unexpected happened. During the months spent in that camp, the sisters were surprised to find how openly they could hold Bible studies and prayer meetings without interference from their guards. Both Corrie and Betsie were dumbfounded by their unexpected freedom, although it was greatly appreciated.

It wasn't until several months later that they learned the truth. The reason the guards would not enter the barracks was because of the fleas![15] The little pests became just another blessing to count.

Stay Calm and Carry On

Gratitude will help us to stay calm and carry on, as the British said during World War II. The Bible teaches, "God has not given us a spirit of fear, but of power and of love and of a sound mind" (2 Tim. 1:7).

The Lord created your human imagination to be a powerful force.

It can create beautiful visions of a desirable future or it can conjure up worst-case scenarios. These dark products of the imagination can put you in the grip of fear—a place God would never have you go.

As this Scripture verse shows, the power that banishes fear is a sound mind. We maintain a sound mind by "bringing every thought into captivity to the obedience of Christ" (2 Cor. 10:5).

When an unhealthy thought enters your head ("I'm sick"; "All is lost"; "I'm going to die!"), examine it in light of the knowledge of God. Does this thought have any basis in reality? If not, take it captive. Don't give it free rein in your mind. Don't let it lead your imagination away from God's goodness and into unhealthy fear.

When Isobel Kuhn was fighting cancer, she realized the real enemy was something too deep for the surgeon's scalpel. It lay in the invisible world of her imagination. She wrote, "I had to refuse to allow my imagination to play with my future. That future, I believe, is ordered of God, and no man can guess it. For me to let myself imagine how or when the end would come was not only unprofitable, it was definitely harmful, so I had to bring my thoughts into captivity that they might not dishonour Christ."[16]

Gaining a sound and centered mind is not as difficult as you think. If we simply read the Scriptures deeply, thoughtfully, and openly every day, we will invite the Holy Spirit to whisper new strength into our thoughts. He and He alone can tame the reckless power of the human mind. A mind centered on the truth of God is the key to His sustaining grace. He will keep you from losing heart.[17]

The best definition I've ever heard of anxiety is "imagining the future without Jesus in it." Have you done some of that?

When we realize that Jesus is present today and will be present tomorrow, we can be set free from worry. As someone said, "Worry is faith in the negative, trust in the unpleasant, assurance of disaster, and belief in defeat. Worry is wasting today's time to clutter up tomorrow's opportunities with yesterday's troubles."

Do the Next Right Thing

Finally, we have to keep busy with whatever God assigns us day by day.

When we were first quarantined in our home, Donna and I realized how easy it'd be to just float along with no schedule, no plan, no objectives. When your normal routine is taken away, what do you do? It's easy to just drift along. But we quickly realized doing so left us exhausted at the end of the day. You probably discovered the same thing. Living life without a daily plan leads to discouragement and fatigue.

So we learned the power of doing "the next right thing." In other words, we learned to just keep doing the work assigned to us as best we could. The pandemic might change the type or intensity of our work, but as long as God keeps us on earth, He has jobs for us each day.

I found encouragement along these lines in something J. R. Miller wrote: "We try to settle our duty in *large sections*. We think of *years* rather than of *moments*; of life-work rather than of individual acts. It is hard to plan a year's duty; it is easy to plan just for one short day. No shoulder can bear up the burden of a year's cares—all gathered up into one load! But the weakest shoulder can carry without weariness—just what really belongs to *one day*."[18]

Doing the next right thing is great advice, and that's how Jesus teaches us to live. Emily P. Freeman has written extensively about this, and in one of her books, she said:

> So often, right after Jesus performed a miracle, he gave a simple next thing to do.
>
> To the leper, he said to tell no one, "But go and show yourself to the priest" (Luke 5:14).
>
> To the paralytic, he said, "Get up, pick up your stretcher, and go home" (v. 24).
>
> To Jairus and his wife, after raising their daughter from the dead, when he had their full and complete attention, and when chances were

good he could get them to swear their lives away for his sake, he did not perform a lecture about dedicating their lives to him or about what grand plans he had for their girl now that she was alive. Instead, he told them to give her something to eat (8:55). After raising their daughter from the actual dead, the one thing Jesus told them in the face of their rapt attention was to go make lunch. At first glance, that seems like a waste of a captive audience.

Rather than a life plan, a clear vision, or a five-year list of goals, the leper, the paralytic, and Jairus and his wife were given clear instructions by Jesus about what to do next—and only *next*. . . .

But what about for us? Let's take our cues from Jesus . . . by considering what it means for us to do the next right thing *now*. Not the next big thing. Not the next impressive thing. Just the next right thing in front of us.[19]

Emily made this discovery about Jesus and the art of doing the next right thing during her last two years of college. Because parking on campus was a nightmare, she'd arrive an hour early to find a space. During her extra hour she began listening to Elisabeth Elliot's radio program.

One day, Elisabeth quoted an old poem. Though Elisabeth had updated the language slightly, it still had its rustic simplicity. That poem profoundly impacted Emily, and she tracked down the original.

That poem was called "Doe Ye Nexte Thynge," by Minnie Paull, who was a writer, musician, and pastor's wife. Elisabeth's revised version was "Do the Next Thing." This is the poem that impacted Emily P. Freeman, and it has touched me too.

So many people have been helped by this poem, I wanted to end this chapter by giving a portion of it to you:

Fear not tomorrows, child of the King,
Trust them with Jesus, *do the next thing*
Do it immediately, do it with prayer;

Do it reliantly, casting all care;
Do it with reverence, tracing His hand
Who placed it before thee with earnest command.
Stayed on Omnipotence, safe 'neath His wing,
Leave all results, *do the next thing.*[20]

A cashless society. Cryptocurrency. Microchipping people. Is this what the prophets were talking about when they described a future in which those who may buy and sell will have to bear a particular mark: the mark of the beast?

It is getting harder to sort this all out when so many signs are appearing in the financial world. Greed and materialism are ever-present. The gap between the rich and poor is widening at an astonishing rate. Discontent is common when what we have falls short of what we think we should have.

As believers we must face these things with biblical insight and a measured tone. While keeping our eyes wide open to all that is happening around us, we must focus on Christ and trust in Him. The financial world will get more chaotic as we approach the end of the age. But Jesus Christ is the same, yesterday, today, and forever!

Chapter 4

A Financial Prophecy— Economic Chaos

No one may buy or sell except one who has the mark or the name of the beast.

REVELATION 13:17

Stylishly bearded and wearing a baseball cap, Jowan Österlund pulls on a pair of surgical gloves and uses a wipe to sterilize the top of his client's hand. Then with a quick jab, Österlund inserts a preloaded syringe into the man's skin. The man gasps as a tiny microchip, about the size of a grain of rice and encased in silicate glass, enters his body. It invisibly imbeds itself into his hand as the man exclaims, "I'm a cyborg!"

What do you think? Is that clip from a horror movie or a dystopian television show? Or could it be from the nightly news?

You guessed it. This procedure didn't take place in a dark movie or in the middle of a criminal lair. It happened in the clean and bright offices of a company in Sweden specializing in biochips—Biohax International— where Österlund is the CEO. He estimates he has chipped more than six thousand Swedes during the six years his company has been in business.

The microchip he injects into clients uses radio-frequency technology. You might have a similar chip in your dog or cat. Chipping pets is a popular way of tracking them if they get lost. But human microchipping is more sophisticated, and it offers a broader range of applications. The chip can be used to open secure doors or log into computers with only the wave of a hand.

It can also be used for contactless payments. When the chip is linked with bank or credit accounts, users can access funds by swiping their hand over payment terminals. Actual credit cards are no longer needed. The technology has literally gotten under your skin.

And it's coming soon to a hand near you! Imbedded microchips will offer you a world without keys, wallets, or other encumbering items—a world where everything is accessible with just a touch. In the future, such biochips will detect illnesses, monitor your vital signs, and send instant messages to your doctor.

Of course, they could potentially be used to track your movements, reveal your secrets, and inform a totalitarian government what you're feeling and saying. Exciting? Frightening?

Österlund believes his company's success is connected to Sweden's culture of embracing new technology—technology that still frightens people in other parts of the world. "The geopolitical situation historically gives us the kind of initial higher trust in the government," he said. "I think a lot of people would be way more apprehensive in a lot of countries."[1]

Maybe you're thinking, *Doesn't the Bible say something about this sort of thing? Haven't I heard about something being stamped in our hands or foreheads?*

You're right! The evolving biometric chip technology reminds us of a prophecy found in Revelation 13:16–17—a passage predicting something that will happen at the end of history during the great tribulation.

He causes all, both small and great, rich and poor, free and slave, to receive a mark on their right hand or on their foreheads, and that no one may buy or sell except one who has the mark or the name of the beast, or the number of his name.

Could the technology being produced by Österlund and many others be a foreshadowing of this *mark of the beast*? That's worth considering. This technology is emerging more quickly than we realize, and I suspect we'll soon be facing personal choices. The appeal and convenience of these innovations is palpable, and the pressure to submit to it may be powerful, especially if you work for a business, school, or industry in which this becomes the uniform behavior. Its innocent uses may be enticing.

But wait! Imagine this technology in the wrong hands. Could it be leading us toward the days when a centralized government will control, attack, punish, or monitor us? All technology, in the wrong hands, can become a tool of terror. High-tech and scientific innovation is flying into our world like runaway meteors. Even your cellphone is increasingly invasive. Imagine that in the wrong hands.

And the wrong hands are already grasping for control.

So yes, without being dogmatic or alarmist, it feels like biometric chips could be a precursor of Revelation 13. We'll take a deeper look at that passage and its ramifications later in this chapter.

For now, let's consider Österlund's claim that people in some countries might be "apprehensive" about having microchips or similar technology imbedded beneath their skin. Is he correct? Are people pushing back at invasive technology?

It doesn't look like it. I see multitudes of people—entire nations—choosing to hardwire their lives to devices and move from the physical world toward the digital one without looking back. This includes digitizing our relationships, our news, our entertainment, our politics, our health. And yes, even our money.

The move toward electronic finances began in the early 1900s when department stores and a few gas companies began issuing their own proprietary cards. In 1946, John Biggins introduced Charge-It cards, and the Diners Club card showed up in 1950. American Express came along in 1958, and soon thereafter credit card companies introduced the idea—very lucrative for them—of revolving credit. With the onset of the Internet, everything became digitalized. Now, like it or not, we're all relying on the security and trustworthiness of electronic systems and massive banks to manage our savings and handle our finances. Few people are stuffing cash under their beds or stockpiling physical commodities such as gold, jewels, or currency.

Today, as you may know from experience, most workers receive their salaries as direct deposits into their bank accounts, which they access through websites and smartphone apps. We can buy almost anything we want with the click of a mouse or the tap of a finger—downloadable entertainment, mutual funds, household items, and even entire homes.

Cash and checks are practically obsolete. Remember those birthday cards with a special slot for a check or a dollar bill? That's yesterday's gift. Now grandparents transfer money instantly through apps like PayPal or Venmo. A growing number of churches collect their tithes through digital platforms. In fact, it was crucial to many churches during the pandemic when the act of passing an offering plate was deemed a health risk.

That trend has been accelerating in the twenty-first century. According to the 2019 Federal Reserve Payments Study, there were 174.2 billion non-cash payments processed in the United States in 2018, which was an increase of more than 30 billion from 2015. Those payments carried a total value of $97 *trillion*! Also, 2018 was the first time there were more ACH debit transfers (16.6 billion) than check payments (14.5 billion). To give some context, the year 2000 saw only 2.1 billion debit transfers and a whopping 42.6 billion check payments.[2]

Of course, all of those trends received a shot of steroids in 2020. A survey conducted in the middle of the pandemic found that 60 percent of us planned to exclusively use digital or contactless payment methods in the future. Shockingly, a full third of respondents (32 percent) were in favor of removing all paper money and coins from circulation.[3]

One more item deserves mention: the rise of all-digital currencies, also known as cryptocurrencies. While national currencies such as the dollar or the euro are officially backed by government reserves, digital currencies are decentralized. They don't have a physical foundation in gold or other tangible assets. Instead, cryptocurrencies exist entirely in the world of cyberspace. They are produced online, stored online, and spent online.

Incredibly, there are more than 6,500 cryptocurrencies circulating in the world today. The most famous is Bitcoin, but others include Ethereum, Dogecoin, Litecoin, and more.[4]

Many see these digital currencies as the wave of the future. They imagine a world where physical currency has been entirely removed and all transactions are processed digitally. Many voices are even declaring the need for a Central Bank Digital Currency (CBDC), which would be a government-backed cryptocurrency designed to be the legal tender of a nation—or perhaps of the entire world.

As one writer declared, "CBDC brings together the convenience and security of cryptocurrencies and the regulated, reserve-backed money circulation of the traditional banking system. CBDC will likely be a game changer, bringing about a rapid shift to the banking ecosystem as more consumers and businesses adapt to a safe and low-cost way of accruing, storing and exchanging value."[5]

To me, the rise of digital currencies feels more sinister than spectacular—especially with the specter of a government-sponsored form of digital tender. The idea of government officials being able to access the financial records and transaction histories of ordinary citizens is frightening. And the idea of those same officials being able to hack, withdraw, or freeze those funds with impunity is terrifying.

More and more, people in the Western world are buying, selling, and giving not with physical money—coins and bills—but through a series of touches on a small screen. We love the convenience of managing our accounts from our palms. For most of us, this technology is still on the outside of our hand, in our smartphones. But it's only two millimeters from where Österlund would like it to be: under our skin.

What does all this mean for our future? And is it a sign of the end times? How does this affect the followers of the Lamb right now—today? Let's turn to Scripture for some answers.

What Does This Mean?

As we've seen throughout these pages, it's difficult to make definitive statements about future events. There are so many variables at play. Even when we have general principles and prophecies from God's Word to guide us, we must be careful about turning those principles and prophecies into specific predictions about people, places, and events. I don't want to leave the impression a Swedish biochip is necessarily and definitively the biblical mark of the beast. But it's hard not to see some obvious trend lines, and there's one thing I can say with confidence: money will play an essential role in future events, including the end times.

Money has always been important in the past, and everything connected with economics is increasingly important today. It's driving our world. I think we can assume money will remain important in the future, and that it will dominate our world even more in days to come.

The Bible is rich with information on this topic. Specifically, Scripture reveals that money will have an impact on the end times, both leading up to and during the period known as the tribulation. Let's talk about three of the most important financial signs of the end times.

The Addiction to Money

How would you feel if someone offered to give you $3.6 million? Most of us would be elated!

Not Sam Polk. As a Wall Street trader, Sam rubbed elbows with some of the wealthiest people in the world every day. He knew the power they possessed, not just financially, but in every aspect of life. He craved the same kind of significance. It was a world of rare air, a world all its own.

And he was so close! Just a little more, and he'd enter the life he'd always dreamed of living.

But when Sam's boss called him to his office and declared his yearly bonus would be $3.6 million, Sam didn't feel elated. He wanted $8 million, and he felt angry at the idea of a smaller sum.

In his words:

> I was angry because it wasn't big enough. I was 30 years old, had no children to raise, no debts to pay, no philanthropic goal in mind. I wanted more money for exactly the same reason an alcoholic needs another drink: I was addicted.[6]

One day Sam Polk saw himself in the mirror, as it were. He was shattered to see what he'd become. Leaving Wall Street, he started a family and launched a better life for himself. Few people escape the clutches of greed, so I congratulate Sam.

Only God knows how many Sam Polks are in this world—people who are addicted to money, wealth, possessions, and the feelings of power those resources can bring. Let's be honest. There's some of Sam Polk in you and me—in all of us. Only an overriding love of Jesus Christ will keep us balanced.

Here's where biblical prophecy comes in. According to Scripture, people will become increasingly greedy in the last days. The Bible says: "But know this, that in the last days perilous times will come: For men will be . . . lovers of money" (2 Tim. 3:1–2).

It's easy to think of Wall Street when we read those verses, but we must grapple with this personally. Paul said the end times will be a period defined by rejecting what is good and running to embrace what is evil, much of which will be centered on an ever-increasing appetite for money.

That matches what Paul had previously written to Timothy: "For the love of money is a root of all kinds of evil, for which some have strayed from the faith in their greediness, and pierced themselves through with many sorrows" (1 Tim. 6:10).

Listen to John Piper's words about this:

> God deals in the currency of grace, not money. . . . Money is the currency of human resources. So, the heart that loves money is a heart that pins its hopes, and pursues its pleasures, and puts its trust in what human resources can offer. So the love of money is virtually the same as faith in money—belief (trust, confidence, assurance) that money will meet your needs and make you happy.[7]

This is everywhere! So many people try to insulate themselves behind a fortress of materialism. They put their hope in money as a means for buying protection, purpose, power, and pleasure. They wear money on their sleeves like cuff links so others will think more highly of them, or at least be envious of them. They invest everything in what is temporary and completely ignore what is eternal. Our addiction to wealth will only grow stronger as we approach the end of history.

Don't let it happen to you! This is our culture, but it cannot be our character. Later in this chapter, I'll give you some safeguards that have helped me.

The Acceleration of Inequality

The last days will also see increasing inequality. As I've been saying, the tribulation is the coming seven-year period during which God will fully bring His wrath to bear on the evil of the world. Within the book of Revelation, chapters 6–19 describe this future period. At the beginning of this section, in Revelation 6, we read about things that will occur near the beginning of the tribulation, including this:

> When He opened the third seal, I heard the third living creature say, "Come and see." So I looked, and behold, a black horse, and he who sat on it had a pair of scales in his hand. And I heard a voice in the midst

of the four living creatures saying, "A quart of wheat for a denarius, and three quarts of barley for a denarius; and do not harm the oil and the wine." (vv. 5–6)

This passage describes the third "seal" of judgment during the tribulation. It paints a picture of worldwide famine. This is a time of judgment when resources will be sparce, forcing many into poverty, hunger, and despair. In those days, a denarius equaled a day's wages. Alarmingly, verse 6 says a quart of wheat will sell for a denarius during the tribulation period. A quart of wheat wasn't much. Neither was three quarts of barley.

Imagine a day of backbreaking labor and getting only a quart of grain. The New Living Translation puts it this way: "A loaf of wheat bread or three loaves of barley will cost a day's pay. And don't waste the olive oil and wine."

These verses describe a period of time when basic staples and supplies will be outrageously expensive because of the broader condition of the world. But notice, not everyone will be affected equally. The end of verse 6 says, "Do not harm the oil and the wine." While wheat and barley were food for the common people of John's day, oil and wine were more like luxury items. They were primarily reserved for those with more resources.

In short, the tribulation will be a period of extreme economic inequality. Most people will struggle to find basic supplies to meet their needs. Yet a few—perhaps those who gave themselves most fully to an addiction to money prior to the tribulation—will hoard great amounts of wealth for themselves. They will continue to indulge in a luxurious lifestyle even during times of shortage.

Once again, we see these tendencies displayed in today's world. In fact, income inequality has skyrocketed in recent years, both in the United States and around the world.

According to the Credit Suisse Global Wealth Report, 1 percent of the world's current population owns about 44 percent of the world's wealth. One percent! And the inequality increases the higher you go up the scale. For example, people who own more than $30 million make up .002 percent of the global population. But those people hold 6 percent of global wealth.[8]

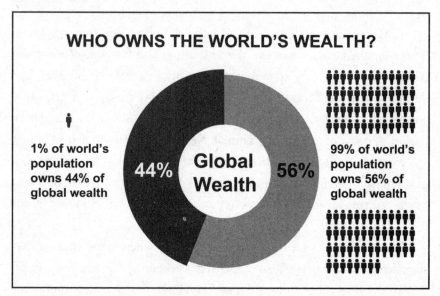

WHO OWNS THE WORLD'S WEALTH?

1% of world's population owns 44% of global wealth

44% Global Wealth 56%

99% of world's population owns 56% of global wealth

Because financial inequality exists in our world, growing economies don't necessarily benefit everyone—especially those who occupy the bottom rungs of the ladder. In the past forty years, for example, wages for average workers have risen about 11 percent—while wages for CEOs have risen a shocking 1,000 percent. When you run a comparison today, CEOs earn 278 times what their employees earn in a given year.[9]

This is another area in which COVID-19 fired up the wrong rockets. While millions of Americans lost their jobs in 2020, the net worth of American billionaires actually rose 35 percent, from $3.4 trillion in January 2020 to $4.6 trillion by May 2021. As might be expected, the wealthiest saw the biggest profits during the crisis. Jeff Bezos saw his personal fortune rise an astonishing $86 billion in just over a year to become the first person in the world to be worth more than $200 billion.[10] He has more dollars than the Amazon has drops of water.

As the old saying goes, "The rich get richer and the poor get poorer."

We're seeing the truth of that statement today, and we will see even greater levels of inequality as we draw closer to the tribulation.

The Adoration of the Antichrist

The twentieth century was littered with some of the worst deceivers and cultists in history. The most recognizable names include Jim Jones, David Koresh, Charles Manson, and Marshall Applewhite. And of course, hundreds of others have used their personalities and influence to corrupt those wandering into their orbits.

A recent example is a man named Keith Raniere, leader of the NXIVM cult in New York. On the surface, NXIVM branded itself as a self-help organization. The company's stated mission was to "raise human awareness and celebrate what it means to be human." Beginning in the 1990s, Raniere and his cronies produced regular seminars—many of which cost tens of thousands of dollars to attend—that claimed to help people overcome significant moments of trauma by "integrating" those experiences into their lives. These conferences and other events were attended by an estimated 18,000 people.

Below the surface, however, Raniere and his enablers played a more sinister game. They used their seminars to identify vulnerable women—some as young as fifteen—who were desperate for connection and healing. A sexual predator, Raniere took advantage of these women emotionally, financially, and physically. He required them to submit embarrassing photographs of themselves to keep them from breaking his control over their lives, and he even branded his own initials in the women's skin.

The cult was eventually discovered when several brave victims contacted federal authorities and gave Raniere up. He was sentenced to 120 years in prison.[11]

Just as financial addiction and rising inequality conjure up scenes of the future, these cult leaders foreshadow the intense adoration people will feel for the Antichrist and his minions during the tribulation. The

Man of Lawlessness will be the personification of charisma. People will do anything for a glimpse of him.

But the Bible gives a clearer glimpse of him. Revelation 13 calls him a beast "rising up out of the sea" (v. 1). This ultimate dictator will rule the world during the last days. He'll not be alone. A few verses later, John saw a second beast, this one "coming up out of the earth" (v. 11). This beast is called the False Prophet. He will have one supreme duty—to point humanity toward the Antichrist. It will be a twisted inversion of how the Holy Spirit points people toward Jesus Christ.

In John's vision, we're told this beast "had two horns like a lamb and spoke like a dragon" (v. 11). In other words, Satan will cause his False Prophet to appear like a meek and gentle lamb, when in reality he will have the heart of a destroyer.

Satan will be the power behind it all. The Antichrist will be the political leader during the tribulation, and the False Prophet will be his spiritual and economic leader. He'll be able to accomplish incredible things such as bringing the Antichrist back to life after a mortal wound and enabling an idolatrous image to speak. The False Prophet will also lead people into the worship of the Antichrist. His influence will be supernatural and demonic.

For our purpose here, I want to direct your attention to the False Prophet's economic power. Consider what he will be in charge of:

> He causes all, both small and great, rich and poor, free and slave, to receive a mark on their right hand or on their foreheads, and that no one may buy or sell except one who has the mark or the name of the beast, or the number of his name. Here is wisdom. Let him who has understanding calculate the number of the beast, for it is the number of a man: His number is 666. (vv. 16–18)

Millionaire and pauper, freeman and slave, everyone will be compelled to receive this mark of the beast. No one will be exempt. Why? Without this mark, people will be unable to buy or sell anything.

Economic access and opportunity will vanish for anyone resisting the Antichrist and the False Prophet.

What will this mark be? Could it be a microchip in your hand or some other emerging technology, such as we discussed at the beginning of this chapter? Again, it's possible. We don't know for sure because Scripture does not provide details. But I do think it's important to explore the background about what this mark meant for John and the earliest Christians.

The New Testament was originally composed in the common written language of the day, which was Greek. Now, the word for "mark" in first-century Greek was *charagma*. That particular term was always connected with the emperor of Rome and often contained not only the emperor's name but also his effigy and the year of his reign. (Think of George Washington's face on a dollar bill, for example.) The *charagma* was also necessary for buying and selling, and it was required to be affixed to all kinds of documents to attest to their validity as an official seal.

In a similar way, the mark of the beast will indicate that the one wearing it is a worshiper of the beast—someone who submits to his rule. Those who refuse that mark will be traitors. They will likely starve while on the run and be killed on the spot when captured.

In the words of one scholar:

> What is portrayed is a tremendous union in which capital and labor are both subject to the control and direction of one man. Anyone who is outside that vast combination will be ruthlessly boycotted; no one will work for him or employ him; no one will purchase his produce or sell goods to him. . . . Bankruptcy and starvation face such a man.[12]

Even more frightening, Satan and the Antichrist will create a union between religion and economics during the tribulation period. There will be no room for freedom of worship. No freedom of expression or freedom of ideas. No freedom of choice. In other words, the entire world will be forced into a cult of massive proportions and of almost unstoppable power. The Antichrist will be at the top of this cult, with his False Prophet by his side. Their unbending law will be, "Worship me or die." And they will use economic pressures to flog those who resist them.

Where Do We Go from Here?

Perhaps all this feels ominous to you. Of course it does. Me too. That's natural. After all, we're exploring future events that will be terrible in their scope and significance. Not only that, but we can already see the outer waves of the coming storm. Technology already exists that may make it possible for the economic and religious union summed up by the mark of the beast. Addiction to money is a legitimate problem in many cultures around the world. The existence of economic inequality is here, and the culture is ready for a cult-like figure to emerge.

We can be aware of these trends without being seized with alarm. Fear is not our only option. As a follower of Christ, you are a child of God. You are a chosen member of His kingdom. You are His disciple, and you are His friend. You're part of the family, included among the holy people and the royal nation that's dedicated to changing the world through the gospel of Christ.

You can respond to apocalyptic danger with emphatic determination and timely wisdom. Here's how.

Determine to Count the Cost

Begin by taking a cue from one of the world's best athletes. On June 3, 2017, Alex Honnold shocked the world of professional climbing by "free soloing" El Capitan in California's Yosemite National Park—an achievement many others in the world, including professional climbers, believed impossible.

El Capitan is a 3,000-foot-high wall of granite in the Yosemite Valley. Its height exceeds any skyscraper on earth, including Dubai's Burj Khalifa tower, which soars a half mile into the sky. Because of its pristine beauty, El Capitan is one of the more famous natural landmarks in the world, and it holds a special place for rock climbers. It's the Mount Everest of rock faces.

The best climbers find El Capitan a daunting challenge under the best conditions. But Alex Honnold chose to "free solo" the rock face. That means he climbed El Capitan with no ropes. No safety harnesses. No anchors. The only tools Alex used for his ascent were his hands and feet, along with a single bag of chalk. One mistake during the climb would have sent Alex to his death. Had he been my grandson, I couldn't have watched. The climb took nearly four hours, and every minute was nerve-racking. But when Alex reached the summit, he made history.

As you might expect, Alex did not approach such a high-pressure, high-danger climb lightly. He spent years preparing for his attempt. Yes, years! He planned. He practiced. He prepared for every possible contingency and expanded his skills in every conceivable way.

"In my case, the reason I spent so much time preparing is because it was so scary," he told reporters. "I would think it was insane and it would fill me with dread. With enough preparation, it wasn't scary anymore. I knew I could do it."

He added, "If I had to choose one lesson to take from it, I would choose preparation and putting in the work—not being stopped by something that seems impossible."[13]

In other words, Alex Honnold counted the cost before putting his life on the line. In the Gospel of Luke, Jesus advised His followers to do the same:

> "For which of you, intending to build a tower, does not sit down first and count the cost, whether he has enough to finish it—lest, after he has laid the foundation, and is not able to finish, all who see it begin to mock him, saying, 'This man began to build and was not able to finish'? . . . So likewise, whoever of you does not forsake all that he has cannot be My disciple." (14:28–30, 33)

Following Jesus carries a cost. Throughout history, many Christians have paid that cost with their lives. Others have paid it with their reputations, their convenience, their relationships, their freedom, and even their health and wealth. When Christ is everything, everything else is nothing in comparison.

Maybe you've not lost your wherewithal or your life. Many of us in the West have likely paid a minimal cost to follow Christ. Yet our circumstances may change. At some point, they *will* change, probably sooner rather than later. As the world veers further away from God's values and as time moves closer toward Armageddon, we'll arrive at a moment when proclaiming the name of Jesus requires a sacrifice. Even a significant sacrifice. Maybe everything.

But wouldn't you rather have Jesus than anything this world affords? Let's take this moment to count the cost, realistically but optimistically. We can place on one side of the scale all of the trappings of the American dream and the modern way of living—our riches, our possessions, our comfort, our career, and so on. On the other side of the scale, place the incredible, unthinkable blessing of eternal life in the presence of our Savior.

I know which side of the scale is more valuable for me. I'm confident as you make your own calculations and count your individual cost for following Christ, you'll say with the apostle Paul, "Oh, the depth of the riches both of the wisdom and knowledge of God!" (Rom. 11:33).

Determine to Be Confident

The wonderful news about living for Jesus is that not only can we experience the riches of the wisdom and knowledge of God, we can also feel confident in the reality of God's presence right now. No matter what cost we may pay to follow Christ, we will never sacrifice our connection to Him.

The author of Hebrews put it this way:

For He Himself has said, "I will never leave you nor forsake you." So we may boldly say: "The LORD is my helper; I will not fear. What can man do to me?" (13:5–6)

This is perhaps the most emphatic statement in the New Testament. The Greek contains two double negatives, which means it could be translated this way: *"No,* I will *never* leave you. *No, neither* will I forsake you." No matter what happens in your life, God will always be there. He will never abandon you! Rather than being tempted to yield to culture's continual cry for more, you can declare your confidence in God—and in Him alone. He is your Helper. He is your Sustainer, your Provider. He will always be there.

The confident Christian knows he stands in a place of security. He cannot be touched by anything the Lord does not allow. The confident Christian can stand tall in the midst of trials because he knows God is enough for any and every situation he might face.

I love how David expressed this sentiment: "The LORD is my light and my salvation; whom shall I fear? The LORD is the strength of my life; of whom shall I be afraid?" (Ps. 27:1).

Since we have the Lord, we can never be left without a friend or a treasure or a dwelling place. This should help us feel independent of humanity and all its schemes. When we stand in such awe of the living Lord, the lying world loses its power on us.

Let me say it again: you don't have to be afraid! Even if our culture continues down a path of greed—addicted to an unhealthy, unsupportable love of money—you don't have to walk that path. You don't have to believe the deception that has engulfed everyone else. Don't settle for anything less than the riches of God's goodness, love, mercy, and provision, which He can pour into your life like rivers from heaven! Make up your mind to be confident in God, for the Bible says, "In quietness and confidence shall be your strength" (Isa. 30:15).

Determine to Be Content

Finally, because God will never leave us nor forsake us, we can be content with what we have. As the globe spins around, the worship of wealth will accelerate. But the Bible can keep us from yielding to these pressures. There's one incredible secret I want to give you. On the authority of Scripture, I can tell you how to distance yourself from a materialistic lifestyle. It's by developing one simple, biblical attitude: contentment.

Two Scripture passages instantly come to mind:

- "Let your conduct be without covetousness; be content with such things as you have" (Heb. 13:5).
- "He who loves silver will not be satisfied with silver; nor he who loves abundance, with increase. This also is vanity" (Ecc. 5:10).

Covetousness is subtle because it's a condition within our minds. It's the invisible violation that no one else sees. You can have your act together on the outside, but inside you can be agonizing over, lusting after, and being consumed by the desire to have what someone else has. Coveting is a closeted spiritual crime that, if not checked, will eventually manifest itself externally.

The writer of Hebrews told us how to replace coveting with contentment. The Greek word for *contentment* means "satisfied," "adequate," "competent," or "sufficient." The same term is used in 2 Corinthians 12:9, when God told Paul: "My grace is sufficient for you."

Someone has said, "Christian contentment is the God-given ability to be satisfied with the loving provision of God in any and every situation."

Maybe you're worried about this. You think to yourself, *I wasn't born with contentment in my genes. I don't feel satisfied with my life or even with my possessions. I often find myself wanting more.*

Don't let that bother you, because I have good news! According to Paul's epistle to the church in Philippi, contentment is something we learn. This is the apostle's own testimony:

Not that I speak in regard to need, for I have learned in whatever state I am, to be content: I know how to be abased, and I know how to abound. Everywhere and in all things I have learned both to be full and to be hungry, both to abound and to suffer need. I can do all things through Christ who strengthens me. (Phil. 4:11–13)

Paul wasn't born a saint. He didn't come into the world with a vast reserve of contentment. Instead, he learned contentment through experience—including both comfort and hardship. He learned contentment by honestly evaluating the value of wealth versus the value of his connection to Christ. And he learned contentment through the continual influx and influence of God's Spirit in his life. He seemed to be equally joyful staying in a friend's villa or chained in a Roman cell.

The same can be true for you.

Remember the story of Sam Polk from earlier in this chapter? The man who was angry when his Wall Street bosses offered him a bonus of $3.6 million? Incredibly, even Sam Polk learned the value of contentment.

As he became enmeshed deeper and deeper into the culture of Wall Street, Polk eventually saw the hollowness of it all. He saw the way veteran traders seemed incapable of thinking about others or evaluating the impact their actions had on "regular" people. All they could think about was money. And more money. And more of everything money could buy.

"My dream was to be a billionaire," Polk said. "A billionaire was a hero. The fact that my boss (who was a billionaire) was self-seeking made me realize that there was no end point."

With the help of a counselor, Sam began to see what was happening in his own heart. "I was trying to fill this hole inside me, this sense of worthlessness," he said. "The only way I thought I was valuable was . . . millions of dollars, a big loft apartment on Bond Street; those things you get when you are on Wall Street. Then I realized the hole is still there."

As I mentioned earlier, Sam Polk eventually left his Wall Street job, though he had to return nearly $2 million in bonus money. He saw the danger of what he was becoming, and he let go of his precious money in order to find freedom. To find contentment. Afterward, Polk founded a not-for-profit organization called GroceryShips, which allowed him to provide healthy food and a plan to escape from obesity for residents of impoverished neighborhoods.[14]

Yes, our world's approach to money is troubling. Even alarming. But we can avoid the danger confronting our culture when we determine to count the cost (and the benefits!) of following Christ; when we choose to remain confident in His presence; and when we learn to be content with His provision in our lives.

As someone said, "You can take the world, but give me Jesus!"

Perhaps little is more heartbreaking and discouraging in the Christian's life than to watch someone fall away and abandon the faith. From our friends and family to prominent pastors and authors, more and more professed believers seem to be losing their first love, changing their minds, and following after the idols of self-reliance, fame, and money.

What does this mean for God's church? Should it cause us to doubt the truth of the gospel? How do we keep ourselves from falling away as well?

In this chapter we confront the discouraging news of modern-day apostasy and discover that this problem is one of the signs of the end times. As we see others' lights beginning to flicker, we must take heed ourselves and remember that He who has begun a good work in us has promised to complete what He started.

Chapter 5

A Theological Prophecy—The Falling Away

That Day will not come unless the falling away comes first.

2 Thessalonians 2:3

Imagine writing your first book at age twenty-two and watching it land on bestseller lists everywhere. A few years ago, that happened to an American pastor. His book conveyed biblical advice about love and relationships, and it encouraged thousands of young people to make better choices. Here's a quote from its pages: "The world takes us to a silver screen on which flickering images of passion and romance play, and as we watch, the world says, 'This is love.' God takes us to the foot of a tree on which a naked and bloodied man hangs and says, '*This* is love.'"[1]

Those phrases pack a punch! It's no wonder this pastor became known for his speaking, writing, and counseling, as well as for nearly two decades of pastoral ministry in a local church. But in 2019, he announced his marriage had come to an end. Then, in a follow-up post on Instagram, he disclosed something even more troubling:

> I have undergone a massive shift in regard to my faith in Jesus. The popular phrase for this is "deconstruction," the biblical phrase is "falling away." By all the measurements that I have for defining a Christian, I am not a Christian. Many people tell me that there is a different way to practice faith and I want to remain open to this, but I'm not there now.[2]

That cuts me to the heart, especially because he isn't alone. Many others seem to be falling away from Christ and His gospel. I saw a recent op-ed with this title: "Everyone Is Leaving Christianity. Few Know Where They're Going."[3]

This departure from biblical faith is happening so often that a new word has been coined. These defectors are no longer evangelicals; they are *ex*vangelicals.

Why is that? And what does it mean?

This "falling away" is not a new phenomenon. Throughout history, many have taken up the banner of Christ only to lay it down again. Even the first generation of Christians faced this challenge.

Do you know about Demas? When Paul wrote to the Colossians and to Philemon, he sent them greetings from his coworker Demas, who was at his side (Col. 4:14; Philem. 1:24). Yet in his final letter, Paul told Timothy, "Demas has forsaken me, having loved this present world" (2 Tim. 4:10).

Another book in the Bible is devoted to this topic—the short epistle of Jude, written by our Lord's half-brother, the son of Joseph and Mary. It's the next-to-the-last book of the Bible, and Jude stated his purpose succinctly: "To contend earnestly for the faith which was once for all delivered to the saints" (v. 3).

It helps me to realize the apostles faced the same problem of falling away we're seeing today. Yet the trend toward apostasy seems to be accelerating in our times. I'm almost hesitant to read Christian news sites because I don't want to hear of another pastor failing or another prominent believer rejecting the faith. Recent headlines aren't encouraging, and neither are the statistics.

There are more than 72 million Millennials in America—almost a quarter of the population.[4] An increasingly large percentage of that generation has walked away from faith of any kind, choosing to identify as "religious nones." In 2008, researchers noted that close to a third of Millennials (31.9 percent) described themselves as religiously unaffiliated. Just ten years later, that number was 42.7 percent.[5]

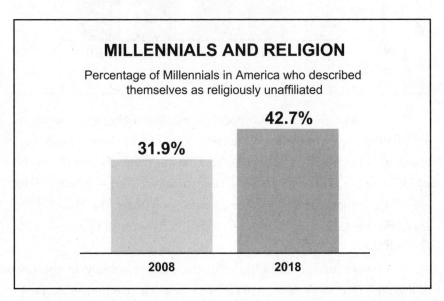

MILLENNIALS AND RELIGION

Percentage of Millennials in America who described themselves as religiously unaffiliated

42.7%

31.9%

2008   2018

There are more troubling numbers. Church membership in America has suffered a decades-long decline. When Gallup first measured US church membership in 1937, the number came in at 73 percent. Even in the early 1980s, more than 70 percent of American adults were church members. In the year 2000, it was 65 percent. By 2010, it was 59 percent. In 2020, it was 50 percent. Now less than half of Americans belong to a local church, with corresponding declines in regular church attendance.[6]

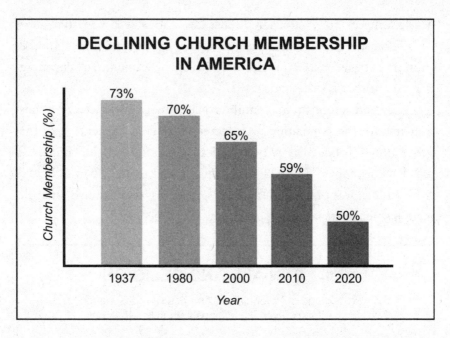

DECLINING CHURCH MEMBERSHIP IN AMERICA

But the core issue isn't that people are falling away from church, or even falling away from faith. We're talking about falling away from Jesus Himself. We're talking about branches that cut themselves off from the vine. These are people who have—these words are stark—"trampled the Son of God underfoot . . . treated as an unholy thing the blood of the covenant that sanctified them, and . . . insulted the Spirit of grace" (Heb. 10:29 NIV).

Remember Judas the disciple? He's the clearest example of apostasy in the Bible. He was among Jesus' inner circle. He had greater access to Christ than almost any other person in his day—walking and talking with the Savior, witnessing the miracles, and watching lives be transformed. Yet Judas still fell away.

So did a pastor here in California. After several instances of publicly criticizing the Bible's views on sexuality, this man was asked to resign from the church. He also lost his teaching positions at two Christian universities. As a result, he decided to live for a year without God. In his words, he planned to "try on" atheism as a New Year's resolution.

"For the next 12 months I will live as if there is no God," he wrote. "I will not pray, read the Bible for inspiration, refer to God as the cause of things or hope that God might intervene and change my own or someone else's circumstances."[7]

At the end of his experiment, he officially rejected his lifelong belief, declaring on National Public Radio, "I don't think that God exists."[8]

Again, this man didn't simply fall away from the church and from the faith. He chose to abandon the Savior, and it left him with nothing except atheism—which, literally, is faith in nothing.

I've been appalled in recent years when would-be shepherds of God's flock have questioned foundational elements of Christian doctrine, including:

- **The divinity of Christ.** In the earliest days of Christianity, a heretic named Arius gained popularity by teaching Jesus was not of the same nature as God the Father. Arius claimed Jesus was merely a man, and his teaching threatened to overwhelm the church until this heresy was rejected at the Council of Nicaea. Yet Arianism has found new life today in those who claim Jesus was a great moral teacher and a wonderful example to follow, but nothing more. They reject the biblical truth that Jesus is both fully human and fully God.
- **The resurrection of Christ.** If you were to visit many seminaries today, you might be surprised by the number of professors who reject the supernatural events of Scripture. They view key moments such as the parting of the Red Sea, the rescue of Shadrach, Meshach, and Abednego from the fiery furnace, the virgin birth of Jesus, and, yes, even the resurrection of Christ as mere fables. Stories that teach a good lesson, but nothing more.
- **The biblical view of sexuality and marriage.** Perhaps more than any other issue, the Bible's clear and unwavering stance on human sexuality has clashed with Western culture's insistence on tolerance at any cost. Rather than risk being seen as intolerant, churches and denominations have rejected Scripture in order to embrace the shifting sands of secularism.

- **Salvation through Christ alone.** I'm dismayed at the number of church leaders who reject the words of Jesus: "I am the way, the truth, and the life. No one comes to the Father except through Me" (John 14:6). Instead, they claim Christ as a way to heaven among many other ways, and in doing so they lead many astray.

If Jude were alive today, he would take notice. So should we.

But don't despair. There's hope even in the face of apostasy. God knows those who are His, and He will bring them home safely. Jesus said, "I give them eternal life, and they shall never perish; neither shall anyone snatch them out of My hand. My Father, who has given them to Me, is greater than all; and no one is able to snatch them out of My Father's hand" (John 10:28–29).

Paul expressed the same hope, declaring, "He who has begun a good work in you will complete it until the day of Jesus Christ" (Phil. 1:6).

And don't forget Jude, who ended his book praising "Him who is able to keep you from stumbling, and to present you faultless before the presence of His glory with exceeding joy" (v. 24).

What Does This Mean?

When I was getting started in ministry, apostasy was a hot topic. Or perhaps I should say "so-called apostasy." There was the so-called apostasy of long hair on men and short skirts on women. There was the so-called apostasy of dancing and attending movies. There was the so-called apostasy of having fellowship with other Christians who did not perfectly line up with all of your personal convictions.

Sometime after enrolling in seminary, I discovered what apostasy really is. Indeed, I found it to be something much more deadly than anything I mentioned above. In fact, true apostasy is far more lethal than all of them put together.

THE DENIALS OF END TIME APOSTATES

- Denial of God – 2 Tim. 3:4–5
- Denial of Christ – 1 John 4:3
- Denial of Christ's Return – 2 Peter 3:3–4
- Denial of Faith – Jude 3–4
- Denial of Sound Doctrine – 2 Tim. 4:3–4
- Denial of the Separated Life – 2 Tim. 3:1–7
- Denial of Christian Liberty – 1 Tim. 4:3–4
- Denial of Morals – Jude 18

To be clear, apostasy is not the same thing as atheism. By apostasy, I'm not referring to people in general who reject Christianity or deny the truth of the gospel. Apostasy doesn't reflect the rise of atheism in and of itself, nor does it apply to everyone who chooses religious systems other than Christianity.

Instead, the concept of falling away has a narrower focus. It applies specifically to apparent Christians—to those who claim to follow Jesus, but then turn their backs on Him. Here is the best definition I have found for the term apostasy:

The Greek word for apostasy is found only twice in the New Testament (Acts 21:21, II Thess. 2:3). . . . . The word means 'a falling away from,' a deserting or turning from a position or view formerly held . . . Spiritual apostasy occurs when a person who once claimed to be a believer, departs from what he formerly professed to believe. An apostate is not one who was saved and then lost his or her salvation. An apostate, though having claimed to be a believer, never was saved in the first place.[9]

Every apostate is an unbeliever, but not every unbeliever is an apostate. Do you see the difference? There are many people who have never had the opportunity to hear the gospel, even in part. They are unbelievers because they have not heard. But an apostate is well acquainted with the gospel. He or she knows more than enough to be saved and, yes, has even professed to follow Christ. But at some point, they turn their backs on the Savior. Their commitment wasn't real, and their decision wasn't authentic. Those who are Christians in pretense are non-Christians in reality, and sooner or later reality wins.

Why am I talking about this theme of falling away? Because the proliferation of apostasy is an important, but often overlooked, piece to the end times puzzle. As we know from Scripture, one of the signs of the imminent return of Christ is a rising number of self-proclaimed Christians who ultimately reject Christ.

The Bible says, "Now, brethren, concerning the coming of our Lord Jesus Christ and our gathering together to Him, we ask you, not to be soon shaken in mind or troubled, either by spirit or by word or by letter, as if from us, as though the day of Christ had come. Let no one deceive you by any means; *for that Day will not come unless the falling away comes first,* and the man of sin is revealed, the son of perdition (2 Thess. 2:1–3, emphasis added).

This is indeed a prophecy about tomorrow that has implications for us today. This falling away that Paul was writing about is not just some gradual defection from Christ. Paul called this *the* falling away. This will be a specific, recognizable departure from the faith during the tribulation.

Let's bring it a little closer. According to the Bible, the tribulation period will begin immediately after the rapture of the church. Paul told the Thessalonians that the tribulation could not begin until the Antichrist was revealed and the falling away occurred. Here is the order of events: Christ comes to rapture His saints to heaven. At that moment, tribulation breaks out all over the earth and the Antichrist is unmasked. Finally, at the same time, the falling away occurs.

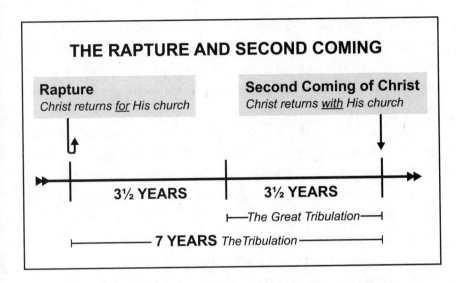

We know from our study of prophecy that the rapture is a sudden signless event. Nothing needs to happen for Christ to return for His own. But here is what we are prone to miss if we do not think carefully. If the rapture could happen at any moment, the "falling away" could also happen at any moment. In fact, what we have been describing, what is happening right now, could very well be the front edge of the "falling away" that Paul was explaining to the Thessalonian believers.

The point I'm making is this: we see the acceleration of people falling away happening now. Apostasy is on the rise even as you read this. To me, it's another sign that we're moving toward the end with increasing speed.

Paul wrote his words about "the falling away" to the church in Thessalonica, which was facing heavy levels of persecution. The Christians there believed the last days were upon them. Paul told them not to be troubled, for all Christians will encounter difficulties, even persecution. The thing to watch for, Paul said, was increased apostasy. That is a predictive sign of the approach of Christ's return and of God's final judgment. Before the return of Christ, a great falling away will occur.

I hope to see a great spiritual revival before the rapture. It can happen. But there's no specific evidence in Scripture that a spiritual awakening must occur before Christ comes for His church. On the contrary, Paul's words in 2 Thessalonians 2:3 reveal that unbelief will continue to rise on a global scale, including increased apostasy within the church, until a tipping point is reached prior to the day of God's judgment.

John said, "It is the last hour; and as you have heard that the Antichrist is coming, even now many antichrists have come, by which we know that it is the last hour. They went out from us, but they were not of us; for if they had been of us, they would have continued with us" (1 John 2:18–19).

In His Olivet Discourse, Jesus said, "And because lawlessness will abound, the love of many will grow cold" (Matt. 24:12).

How can this happen? How could anyone who has tasted the goodness of Christ ever choose to fall away? There are many reasons, of course, but let's focus on three specific ones.

Some Fall Away Because They Are Deceived

Zach Avery is young, sharp, talented, and good-looking—qualities he plied in Hollywood to build an acting career. You can see his face in about fifteen movies. But Hollywood is a tough town. To support himself, Zach started his own entertainment company known as One in a Million Productions. It was an exciting venture. According to news accounts, he met potential investors, told them about his company's agreements with Netflix and HBO, and promised them a 40 percent return.

Between 2014 and 2019, Avery raised more than $690 million.

But nothing was real. Avery had no relationship with Netflix or HBO. He fabricated the story and used the money from new investors to pay older ones. It was a classic Ponzi scheme. According to the Securities and Exchange Commission, Avery squandered much of the money on a lavish lifestyle, including a six-million-dollar mansion, costly home decor, and extravagant trips.

His investors lost millions, and the actor now has a starring role in a federal courtroom.[10]

There are many deceivers in our day, but the most dangerous ones aren't the cheats who take our money, as bad as that is. It's the ones who operate in the spiritual realm. According to the Bible, spiritual deception will cause many to fall away from Christ in the days leading up to the end times.

Look at this passage: "Now the Spirit expressly says that in latter times some will depart from the faith, giving heed to deceiving spirits and doctrines of demons, speaking lies in hypocrisy, having their own conscience seared with a hot iron" (1 Tim. 4:1–2).

According to this passage, unseen demonic forces are operating in our world, enticing and deceiving people into abandoning their faith in Christ. Their influence, even in the church, will only increase as we draw closer to the end of history.

The passage in 1 Timothy also warned of false teachers who traffic in "lies" and "hypocrisy." These men and women attempt to cause spiritual damage for their own benefit—typically for their own financial profit. These people are cold, callous, and calculating. Paul said their consciences have been "seared." They have lost moral sensitivity, and their spiritual compasses are defective.

Such people are operating within the church today. They promise miracles for money. They constantly push for power. They twist the Word of God. Their drive to deceive will continue escalating with each passing year.

Some Fall Away Because They Are Disillusioned

In Luke 8, Jesus told a parable illustrating the reasons people would fall away from the gospel. He said a farmer went out to sow seed, and he broadcast it over a wide area. Some fell on the pathway or road, where it was trampled down. Other seed fell on rocky soil. As soon as the plants sprang up, they withered away, having no root. Other seed fell in a thorny patch and were choked by briars. But some of the seed fell on prepared soil, yielding a great harvest.

When the Lord's disciples asked Him to explain the parable, He revealed that the seed represented the gospel message. He said:

> Those by the wayside are the ones who hear; then the devil comes and takes away the word out of their hearts, lest they should believe and be saved. But the ones on the rock are those who, when they hear, receive the word with joy; and these have no root, who believe for a while and in time of temptation fall away. Now the ones that fell among thorns are those who, when they have heard, go out and are choked with cares, riches, and pleasures of life, and bring no fruit to maturity. (vv. 12–14)

Notice the first reason people reject the gospel is that "the devil comes and takes away the word out of their hearts" (v. 12). That's deception—the deceiving spirits and demons I mentioned earlier.

The second reason is more complicated. Jesus described those who hear the good news and "receive the word with joy" (v. 13). These people are genuinely excited about Christianity. They've seen the brokenness of the world and they've felt the brokenness in their own spirits. They know there must be something better.

These people encounter the truth and receive the message with joy and hopefulness. They see a pathway to peace and purpose and meaning. It's what they've been searching for!

John Starke said, "A nominal Christian finds Christ useful. A true Christian finds Christ beautiful."[11]

Sadly, stony-ground believers "have no root." In times of temptation they fall away. Many of these people are looking for a solution rather than a Savior. They want their problems to go away without surrendering their lives to Christ. They want the blessings of belief without the burden of swimming against the cultural stream. They like the idea of the gospel, but they lack a personal commitment to Christ.

Sooner or later, they begin to feel disillusioned, disenchanted, even disappointed. They fall away.

It's been relatively easy to live as a Christian in America throughout recent decades. I know that from experience. However, the days are coming—in many ways they're already here—when lifting up the banner of Christ will cost something. This will be especially true as we draw closer to the period known as the tribulation. An increasing number of cultural Christians with little or no roots in the gospel will decide the cost is too great, and they will turn their backs on Christ.

Some Fall Away Because They Are Distracted

Jesus' third explanation for the Parable of the Sower points to another reason why apostasy has been prevalent throughout history: "Now the ones that fell among thorns are those who, when they have heard, go out and are choked with cares, riches, and pleasures of life, and bring no fruit to maturity" (Luke 8:14).

Many fall away from Jesus simply because they get distracted. When forced to choose between the spiritual blessings of following Christ and the physical "cares, riches, and pleasures of life," they're unable to see past their own noses. The pull of desire is too strong, and they let go of their faith in order to grab all the world offers with both hands. They may play the Christian game for a period of time, but they are ultimately revealed as impostors.

I know that's not a pretty picture, nor is this an easy subject to discuss. But God has chosen us to be here as His witnesses at this critical time. So, as Francis Shaeffer asked, "How should we then live?"

Where Do We Go from Here?

It's easy to become discouraged when we consider the prevalence of apostasy in the church and in our world. This is especially true when we hear stories—whether in the news or in our personal lives—of people we admire who fall away from Christ. If we're not careful, we can begin to think of apostasy almost as a disease. Something that can be "caught" like a cold or a flu, or, yes, like COVID-19.

But apostasy isn't caught like an illness. It's not something that happens to you out of the blue. It's a choice. A decision you make based on your own values and priorities.

So, what can we do to protect ourselves from that ever happening to us? How can we make sure that we are never among those who fall away? I'd like to suggest three things you can do to immunize yourself against this danger.

Examine Yourself

Jeff Graf oversees much of the college ministry for the Navigators, a ministry that emphasizes Christian discipleship. One day Jeff was approached in the student union at South Dakota State University by a young man named Thomas. The night before, Thomas had attended a weekly meeting when the speaker said it was dangerous to assume you are saved if you have never personally asked God to forgive your sins and trusted in Jesus Christ as your Savior.

Those words pricked Thomas's heart, and he was very troubled. He asked Jeff about it, and Jeff opened the Scriptures and talked with him about it. Growing up, Thomas had known about God. He had gone to church, worked at a Bible camp, and attended Bible studies in college. But he suddenly realized he had been going through the motions but was missing out on Christ. He told Jeff, "All these years I thought I was a Christian, but I've never really asked God to forgive me for my sins."

Jeff had the joy of praying with Thomas as the young man truly turned his life over to Christ and was born again.[12]

In 2 Corinthians 13:5, Paul wrote: "Examine yourselves as to whether you are in the faith. Test yourselves. Do you not know yourselves, that Jesus Christ is in you?"

The most important thing you can do in response to this chapter is to make sure that you are a Christian. You are not a Christian just because you grew up in the church. You are not a Christian just because your parents are Christians. You are not a Christian because you have lived a good life. And you are not a Christian because you have served in the church and done great things for God.

One of the most sobering passages in the Bible is found in Matthew 7, where Jesus said: "Not everyone who says to me, 'Lord, Lord,' shall enter the kingdom of heaven, but he who does the will of My Father in heaven. Many will say to Me in that day, 'Lord, Lord, have we not prophesied in Your name, cast out demons in Your name, and done many wonders in Your name?' And then I will declare to them, 'I never knew you; depart from Me, you who practice lawlessness!'" (vv. 21–23).

Jesus was not saying that good works don't matter. He was warning that good works will not get you into heaven. We do good works because we are saved, not in order to be saved.

On the one hand, we don't want to have a false assurance of salvation. But on the other hand, we do want a firm assurance that we're saved. I believe God will run alongside you, as it were, and help you find that balance if you'll ask Him. The psalmist taught us to pray, "Search me, O God, and know my heart; try me, and know my anxieties; and see if there is any wicked way in me, and lead me in the way everlasting" (Ps. 139:23–24).

I've been a pastor for many years, so let me act as if I were your pastor for a moment. Ask God to help you examine your heart. Tell Him you want to be certain of heaven. If you know your spiritual birthday and you're utterly certain you are a follower of Christ, then thank Him for it. Not every Christian can remember the exact moment when they received Jesus as their Lord and Savior. That doesn't mean you aren't born again. But if you're uncertain about it, take a moment right now to repent of your sins, place your faith in Christ, and trust Him for His total forgiveness. Claim the promise of eternal life. You might want to kneel down and pray aloud. Perhaps you want to ask someone to pray with you. Tell the Lord that if you have never truly received Christ as Savior, you want to do so right now! Then claim His assurance!

After your prayer, write down the time and place on the first page of your Bible or even on the flyleaf of this book. Then read these twenty words from Jesus aloud: "And I give them eternal life, and they shall never perish; neither shall anyone snatch them out of My hand" (John 10:28).

Encourage Yourself

That leads me to the second bit of advice I want to give you: encourage yourself. Encourage yourself in the Lord. We learn this technique from David, who came to a very disheartening moment in his life. While fleeing from King Saul through the cavernous deserts of lower Israel, David became weary. Then he encountered waves of bad news that would have sent the strongest soul over the brink. He also realized his own men were turning on him, and his plight was truly desperate. At that moment, according to 1 Samuel 30:6, "David encouraged himself in the LORD his God" (KJV).

If we learn to do this, we will never fall away—and the devil can't push us around.

Derrick and Shannon Williams were thrilled when they learned a baby was on the way. But then everything went wrong. Shannon nearly miscarried, and she spent ninety-six days on bedrest. At the hospital, doctors came in regularly with bad reports. One doctor told her, "Please don't get your hopes up high. I doubt if your baby will live for a week after he is born." They told her the little boy would never breathe on his own. The baby—named Emmanuel—weighed in at two pounds and thirteen ounces at birth, and he was diagnosed with autism.

"Each and every day I had to encourage myself in the Lord," Shannon recalled. "In fact, I had encouraging and applicable Bible scriptures taped all over my hospital walls. I would read them, quote them, confess them several times a day. The Bible was literally my life source. It gave me life when I was surrounded by death. It sustained me and it protected me from the lies, tricks and snares of the devil."[13]

That is God-encouragement, coming to us via self-encouragement. We can learn to encourage ourselves in the Lord. When we listen to the devil, we're led in the wrong direction. When we listen to friends, we get mixed advice. When we listen to our doubts, fears, worries, and feelings, we grow confused. Sometimes there's no one to preach to us, so we must say, like the psalmist, "Why are you cast down, O my soul? And why are you disquieted within me? Hope in God" (Ps. 42:11).

Sometimes we try too hard to squeeze encouragement from someone else. There are some needs only God can meet. It's unfair to expect our husband or wife or pastor or friend to do for us what only the Lord Himself can do. Instead of succumbing to discouragement and despair, we can strengthen ourselves in the Lord.

When your faith is faltering, that is when you need to turn to God. There may not be anyone else around in whom you can place your trust, but you can trust God. So, place your faith in Him and encourage yourself in your faith and strengthen yourself in your faith.

Nancy DeMoss Wolgemuth wrote, "I have learned to encourage myself in the Lord by meditating on specific promises from His Word and affirming they are true, regardless of what I may feel at the moment. I carry a list of some of those promises in my Bible and often turn to them to strengthen and encourage my heart."[14]

Exercise Yourself

Finally, if you want to stay confident and strong, it is important to keep growing in your faith, and that requires exercise.

According to *Business Insider*, LeBron James spends about $1.5 million each year caring for his body. Where does the money go? LeBron keeps his home gym updated. He's said to have replicated the Miami Heat and Cleveland Cavalier's gyms in his home. He has a cryochamber in his home, which uses liquid nitrogen to give him something akin to an ice bath. He also has a hyperbaric chamber that puts more oxygen in his body. He doesn't hesitate to hire and pay for the best trainers, massage therapists, and chefs in the world. He eats only the best and healthiest foods. And he invests in compression gear to wear on airplanes.

LeBron spares no expense to keep his body working like a sleek machine. His former teammate Mike Miller said, "He puts a lot of money behind taking care of his body. A lot of people think it's a big expense, but that big expense has allowed him to make a lot more money for a long period of time."[15]

If a basketball player is that concerned about taking care of his body, shouldn't you and I be diligent to take care of our souls? The Bible says, "For bodily exercise profits a little, but godliness is profitable for all things, having promise of the life that now is and of that which is to come" (1 Tim. 4:8).

Stagnant faith is the devil's playground, and he will fill your heart and mind with doubts. Just when you really need God, it will occur to you that He has not been very important to you of late.

Andrew Murray wrote this powerful paragraph:

> In commerce, in study, in war, it is so often said there is no safety but in advance. To stand still is to go back. To cease effort is to lose ground. To slacken the pace, before the goal is reached, is to lose the race. The only sure mark of our being true Christians, of our really loving Christ, is the deep longing and the steady effort to know more of Him. Tens of thousands have proved that to be content with beginning well is but the first step on a backward course, that ends in losing all. . . . Let us press on.[16]

The apostle Peter said, "Therefore, brethren, be even more diligent to make your call and election sure, for if you do these things you will never stumble" (2 Peter 1:10). "These things" refers back to eight character qualities listed in verses 5–7: faith, virtue, knowledge, self-control, perseverance, godliness, brotherly kindness, and love. Could Peter have been more emphatic? If we keep growing in these traits, we'll never stumble.

Now, let me make one thing clear. When Peter said we will never stumble, he didn't mean we will never make a mistake or commit a sin. He meant we'll never shipwreck our faith. We'll never fall away from Christ.

That becomes clear in the New Living Translation: "So, dear brothers and sisters, work hard to prove that you really are among those God has called and chosen. Do these things, and you will never fall away."

Earlier I mentioned the book of Jude, a small one-page letter near the end of the Bible. It's all about the dangers of false teachers and the temptation to fall away. Reading Jude can help us make the right choices when facing pressure. His words are critical for those of us living in a culture and in a church defined by increasing apostasy.

Jude wrote to Christians experiencing double pressure. They faced extreme persecution, and they were under spiritual attack from heresies of all kinds. Most of the influential leaders of the early church had been martyred—including Peter, Paul, and James—which left both churches and individual Christians feeling vulnerable.

In the darkness of that moment, Jude's epistle provided a ray of hope. In just two verses near the end of his tiny epistle, Jude explained to Christians how to remain committed to Christ during a time of increased apostasy: "But you, beloved, building yourselves up on your most holy faith . . . keep yourselves in the love of God" (vv. 20–21).

Jude was speaking to Christians, and the phrase *building yourselves up* conveys the idea of continuation. Jude was not speaking of a one-time event, but rather a life-long process. In other words, Jude told us to keep building ourselves up.

You will notice that these passages use the word *yourself* or *himself*. You must not wait for someone else to do this for you. This is your responsibility.

You must continue to cultivate your relationship with the Lord. Your walk with God is not static. You are either growing in Him or you are beginning to grow cold toward Him.

This is why God warned the church in Ephesus, "Nevertheless I have this against you, that you have left your first love. Remember therefore from where you have fallen; repent and do the first works" (Rev. 2:4–5).

Examine yourself, encourage yourself, and exercise yourself in the Lord. And most of all just keep going and growing. Don't stop! Don't look back! Just keep walking with the Lord.

A young girl named LeeAdianez Rodriguez-Espada arrived late for the Wegmans Family 5K on a brisk spring morning in Rochester, New York. She was twelve years old at the time. Her mother dropped her off at the starting line before leaving to find a parking spot, then settled in at the finish line to cheer for her daughter as she finished the race. The mother expected to wait about an hour.

At the starting line, LeeAdianez realized the race had just begun, so she joined the other runners at the back of the pack. Concentrating on putting one foot in front of the other, it wasn't until around mile four that she began to realize something was wrong. The finish line was nowhere in sight.

After asking a few of her neighboring runners how much longer the race would take, LeeAdianez realized her mistake. She was not part of the Wegmans Family 5K. She had instead entered the Flower City Half Marathon! This race was not five kilometers, but over thirteen miles!

Incredibly, she decided to keep going.

By this time, the young girl's mother was beginning to panic. She contacted the race organizers, and a police officer eventually found her daughter on the half-marathon course. Even then, twelve-year-old LeeAdianez refused to quit. Eventually, she crossed the finish line after running a full ten miles more than she originally planned.

LeeAdianez's mother was waiting for her there, crying tears of joy. "I see her with a medal and I thought, 'Oh my gosh, she ran the other one, like for real,'" she said. "She decided to just keep running and not give up."[17]

That is my challenge for you today. When you feel the pressure to let go of your faith, decide instead to keep running and never give up! Remember, this is your choice. Jesus is with you. He will keep you from falling, and He will empower you. He has every intention of presenting you faultless before the Father once your race comes to an end.

Until that moment, keep going. Keep running. And keep building up your faith and the faith of those around you.

May the Lord bless you with this benediction:

> Now to Him who is able to keep you from stumbling,
> And to present you faultless

Before the presence of His glory with exceeding joy,

To God our Savior,

Who alone is wise,

Be glory and majesty,

Dominion and power,

Both now and forever.

Amen.

JUDE 1:24–25

Our world is changing and not for the better. People are be-coming more callous, selfish, violent, and angry. Attitudes and behaviors deemed unthinkable even a decade ago are now considered acceptable. Common courtesy is increasingly un-common. Cordiality is no longer in our lives or in our vocabu-laries. This world is broken—and it seems to be getting worse.

As individuals, families, and a society we are experienc-ing a breakdown that feels irreversible. Increasingly we priori-tize self, money, and pleasure over God. As we stretch toward what the Bible refers to as the last days, we find ourselves trying to navigate our way through a very unfriendly world—a world of people that the Bible actually describes as growing "worse and worse" (2 Tim. 3:13).

How do we survive in this growing hostility, and more im-portantly, what can we do as followers of Christ to stem the tide of evil in our land?

Chapter 6

A Biographical Prophecy—End Times People

Evil men and impostors will grow worse and worse,
deceiving and being deceived.

2 TIMOTHY 3:13

Shon Hopwood grew up in a Christian home in rural Nebraska with parents who had started a local church. He was the oldest of five children. He was bright, excelling on standardized tests. He played basketball in high school and won a scholarship to Nebraska's Midland University. But in his teens Hopwood grew disillusioned with his basketball skills, stopped going to classes, and dropped out of school.

He soon joined the United States Navy and ended up in the Persian Gulf guarding warships with shoulder-mounted Stinger missiles. But Hopwood developed acute pancreatitis, almost died in a Bahrain hospital, and left the Navy with an honorable discharge.

That's when lostness overtook the young man. His alcohol and drug use grew into raging addictions, and he became depressed.

One day while drinking with a friend, they decided to rob a bank together. Why not? They could use the money. They ended up robbing five banks while armed. Afterward, Hopwood squandered the money on parties.

Eventually Hopwood's life came crashing down in the lobby of the DoubleTree Hotel in Omaha, Nebraska, when FBI agents tackled and arrested him. A year later, terrified, he stood before a federal judge who sentenced him to more than twelve years in prison. Shortly thereafter, he was on a prison plane, handcuffed, shackled, and heading to a federal penitentiary. He was only twenty-three, and his life was growing worse and worse by the day.[1]

I'll tell you what happened to Shon Hopwood a bit later, but his story raises questions for us. Why do people go the wrong way? Why do good people do bad things?

For thousands of years, people have been debating those types of questions. Sociologists and laypeople expend huge amounts of air and ink trying to determine if human beings are basically good or fundamentally evil.

For much of his life, retired British physician Theodore Dalrymple believed in the basic goodness of humanity. During his career, the doctor worked in hospitals and prisons, and he traveled to countries where dictators massacred their own people. Initially he believed widespread evil was impossible unless tyrants were everywhere. Slowly, though, he changed his mind as he listened to the stories of his patients. Evil, he decided, is something inside of us—something we all can freely choose.[2]

"Never again will I be tempted to believe in the fundamental goodness of man, or that evil is something exceptional or alien to human nature," Dalrymple said.[3]

The Bible has a word for what Dalrymple witnessed: sin. According to Scripture, sin is the fundamental problem of every person. Romans 3:10–12 says, "No one is righteous—not even one. No one is truly wise; no one is seeking God. All have turned away; all have become useless. No one does good, not a single one" (NLT).

Pastor Kevin DeYoung wrote:

Sin is in every human heart. It is the villain with a thousand faces. It's the man who gets a woman pregnant and leaves town. It's also the reputable family man who cuts down his wife and ignores his kids. It's the mean-spirited woman who talks bad about everyone, but it's also the sweet lady who never says an unkind word but harbors all kind of resentment and grudges. It's the kid who swears at his parents and blows off everyone who tries to help. It's also the kid who gets straight A's, keeps curfew, and smiles at church, but is one enormous bundle of pride and self-righteousness.[4]

Our problem, then, isn't just that we live in a sinful world, but that we live in a world of sinful people. Our sin affects everything.

The Bible makes it clear we are all corrupted by sin. That corruption entered our bloodstream through Adam and Eve, who rebelled against God in His garden. The blood disease of sin has descended through the generations, and it infects us today. The Bible says, "Therefore, just as through one man sin entered the world, and death through sin, and thus death spread to all men, because all sinned" (Rom. 5:12).

The prophet Jeremiah wrote, "The heart is deceitful above all things, and desperately wicked; who can know it?" (17:9). Because we've been stained by sin in this way, we can produce nothing good on our own— either as individuals or collectively. Jesus said, "For without Me you can do nothing" (John 15:5). The blood of Christ and the Spirit of God must unleash their power in our lives if we're to be godly people.

This is the war zone we call planet Earth. We're pushed and pulled between goodness and evil, between love and hate, between creation and destruction. You and I are Christ-followers in a fallen world. This has been true for God's people throughout the centuries.

But can you feel it? Something has changed.

The bad is getting worse. Godlessness is overtaking every institution, every platform, every square inch of our culture. Decency is crumbling like wooden planks infested by termites. The pathway ahead is increasingly unsound and may snap at any moment.

Just consider the story of Xiao Zhen Xie, who lives in San Francisco. Xie is seventy-five years old, and she was the victim of a brutal attack while she was walking on Market Street in the middle of the day. A young man struck her in the face without provocation. Without warning. Without mercy.

The assailant did not know with whom he was dealing, because within seconds of the attack Xie had found a wooden board close by on the ground and began pummeling her attacker as a means of defending herself. In fact, when police arrived, they found the young man lying on a stretcher and Xiao Zhen Xie standing over him to make sure he didn't escape!

Still, Xie was left bloodied and traumatized by the attack. Worse yet, police discovered that this same attacker had beaten an eighty-three-year-old man earlier that day.[5]

How can we account for such reckless disregard for humanity? Such casual cruelty?

Yes, evil has always been part of human society—including extreme acts of violence and brutality. Satan and his demons have been present in our world for as long as human society. People have been driven to commit atrocities, both small and large. World history is an album of infamy. Yet I sense things have reached a tipping point.

Gun violence. Depression. Obesity. Homicide. Addiction. Choose the negative headline, and chances are it has been increasing dramatically over the past decade.

Why? Because something is broken in us.

What Does This Mean?

I want to show you a prediction about the last days that will put all of this into prophetic context. I want to quote from a letter written by another prisoner, this one on death row. He wasn't there for robbing banks, but for preaching the gospel. The apostle Paul wrote his final letter to Timothy, his son in the faith, from a Roman cell. Near the end of his letter, Paul drew a surprisingly detailed picture of how people will behave prior to the tribulation.

"But know this," he wrote, "that in the last days perilous times will come: For men will be lovers of themselves, lovers of money, boasters, proud, blasphemers, disobedient to parents, unthankful, unholy, unloving, unforgiving, slanderers, without self-control, brutal, despisers of good, traitors, headstrong, haughty, lovers of pleasure rather than lovers of God, having a form of godliness but denying its power" (2 Tim. 3:1–5).

And notice what he added in verse 13: "But evil men and impostors will grow worse and worse, deceiving and being deceived."

"Worse and worse!" With those three short words, Paul predicted people will descend into rampant and accelerating godlessness as we approach the tribulation. Please note the apostle's focus was not on bad times, but on bad people. As John Calvin wrote, "The hardness or danger of this time is in Paul's view to be, not war, famine or diseases, nor any of the other calamities or ills that befall the body, but the wicked and depraved ways of men."[6]

Paul gave us nineteen specific character descriptions of what people will be like. In other words, here in 2 Timothy 3, the Lord gave us nineteen expressions to depict the nature of godlessness in the last days. I can't bore into all nineteen words and phrases, but I can show you a pattern—Paul's words move from selfish people to splintered families to shattered societies.

Selfish People

Right up front, the Lord told us that the last days will be populated by people who are lovers of themselves (v. 2).

Do you remember Narcissus from Greek mythology? According to the legend, Narcissus was a hunter who was extremely handsome. Women constantly fell in love with him, but he spurned their advances and disdained all who tried to approach him. One day Narcissus came to a clear pool in the middle of the woods. He saw his reflection and immediately fell in love with his own face. When he realized what was going on—that he had not encountered another person, but only himself—he took his own life in a burst of despair.

That's the origin of our modern word *narcissism*, the excessive love of self. According to Paul, the days before the tribulation will be perilous because people will love only themselves. They will accordingly be "boasters, proud, blasphemers" (v. 2).

These people love to talk about themselves and to build themselves up. Such people want everyone else to love them as much as they love themselves. They write their own press reports and pad their own resumes. When you finally meet the person in question, you hardly recognize them.

These are proud or haughty people, which means they're disdainful toward others. Looking down on others comes as naturally to them as it does to a pigeon atop a statue.

The word *blasphemers* is a theological term referring to verbal abuse toward God. The original Greek word also included the idea of slander. Those who harbor a disproportionate love for themselves, being boastful of themselves and disdainful of others, expend a lot of energy seeking to reduce everyone around them. They're intent on pushing others aside so they can stand taller.

Robert Ringer was an early apostle of this aggressive form of narcissism. Decades ago, he published a book called *Winning Through Intimidation*. He encouraged people to view themselves as wolves or foxes, seizing what they wanted and dominating those around them. His next book was the aptly titled *Looking Out for #1*. Both books were *New York Times* bestsellers.

Robert Ringer is seen as a visionary entrepreneur. In reality, he simply sold readers on the value of plain old selfishness. "Clear your mind, then," he wrote, "forget the 'moral' standards others may have tried to cram down your throat and do what is best for you."[7]

Perhaps nothing represents modern narcissism better than social media. Facebook, Twitter, YouTube, and Instagram allow us to constantly crow about our own success while simultaneously slashing away at the achievements of others, often through anonymous comments and online bullying. Social media is a stronghold for selfish people.

Unfortunately, selfish people rarely keep to themselves.

Splintered Families

The increasing selfishness of the last days will manifest itself in selfish people, and those selfish people will unavoidably result in damaged families. People will focus less on loved ones. Their time, energy, and passion will be tied up in themselves. The result? The days prior to the tribulation will be strewn with broken homes.

There are five descriptive terms in 2 Timothy 3 that highlight the damage broken people will perpetrate on their own families in the last days. People will be:

- Disobedient to parents
- Unthankful
- Unholy
- Unloving
- Unforgiving

When ancient Greek writers wanted to say something negative, they took a positive word and put a letter in front of it called the *alpha privative*. That letter negated the positive word. You see the same principle in English when we say something is "distasteful." We take the word *tasteful* and put a prefix in front of it, and that prefix negates the word.

All five of Paul's terms listed above included the alpha privative. All five describe a positive attribute that has vanished from most families during the last days.

Children will be *disobedient*. Willfully, they will do what they want to do, casting off oversight and authority. They will ignore the instruction of Scripture that says, "Children, obey your parents in the Lord, for this is right" (Eph. 6:1).

They will be *ungrateful*. Gone will be a thankful spirit between children and their parents, and that lack of gratitude will extend to other relationships as well.

The third word is *unholy*. In this context, that implies lack of respect. There will be no respect within the structure or framework of the family. The picture is of someone who throws off the oversight at all levels of authority and harbors a growing sense of rebellion and independence. Ask most schoolteachers and educators in America today, and they'll tell you all you need to know about the culture of disrespect.

Next, we come to the word *unloving*. Normal human affection will wither away. This word is translated elsewhere in the New Testament as "heartless." Homes will become hard places ruined by harsh hearts, which will spill over into the whole society.

The final word is *unforgiving*, which could also be translated "truth-breaker." This refers to people whose rebellion becomes stubborn and hardhearted. The root of bitterness within them grows into an emotional forest of poisonous trees bearing toxic fruit. They lack the capacity to forgive others, which paradoxically means they live as though they themselves could never be forgiven for all the harm they've caused.

By now, maybe you need a breath of fresh air. So let's take a moment and turn this around. If the ungodly world is characterized by these negatives, how should God's people live in the midst of it all? It's very simple. Our grammar should be different. We should leave off the alpha privative. In Christ, it's not appropriate to negate virtue. Our homes should be filled with obedience between children and parents. Families should be filled with gratitude and defined by respect. They should exude a natural love and affection. And we should be able to trust one another.

We have to work hard to avoid the alpha privative lifestyle. We must be doggedly committed to biblical marriages and to kingdom families.

Whatever has happened to you in the past, start where you are today and, with God's help, make your home a place indwelled by Jesus Christ.

Shattered Societies

Dr. Tony Evans is a pastor who has a way of expressing truth that is both poignant and memorable. For example, look at what he said in a recent sermon about the ripple effect that selfish or sinful individuals will produce in the larger pool of society:

> If you're a messed-up man and you have a family, you're going to help make a messed-up family.
>
> If you're a messed-up man contributing to a messed-up family, and your messed-up family goes to church, then your messed-up family's gonna make its contribution to a messed-up church. . . .
>
> If you're a messed-up man contributing to a messed-up family resulting in a messed-up church causing a messed-up neighborhood, and your neighborhood's part of a city, well, now your messed-up neighborhood's gonna make its contribution to a messed-up city. . . .
>
> If you're a messed-up man contributing to a messed-up family resulting in a messed-up church causing a messed-up neighborhood that resides in a messed-up city that's part of a messed-up county, and your county's part of the state, well, now your messed-up county's gonna make its contribution to a messed-up state.
>
> If you're a messed-up man contributing to a messed-up family resulting in a messed-up church causing a messed-up neighborhood that resides in a messed-up city that's part of a messed-up county contributing to a messed-up state, and your state's part of the country, well, now your messed-up state's gonna make its contribution to a messed-up nation.
>
> If you're a messed-up man contributing to a messed-up family resulting in a messed-up church causing a messed-up neighborhood that resides in a messed-up city that's part of a messed-up county

that's contributing to a messed-up state that's contributing to a messed-up country, and your country's part of the world, well, now your messed-up country is gonna make its contribution to a messed-up world.[8]

Dr. Evans is describing the same progression as the apostle Paul in 2 Timothy 3:1–5. Paul began by describing the selfishness of end times people. That selfishness will contribute to the decline of end times families. And the more broken families you find within a society, the more broken that society will become.

That's what we see in the final section of those nineteen descriptors. The culture of the last days will be dominated by "slanderers, without self-control, brutal, despisers of good, traitors, headstrong, haughty, lovers of pleasure rather than lovers of God, having a form of godliness but denying its power" (vv. 3–5).

Where Do We Go from Here?

How do Christians live in such a place—in this world where selfishness reigns and immorality increases? How can we be a different kind of "end times people" in a dark world?

Let's take a page from Benjamin Franklin. In his autobiography, Franklin described the darkness that filled the streets of Philadelphia in his day. It was pitch black at night, and people were stepping into mud puddles and stumbling over rough stones. Even worse, crime was increasing. It wasn't safe to be out after sunset. Franklin waged an intense campaign to persuade everyone to light the area outside their own house, but he got nowhere. Finally, he just did it himself—but only in front of his own house. He planted a pole in front of his porch with a kerosene light on top. That night in the city of Philadelphia, there was one house bathed in a warm glow. The lamp cast light on the street, giving passersby a feeling of well-being and safety.

The next night, another house had a lamp, then another. Pretty soon, almost the whole city was lighting the walkways in front of their houses at night. Franklin learned something: our example is often greater than our admonitions and campaigns.

That's what we need to learn too.

With that in mind, I want to lift you out of 2 Timothy 3 and take you into Ephesians. This is the passage that says: "For you were once darkness, but now you are light in the Lord." That sentence—Ephesians 5:8—is short enough to memorize, but powerful enough to illumine the pathways around your life.

Remember the Grace You Received

How do we walk in the light when our society is defined by end times people?

First, by experiencing God's grace through an encounter with the Lord Jesus Christ. Metaphors involving light pervade Scripture, and Ephesians 5:8 describes the difference that comes over us when we have a grace experience with Christ. Before that moment, we live in darkness as deep as underground caverns. We are spiritually, morally, personally, and eternally in pitch blackness. The moment we come to Christ, He pushes down the lever that connects us to the throne of grace and switches on a billion megawatts of light inside us.

This experience is so vivid that many Christians describe their moment of grace in bright terms. Cameron Cole was a missionary kid who grew up in Turkey and Thailand. Though his parents were Christians, Cameron wanted nothing to do with the Lord. He was self-absorbed. But during Cameron's senior year, a speaker came to his high school and spoke every day for a week.

"It was during this week that the light switched 'on' in my heart," Cameron said, "and I began to see this Jesus and understand that the way to life and joy and peace is His way. The truth that all my awful decisions and hurtful words could be washed away forever by faith in Jesus was the sweetest news I had ever heard, so I began to follow Him and dig into His word."[9]

Today, Cameron and his wife are serving a church in Texas, and he's always eager to tell others about the day Christ lit up his life.

The same happens inside each of us the more we remember the grace we have received.

Reflect the Light You Have Become

That brings us to our next tactic for living in these dark times: We must exude God's light. We have to convey it, reflect it, and radiate it. That's what we read in Ephesians 5:8–10: "Walk as children of light (for the fruit of the Spirit is in all goodness, righteousness, and truth), finding out what is acceptable to the Lord."

I'm concerned about the way this present darkness is casting its shadows over many churches and over many Christians. Too many people in our community of faith are trying to blend the light and the darkness, trying to achieve a sort of grayness. That doesn't work. It's a devilish lie to believe we can be Christians without being different and distinct from the world.

As followers of Jesus, we have left the kingdom of darkness, and we are now children of light. So now we must walk—we must live—as children of light. Psalm 34:5 says, "They looked to Him and were radiant, and their faces were not ashamed."

Isaiah 60:5 says, "Then you shall see and become radiant, and your heart shall swell with joy."

What exactly does that mean? We don't need to theorize about it. Paul told us plainly in his parenthetical statement in Ephesians 5:9. Those who are radiant and who walk in the light demonstrate the fruit of the Spirit in all goodness, righteousness, and truth.

People of goodness. Those who are walking in the light are supposed to be good. This has to do with your relationships with other people. You've been translated out of the darkness of deceitful and destructive relationships. Now you're going in a different direction. You share the essential goodness of Christ through His Spirit, who is working within you. This goodness is a characteristic of those who have been delivered from the darkness and are now walking in the light.

Elsewhere in the Bible, we see it stated like this: "See that no one renders evil for evil to anyone, but always pursue what is good both for yourselves and for all" (1 Thess. 5:15).

Before, you were pursuing the evil as fast as you could. Or maybe it was pursuing you. But now you've become a Christian, which prompts you to look for ways to do good things. You are pursuing good for yourself and for all people.

I just read about two sisters—twins—who are ninety-seven years old. When they were eighty-five, someone at church told them about a child who was sick. The sisters bought a teddy bear and crocheted a custom wardrobe for the stuffed animal, which they gave to the child. That began a ministry of teddy bears. For the last twelve years, these two sisters have devoted their days to sewing and crocheting custom outfits for teddy bears. They buy the bears and make outfits according to the needs or age or condition of the child. They also pray over the children—and even over the bears.

"We can't get out much anymore," said one of the sisters. "But we can still do things to bring a smile to people. . . . It takes pretty much all day to make an outfit for one bear, but I don't mind. I've got the time. We just want to bring some happiness to kids, some who don't have too much."

These superb sisters even give bears to high school seniors who are going off to college. Those bears are dressed in the colors of their high school, complete with cap and tassel. "There is a lot of prayer that goes into a bear before it leaves us. Since we know who will be receiving the bear, my sister and I are able to pray over the bear as I'm crocheting the outfit."[10]

What can you call that except—goodness! It's a quality we can never outlive.

People of righteousness. If our relationship with other people is one of goodness, our relationship to God is one of righteousness. Paul told Timothy, "But you, man of God, flee from all this, and pursue righteousness" (1 Tim. 6:11 NIV). Later he repeated the command: "Flee the evil desires of youth and pursue righteousness" (2 Tim. 2:22 NIV).

Notice that verb—*pursue*. It means "to chase after" and "to hunt down." It gives me the impression that when we have walked out of the darkness into the light, we are on a pursuit. We are pursuing, trying to chase down, running hard after righteousness. In thinking about this, I confess I've asked myself if that's really what I'm doing. Does that describe my life? Or am I just kind of floating along with what's going on in my busy world? Those are questions for us all in times like these.

Dr. R. C. Sproul described a night when he was almost asleep in his college dormitory room. He was a new Christian, but he had a lot of questions. Suddenly he was wide awake, feeling he had to get up and get out of the room. "The summons became stronger, more urgent, impossible to ignore." He rose, dressed, and stepped out of the dorm into the cold snow of the evening. It was midnight, and the moon cast a ghostly pall on the college buildings. Making his way to the Gothic chapel, he swung open the doors and entered. The door slammed shut behind him, startling him. His eyes adjusted to the darkness, and the moon seeped through the muted stained-glass windows. His footsteps echoed hauntingly as he made his way down the aisle and knelt at the chancel. A sense of fear fell over him, but then came a sense of peace. In that moment, somehow, he yielded all his questions to God and realized his entire life was to be a glorious pursuit in knowing ever more intimately the God of all holiness.

"I was alone with God," he recalled. "A holy God. An awesome God. A God who could fill me with terror in one second and with peace in the next. . . . Within me was born a new thirst that could never be fully satisfied in this world. I resolved to learn more, to pursue this God who lived in dark Gothic cathedrals and who invaded my dormitory room to rouse me from complacent slumber."[11]

Oh, that we would all have that kind of experience! In these perilous days, we need to chase after, to hunt down righteousness in all our habits—and a righteous God in our daily experience.

People of truth. Walking in the light also makes us people of truth.

Men and women of integrity. Our outward persona must be matched by inward reality.

Around the world, there are fourteen mountain peaks that rise to 8,000 meters, which is nearly five miles above sea level. Forty-four people claim to have reached the summit of all fourteen. But did they really do it? Damien Gildea, an Australian climber and writer, isn't so sure. He's causing a turmoil in the world of mountain climbing because he and his researchers are trying to verify the claims. He matches the words of the climbers with pictures and news reports of their adventures, as well as GPS indicators. Some of the climbers came close to the top, but the last few feet were too dangerous. Others took paths that made it difficult to know exactly where the summit was. Some stopped at what seemed to be the highest point, but it wasn't. One of the forty-four has already withdrawn his claim.

"No one's trying to take away the fact that they've gone a long way up a big mountain," Gildea told ABC News. "I know how hard it can be. And we all make mistakes, particularly when you're cold and tired and you're up at high altitude. But these people are basing their reputations . . . on a claim, and that's a claim to have gone to the top of the mountain."[12]

If you're like me, reading that pings at the conscience. As Christians, do we sometimes misrepresent ourselves or fudge the truth? How often do we exaggerate? How many white lies are floating around in our world?

We not only want to avoid dishonesty, but we also want to bring the truth—Truth with a capital *T*—into every situation. We want to awaken each morning and say, "Lord, I have a lot of things going on today. Help me to take You with me wherever I go. And help me to bring Jesus and His truthfulness and openness and honesty into every situation, with kindness and love."

Castlefields Church in the center of Derby, England, has a section on its website for its members to share how they found the light of Christ. Amanda grew up without a Christian background, except for a great-aunt who would talk about the Lord and give out Bibles. When Amanda was twenty-five, she was studying at a university, feeling depressed, and having trouble finding employment. While walking home on a cold February evening she heard someone singing behind her. He was singing loudly. Amanda turned around and said, "Why are you so happy?"

He said, "I'm praising the Lord, he makes me so happy." Turns out the man was a Nigerian evangelist. Over time, he answered her questions, gave her literature, and pointed her to passages of Scripture. He explained the gospel simply enough for her to understand it. One evening, she said, "Something supernatural happened, a light switched on and I believed Jesus had died on the cross for my sins. It all became so personal. I gave my life to Jesus that February night in 1998. Jesus became my Lord and Saviour."[13]

Notice that same phrase—*a light switched on.*

When I read that story, I could almost hear that Nigerian evangelist singing as he walked through the dark streets of Derby on that cold February night. His faith lit up the sidewalk, and he was living out the words of Christ: "You are the light of the world. A city that is set on a hill cannot be hidden" (Matt. 5:14). He was proclaiming "the praises of Him who called you out of darkness and into His marvelous light" (1 Peter 2:9).

Reveal the Darkness You See

The Ephesians passage goes on to tell us something else: "And have no fellowship with the unfruitful works of darkness, but rather expose them. For it is shameful even to speak of those things which are done by them in secret. But all things that are exposed are made manifest by the light, for whatever makes manifest is light. Therefore He says: 'Awake, you who sleep, arise from the dead, and Christ will give you light'" (Eph. 5:11–14).

Turn over a large rock on a bright day, and you'll see a whole world of bugs and pests fleeing in all directions. These creatures prefer the darkness, and the light expels them. In the same way, the world may be ill at ease when we walk in the light and seek, through our lives, to reveal Christ's holiness.

Did you notice how this happened naturally after you gave your life to Jesus Christ? All of a sudden, the people around you started looking at you differently. *What's wrong with him? He doesn't laugh at my dirty jokes anymore. What's wrong with her? She doesn't like to party on weekends now.*

We reply, "Well, you know what? I'm now a child of the light, and I can't have fellowship with the unfruitful works of darkness." Some people will turn away from us. Some will remain friends, but our joint activities will become different. And some of them will follow our trail of light and find Christ for themselves.

The word *fellowship* in Ephesians 5:11 is translated from the Greek word *sunkoinoneo*. The last part of the word means *fellowship*, but the prefix, *sun*, is the Greek word for *with*. It means participating with someone in doing something. This verse tells us that once we become a child of the light, we can no longer participate with those who are doing the works of darkness.

That doesn't mean we reject these people, or stop loving them, or exclude them from our lives. It does mean we no longer participate with them in things that are unworthy of our walk with Christ. We are still *in* the world, but we're no longer *of* the world. We are lights in the world. As Jesus warned us, some people love darkness more than light. He said, "For everyone practicing evil hates the light and does not come to the light, lest his deeds should be exposed. But he who does the truth comes to the light" (John 3:20–21).

I've had the same barber for many years. One day when I went for a haircut, the man in the chair next to me became increasingly vulgar and filthy in his talk. I could see my friend in the mirror. He was trying to gesture and intervene. He was determined to signal to the man that there was a pastor in the shop. He was uncomfortable with that kind of language flying through the air while I was present.

Why was that? I'm just another person. I'm one of scores of people in that shop every week. But that's not entirely true, is it? You and I are children of light. We don't want to be offensive, make people uncomfortable, or drive people away. Yet we can't help being lights in the darkness wherever we go. And that light casts its rays around us wherever we are.

When Almighty God comes into your life, He changes you, doesn't He? He makes you an agent of change. He gives you a new description—you're now a child of light. He gives you a new direction—you walk in light. You have a new desire—pursuing the will of God for your life. You have a new distinction—you no longer walk according to the unfruitful works of darkness. And you have a new duty—to spread the light.

Everyone is longing for some light. The world and its darkness are closing in on us. But when Jesus Christ comes into your life, He switches on the light that can never be turned off!

And that brings me back to Shon Hopwood, whom we last saw entering federal prison at age twenty-three. As time went by, Shon got a job in the prison library where he began reading books about the law. As he learned about the law, he began taking on cases for fellow prisoners, writing petitions they could use in federal courts. They called him the "jailhouse lawyer." Shon also began corresponding with a friend named Annie, his secret crush through high school. Furthermore, his parents let him know they continued to pray for him, and his mom kept sending him Christian books.

One day Shon's prison friend Robert had a life-changing experience with Jesus Christ. Shon took all that in, and he found it increasingly difficult to rationalize his darkened life. After Shon was released from prison in 2009, he and Annie got engaged. They asked pastor Marty Barnhart to officiate the wedding, but Barnhart wanted to talk with them first. He asked them what they believed about Jesus, and he said they could be forgiven by the shed blood of Christ. The pastor's exact words were: "Yeah, even you, Shon." Shon described what happened next:

> The next day I couldn't escape the feeling that God had been pursuing me for a long time and that if I'd just abandon my stubbornness and selfishness, and hand everything over to him, I would find redemption.
> What does it mean to be redeemed? And how do you redeem

yourself after robbing five banks? The answer is, you don't. The answer is that you need some help.

In Ephesians 1:7–8, Paul writes that in Christ "we have redemption through his blood, the forgiveness of sins, in accordance with the riches of God's grace that he lavished on us." To put it differently, because of our sins, none of us—and surely no former prisoner like me—can be redeemed on our own. We need the gospel of grace, which says that each of us matters and has worth because we're made in the image of God. Grace says we are not defined by our failures and our faults, but by a love without merit or condition.

God's grace was enough to redeem me.

Shon and Annie asked Christ to come into their lives, they were married, they were baptized, and they moved to Seattle so Shon could attend the University of Washington Law School. Today Shon is a professor of law at Georgetown University in Washington, DC, where he is spreading light every day.[14]

We're living in a messed-up world filled with self-centered, self-absorbed, self-indulgent people. The Bible warns that in the last days perilous times will come. Society will go from bad to worse. But remember, the city of Ephesus was also a place of darkness in Paul's day, yet he viewed the Christians there as children of light. Their presence lit up the city streets with the glow of Jesus.

Even in dark days, you can experience God's grace, exude His radiance, and exhibit His holiness. So, brighten up! God wants His people to be light on their feet, so to speak.

In a world increasingly dominated by end times people, He has empowered you to shine.

---◇---

It is one of the great ironies of our age that while we are living during a time when almost any behavior is celebrated no matter how sinful, we are simultaneously living in a time where any small misstep, public or private, could be the catalyst of our own social and financial ruin.

That is the phenomenon in which a person may have made an innocuous comment or even a statement of truth only to be pounced on by an online mob and called upon to apologize, step down, resign. Some people lose their jobs; some even receive death threats. Whether the person being attacked actually did anything wrong is irrelevant, as is whether or not they apologize. Even if their innocence is later proven in court, the damage has been done.

Several writers of the New Testament made end time prophesies about the rise of this type of brokenness. What they prophesied about tomorrow is increasingly happening today!

Chapter 7

A Political Prophecy—
Cancel Culture

*"Many will be offended, will betray one another, and
will hate one another. Then many false prophets will
rise up and deceive many. And because lawlessness will
abound, the love of many will grow cold."*

MATTHEW 24:10–12

Except for 1968 with its riots and assassinations, I can't remember a more
challenging year for America in my lifetime than 2020. Between the pandemic, the flaring of racial tensions after the death of George Floyd, a
floundering economy, skyrocketing murder rates, and the impeachment
of President Donald Trump, people had a lot to argue about. Of course,
the US presidential election added fuel to those fires.

In the midst of that tension and animosity, pastor Chris Hodges of
Birmingham, Alabama, logged onto his Instagram account one day and
clicked "like" on a small number of posts from a conservative author
and speaker. Can you imagine something so innocuous causing trouble?
Well, it did.

A high school English teacher living in Birmingham saw what pastor Hodges had done and felt uncomfortable. She created a Facebook post to address that discomfort, including an image of Hodges's name next to the notorious "likes." She later ironically told reporters, "I would be upset if it comes off as me judging him. . . . I'm not saying he's a racist. I'm saying he likes someone who posts things that do not seem culturally sensitive to me."

In less than two weeks, the Birmingham Housing Authority voted to cut ties with Pastor Hodges and the Church of the Highlands, no longer allowing the church to rent space for one of its campuses. The Housing Authority also cut ties with Christ Health Center, a separate ministry founded by Church of the Highlands to provide free health services for residents of public housing.

Now, stop and think about that. A local government shut down a free clinic for the poor in the middle of a public health crisis! Why? In their words, "Pastor Hodges' views do not reflect those of HABD and its residents."[1]

That wasn't the end. The Birmingham Board of Education also voted to cut ties with Church of the Highlands after the so-called scandal. For several years, the church had rented two high school auditoriums to serve as additional campuses on Sunday mornings, paying more than $800,000 for that privilege. No more. The leases were terminated immediately.[2]

Ed Stetzer was quick to point out the sad irony of these decisions, given all the ways Hodges and his church have contributed to the Birmingham community and beyond. He wrote:

> [Chris] has . . . led his church to be the largest diverse church in Alabama, to engage the poor and marginalized, and to minister widely and well in his community. He and the church he leads has served the poor, engaged the sick, volunteered in the schools, and more. During the pandemic, Church of the Highlands has served thousands of meals, made masks, hosted blood drives, and helped other churches

with online services. He also liked some social media posts. Get the pitchforks.[3]

The long and short of it was that Pastor Hodges had been "canceled" because he liked a few posts from a popular conservative pundit.

The word *cancel* once described what we did to magazine or newspaper subscriptions, or to what happened to a faltering television program. Now it's what we do to people. In our society, canceling someone is a punishment for doing something, saying something, or even thinking something that violates a set of unwritten rules currently in play throughout much of the liberal world. These punishments are typically carried out in three stages:

1. There's an attempt to publicly humiliate the person by flagrantly exposing the supposed wrong he or she committed.
2. Once the person has been exposed, he or she is pushed mercilessly to confess and apologize. Whether that person has actually done anything that requires regret is irrelevant. Simply to be accused means a retraction and an apology is expected.
3. Regardless of whether the accused apologizes or not, attempts are made to remove that person from public life and from all public conversation once and for all. As a result, people are fired, mocked, threatened, de-platformed, and delegitimized in every way.

Professor Evan Gerstmann said, "There is no single accepted definition of cancel culture, but at its worst, it is about unaccountable groups successfully applying pressure to punish someone for perceived wrong opinions. The victim ends up losing their job or is significantly harmed in some way well beyond the discomfort of merely being disagreed with."[4]

What does it take for a person to be canceled? We'd like to know because most of us would rather avoid the experience. But no one knows what it takes to be canceled. At least, not specifically. As I said, the boundaries that govern this new way of life—what many are calling "cancel culture"—are unclear. The rules are unwritten, and it reminds me of a car driven by an inebriated person, swerving from lane to lane. We'd best stay out of the way, if possible.

Yet it's not always possible. People have been canceled for a broad range of offenses—everything from being accused of rape to voting the wrong way to expressing unpopular opinions. Or even liking social media posts that make other people feel "uncomfortable."

One of the more frightening aspects of cancel culture is that its tendrils extend even to regular members of society. You don't have to be famous to be canceled. For example, Mary Purdie is a local artist who was accused of plagiarism when a piece she designed went public. The accusations were false, but that didn't matter to the hundreds of people who posted hateful comments on her Instagram account and found other ways to harass her. She even attempted to apologize for a possible misunderstanding, but, in her words, the apology was "torn to threads."

"I've survived five miscarriages and breast cancer," Purdie told *Good Morning America*, "and this was still the worst thing that's happened to me."[5]

If this culture sounds unreasonable to you—even unbiblical—you're correct. When Jesus was asked to identify the most important commandment in the Bible, He replied with a two-for-one special: "'You shall love the LORD your God with all your heart, with all your soul, and with all your mind.' This is the first and great commandment. And the second is like it: 'You shall love your neighbor as yourself'" (Matt. 22:37–39).

I can think of few things less loving than publicly excoriating random people, even trying to get them fired and shamed and silenced, all for the sin of daring to disagree with a prevalent opinion. Yet that's what cancel culture demands.

It bears noticing that Jesus spent a lot of time with people in His day who had been canceled, so to speak. Remember the woman at the well? Women were considered second-class citizens in the ancient world, and Samaritans were scorned. Even her own people shunned her, which is why she came alone to draw water from the community well during the heat of the day. Yet Jesus approached her. He spoke kindly to her. He even offered her the water of life, saying: "Whoever drinks of this water will thirst again, but whoever drinks of the water that I shall give him will never thirst. But the water that I shall give him will become in him a fountain of water springing up into everlasting life" (John 4:13–14).

Jesus touched lepers who were untouchable according to the law. He welcomed sinners who were despised. He blessed children when others tried to nudge them away. He expressed compassion for a woman taken in adultery, and He accepted the worship of a woman criticized for pouring perfume on His feet. He touched the eyes of the blind and the ears of the deaf. He cast demons from the violent. During His final hours He comforted a criminal nailed to a cross beside Him. After His resurrection, He reassured a doubting disciple and reestablished the one who had denied Him.

Jesus had no place in His heart for the cancel culture, but He was wonderful at demonstrating God's love and grace to everyone. He still is.

What Does This Mean?

It would be nice to think cancel culture is a temporary phase our world is going through. But society is becoming more intolerant and polarized by the day, and I'm not sure we'll see a reversal of these trends. The more insidious elements of cancel culture are a malignant form of the spitefulness and self-importance common to all human nature. But what we're seeing today reminds me of what Jesus described in Matthew 24, which was our Lord's sermon about the last days and the great tribulation.

Jesus warned of a coming period of world distress, saying: "For then there will be great tribulation, such as has not been since the beginning of the world until this time, no, nor ever shall be. And unless those days were shortened, no flesh would be saved; but for the elect's sake those days will be shortened" (24:21–22).

As we learned in chapter 3, Jesus predicted a series of signs that will foreshadow the end of history. He spoke of wars and rumors of wars, famines, earthquakes, and pestilences. Then He said: "These are the beginning of sorrows. . . . And then many will be offended, will betray one another, and will hate one another. Then many false prophets will rise up and deceive many. And because lawlessness will abound, the love of many will grow cold" (vv. 8, 10–12).

Read that again, because there are several terms in those verses that represent the ethos of cancel culture.

A Culture of Disdain

First, Jesus talked about how easily people would be offended in the days leading up to the tribulation. Boy, is that ever true today! Recently NFL star Aaron Rodgers got attention when he appeared in a black T-shirt bearing the words, "I'm offended." The sports world wondered if it meant something, or if it meant nothing.

Lots of people seem to be going around with an "I'm offended" attitude. How many groups or products have had to change their names, their symbols, or their mascots out of fear they might "cause offense"? None of us want to be offensive, but doesn't it seem people everywhere are too easily offended? How long before someone sees us reading a Bible on the airplane and feels "uncomfortable"? When will someone take offense when we wear a T-shirt with the slogan "John 3:16" on it? What about the cross around your neck?

Jesus linked being easily offended with hating one another and betraying one another. The Greek word translated "betray" is important. It doesn't mean betrayal in the sense of saying negative things about coworkers so that you get a promotion instead of them. Nor does it mean betrayal in terms of deceiving others or turning on someone who used to be your friend—stabbing them in the back.

Instead, the text is talking about betrayal in the sense of intentionally revealing or exposing something that is hidden. It's the same idea as betraying a secret—or people betraying the Jewish identities of their neighbors to the secret police during the Reichstag leading up to World War II.

In other words, Jesus said society leading up to the end times would be marked by people who actively root up, expose, and betray those around them. Wouldn't you say that kind of betrayal is commonplace in our world today? It is. Wouldn't you say that kind of betrayal makes up an essential ingredient of the toxic stew we call cancel culture? It does.

In many ways, cancel culture is dependent on betrayal. We all have mistakes from our past we'd like to forget. All of us have made choices we regret and decisions we would correct or redo if we had the chance. But in a world fueled by cancel culture, those mistakes are not allowed to remain in the past. People intentionally dig through the histories and biographies and social media posts of others—even those they consider to be friends—in order to drag those mistakes into the present.

Lizzie Troughton is a legal advocate in London who specializes in protecting family life and religious freedom. Her work has included legal consultation with the UK Ministry of Justice and the World Health Organization. Her recent article "Cancelling Christians" is a fascinating dive into our present society. She began by recounting Billy Graham's influence on England. In 1954, over two million people thronged Harringay Arena, and thousands more came to his last British crusade in 1989.

Troughton wrote, "If Billy was alive today, it seems unlikely that he would have the same opportunities. The courting of cancel-culture across the UK is now rapidly denying Christian preachers the opportunity to preach on the streets, make bookings at privately rented venues, and even be indirectly advertised in public. We're not just facing a free speech crisis. We're cancelling *Christians*."

She ended her article with these words: "Christianity has had too long a positive influence in our land for us to let it be unlawfully canceled by people who take offence or simply dislike it."[6]

Another voice of reason is Diana Graber. Back in 2010, Diana's daughter attended Journey School in California. Students and staff there were attempting to confront a major cyberbullying incident—the school's first. Everyone did their best to understand the situation and figure out a way to respond, but there was much uncertainty. This was new ground.

Diana had just finished her master's degree in a new field called Media Psychology and Social Change. She had academic experience helping people adjust to the new world of the Internet and social media, and she was eager to put that experience into practice. Together with Journey School, Diana created a new course called "CyberCivics." The goal was to teach middle schoolers what she called "digital citizenship"—a way to help them make sense of the challenges posed by a digital world, gain a better understanding of ethics and morality, think critically instead of superficially, build their digital reputation, value their privacy, and reject all forms of cyberbullying, shaming, and intimidation.[7]

The vitriol we see on social media today is evidence of something new. Something as simple as it is disturbing. Our children need to be taught not to destroy one another because they are being raised in a culture that glorifies hatred. And abuse. And exploitation.

We are living in a culture of disdain.

A Culture of Deception

In His great sermon on the end times, Jesus also warned of the rise of many false prophets who would deceive multitudes (Matt. 24:11). That's never been easier than today, due to social media. Most at risk are senior citizens, who lost about a billion dollars in 2020 due to online scams. A total of 105,301 people over the age of sixty-five were taken to the cleaners. The average person lost more than $9,000, and almost 2,000 senior citizens lost more than $100,000.[8]

Thomas Mulligan, eighty-five, is a retired surgeon and a devout Christian. One day he received a phone call on his landline from Amazon cyber security representatives who said they needed his help to stop a hacker. Mulligan was eager to help, not realizing he was actually on the phone with the very criminals he thought he was helping to catch. He was being scammed by two brothers in India named Karan and Arjun Mishra.

The brothers told Mulligan to download some software that would allow them to "catch the criminals." That software gave the brothers complete control over Mulligan's computer, including all his records and accounts. Their goal was to drain all of Mulligan's bank accounts and take his last cent, including all his retirement funds.

Fortunately that's not the end of the story. While Mulligan was on the line with the criminals, his cell phone buzzed. It was a man calling himself Jim Browning. Browning is an "ethical hacker," a sort of cyber vigilante trying to help victims. Browning said, "Please don't announce this but I think you're on the phone with people who are trying to steal your money."

Browning, using his own hacking prowess, had been tracking the Mishra brothers and had managed to film the entire encounter. With Browning's help, Mulligan was able to recover most—but not all—of his money. Browning explained that he himself was once scammed, and now he uses his skill to help victims—as many as twenty every week.

As for Thomas Mulligan, he told a journalist, "I thought I was an intelligent person and I was too aware to be caught, but I soon realized people can play on your good nature to scam you. They just seemed so credible that I was fooled."[9]

Fake people, fake reviews, fake products, fake news, fake friends—all of this has come to us via the world of Big Tech. And all of this is contributing to a growing culture of deception.

A Culture of Disconnection

The next logical step? Disconnection. In a culture marked by disdain and deception, people want to withdraw from society in any way possible. Jesus put it like this: "And because lawlessness will abound, the love of many will grow cold" (Matt. 24:12).

Apologist Abdu Murray had this to say about the relationally frightening nature of today's society: "In cancel culture, a single mistake is perpetually unforgivable because it's not simply a guilty *act*. Rather, the mistake defines the individual's identity, turning them into a shameful *person*—someone who can be 'canceled.'"[10]

The culture leading up to the tribulation and the end of history will be characterized by coldness in our feelings for one another and in our dealings with one another. It will be marked by isolation and disconnection. Shame will drive people inward. Bullying will drive them downward. Hatred will drive them backward.

We all know about physical pain and emotional pain, but our society is suffering from social pain. According to *Healthline*, "Social pain involves painful emotions caused by situations involving other people, such as feeling rejected, alone, ostracized, devalued, abandoned, or disconnected."[11]

The COVID-19 pandemic exacerbated the problem, taking people from their schools or places of work and forcing many to live in isolation. But the root cause of disconnection is spiritual in nature. When we are disconnected from God, we don't have the love, joy, peace, patience, or kindness to show to others. We become isolated in our self-centeredness.

We see these realities at play in the cancel culture of our modern world. It's not difficult to understand why such a society would lead to relational indifference and isolation. After all, relationships become risky. A good relationship requires us to be vulnerable, but why would I choose to make myself vulnerable to another person when he or she could use my faults to cancel me?

We're witnessing the consequences of this disconnection firsthand. In fact, isolation has become such a problem in our world that in 2018—before the COVID-19 pandemic—Great Britain created a new position in its government called the "minister for loneliness." Tracey Crouch was the first person to fill Britain's new position, and the prime minister proclaimed in a press release: "For far too many people, loneliness is the sad reality of modern life."[12]

The UK isn't the only place struggling with an epidemic of disconnection. Japan appointed its own minister for loneliness in 2021 to combat a huge rise in suicide rates. And Dr. Vivek Murthy, the two-time surgeon general for the United States, wrote a book called *Together*, giving ideas about how to fight loneliness on a national level. His research showed him that loneliness is "associated with an increased risk of heart disease, dementia, depression, anxiety, sleep disturbances and even premature death."[13]

Shockingly, a recent study revealed that nearly half of Americans have not made a new friend in the past five years. As hatred and deception have increased, love in our world has decreased. Our relationships have gone cold.

Where Do We Go from Here?

Now that we understand more about cancel culture and the dangers it poses, where can we go from here? What does it take to live in such a world? Here's an even greater question. What does it take to live for Christ? What does it take to create a different kind of culture in your home? At work? At church?

The short answer is—a lot! It's not easy to live as members of God's kingdom in a world that is increasingly hostile to His values. This is the shared experience of every generation of Christians since the first one, so we've had two thousand years to prepare for these days. One thing we know: the rewards of following Christ are worth it.

So, let's explore four uncancelable characteristics we can incorporate in our lives to claim those rewards.

It Takes Wisdom

Jesus told us, "Behold, I send you out as sheep in the midst of wolves. Therefore be wise as serpents and harmless as doves" (Matt. 10:16).

Wisdom is a word that confuses people today. Many believe wisdom is the same as saying something snappy or catchy—as in a fortune cookie. Others believe wisdom means speaking and acting in accordance with a larger group. This is the "wisdom of the crowd."

On a practical and biblical level, wisdom looks much different from either of those. True wisdom is the ability to discern what is right, good, just, and proper. Wisdom also conveys that discernment to others as temperately as possible. It makes me cringe to see Christians losing their tempers while trying to share the truth. We can't avoid the culture wars, but the tone of our conversation is critical.

Colossians 4:6 says, "Let your conversation be gracious as well as sensible, for then you will have the right answer for everyone" (TLB).

Dr. Barry H. Corey, the president of Biola University, remembers sitting by his dying father's bedside. "What I recall," Corey said, "is not his courage in death. It is his kindness in life. I had never given serious thought to the revolutionary power of kindness until my father died. Then I started paying attention to the stories told about him. He wasn't quickly forgotten. His gentle influence rippled on and continues to ripple on. The stories were neither about his commanding leadership nor about his well-known status. He didn't start a company, earn much money, make the news, hold public office or write a book. No one would have drafted his Wikipedia page. The stories were about his spirit of kindness."

Dr. Corey continued, "I'm just now beginning to grasp how uncommon kindness is. My father's example doesn't seem to characterize the tone of conversations many Christians are having today in the public square."[14]

We don't need to pick fights with those who disagree with us. On the other hand, we don't need to stay silent when our faith is challenged. There are moments when wisdom would suggest we listen and learn rather than speak and stumble. As Solomon said, "Even a fool is counted wise when he holds his peace; when he shuts his lips, he is considered perceptive" (Prov. 17:28).

There are also moments when followers of Jesus need to stand firmly for the truth. That includes you and me. And when those moments come, I hope we will speak and write and teach and create with the same boldness Stephen demonstrated before his accusers in the Sanhedrin. May it be said of us, as it was said of him, that those who hear our words will be "cut to the heart" (Acts 7:54).

Knowing what to say, when to say it, and how to say it—that is wisdom. And that's what we need!

The book of James contrasts the wisdom from below with the wisdom from above. The wisdom from below is "earthly sensual, demonic. For where envy and self-seeking exist, confusion and every evil thing are there. But the wisdom that is from above is first pure, then peaceable, gentle, willing to yield, full of mercy and good fruits, without partiality and without hypocrisy" (James 3:15–17).

Notice that James contrasted worldly wisdom with sensuality, demonic thinking, envy, self-seeking, confusion, and every evil thing. Those are the fruits of cancel culture. But true wisdom is from above. It is a gift from God, available to all who ask for it. James said, "If any of you lacks wisdom, let him ask of God, who gives to all liberally and without reproach, and it will be given to him" (1:5).

That is my challenge for you as you seek to navigate the troubled waters of cancel culture. Don't be frustrated. Don't get angry. Don't let yourself become caught up in the silly arguments or escalating conflicts that are increasingly common. Instead, ask God to fill you with His wisdom. Ask in faith, believing the truth of His Word. Pray for discernment, and He will give it to you.

It Takes Courage

The Bible says, "Be strong and of good courage, do not fear nor be afraid of them; for the LORD your God, He is the One who goes with you. He will not leave you nor forsake you" (Deut. 31:6).

You and I need to heed those commands if we want to live meaningfully as followers of Jesus in a world influenced by cancel culture. We need courage because, as I mentioned above, there will be times when staying close to Christ means taking a stand.

And that stand will likely come at a cost.

John Piper offered this reminder: "Christian courage is the

willingness to say and do the right thing regardless of the earthly cost, because God promises to help you and save you on account of Christ. An act takes courage if it will likely be painful. The pain may be physical, as in war and rescue operations. Or the pain may be mental as in confrontation and controversy."

Either way, according to Piper, "Courage is indispensable for both spreading and preserving the truth of Christ."[15]

The word *bold* occurs repeatedly in the book of Acts to describe the attitude of the early Christians who were infused with courage by the Holy Spirit. One of my favorite verses is Acts 4:31: "And when they had prayed, the place where they were assembled together was shaken; and they were all filled with the Holy Spirit, and they spoke the word of God with boldness."

Iman was a thief and drug addict in Iran. After he was converted to Christ, it became clear he had the gift of evangelism. One day he was arrested, and his first thought was, "If I'm in prison, it must be because someone here needs to hear about Jesus." He didn't resist arrest nor fight the guards. He was kind. When he arrived in his cell, he gave a fifteen-minute sermon to the inmates he found there, and two men knelt down to receive Christ as Savior.

Iman later said, "I only had those 15 minutes to share the gospel because after I shared the gospel, immediately after, the police came and said, 'You have been very good, and you shouldn't be here. You are very kind to us and we want to release you.'"

When the guard opened the doors, the two saved men hugged him, and all three began crying. The police warden was amazed. "You have only known these people for 15 minutes, and they act like you are family!"[16]

Courage is a God-given personality trait that is crucial in critical times. We see this quality in the life of the Old Testament prophet Jeremiah. He remained committed to God and to his prophetic work even in the midst of extreme criticism. Jeremiah was faithful to his ministry even when those attacks came from his own people. He declared the words of the Lord during a particularly difficult period of Israel's history, and he didn't falter as things grew worse around him.

His hearers tried to cancel him. They said, "Come and let us devise plans against Jeremiah; for the law shall not perish from the priest, nor counsel from the wise, nor the word from the prophet. Come and let us attack him with the tongue, and let us not give heed to any of his words" (Jer. 18:18). Yet Jeremiah persisted in his ministry. He continued to speak the truth as a representative of Almighty God.

You and I need a streak of Jeremiah's sanctified stubbornness in these troubled times. The mob will mock and malign us. Society will shame and slander us. Associations will assault and attack us. The crowds may even want to kill us. Through it all, we must have courage. We must choose to be courageous. Thankfully, that is a choice we do not have to make alone, nor is it a stand we need to take alone. God will be with us. Psalm 27:14 says, "Wait on the LORD; be of good courage, and He shall strengthen your heart."

And remember—courage is contagious. Your courage will spread to others.

Mike Nappa wrote, "True Christianity, courageous Christianity—the kind the apostles Paul and Peter and thousands of other early Christians practiced—isn't for wimps. It's not for the fainthearted, the lukewarm, the moderately committed, or the occasional churchgoer. It's for the passionate, the ones with the courage to say, 'I believe God, and I will dedicate my every waking hour to his purpose, no matter what it costs.'"[17]

It Takes Forgiveness

In a world where the mistakes of the past are fair game for the present, there's no room for forgiveness or even atonement. Instead, those who are canceled are always treated as deserving of scorn, wrath, and judgment.

Thankfully, the Bible offers another way.

Ephesians 4:32 says, "Be kind to one another, tenderhearted, forgiving one another, even as God in Christ forgave you."

Colossians 3:12–13 adds, "Therefore, as the elect of God, holy and beloved, put on tender mercies, kindness, humility, meekness, longsuffering; bearing with one another, and forgiving one another, if anyone has a complaint against another; even as Christ forgave you, so you also must do."

When we forgive someone who has wronged us, we set them free, but we also set ourselves free. Bitterness in our own hearts is like a poison that continually eats away at our joy and happiness. But when we forgive, it's liberating for them and for us.

Erik Fitzgerald is a great example of this. One day Erik's pregnant wife, June, was driving down the road with their young daughter, Faith. A car veered into her lane, and June and their unborn baby were killed. Thankfully, Faith survived the crash. The driver of that other car was Matt Swatzell, a young firefighter who had just endured a twenty-four-hour shift and was exhausted. Only a few miles from his home, he fell asleep behind the wheel.

Erik's grief was immense, and so was Matt Swatzell's. The firefighter survived the crash but was devastated at the pain and wreckage his momentary lapse had caused. That pain might have destroyed him—but for Erik.

As a pastor, Erik had been teaching the necessity of forgiveness for years, and he knew he had to practice what he preached. Erik lobbied the judicial system to reduce Matt's punishment. Then the two men began meeting for breakfast several times a month at a local Waffle House. Erik helped Matt work through his pain and regain his footing.

"You forgive as you've been forgiven," Erik later told reporters. "It wasn't an option. If you've been forgiven, then you need to extend that forgiveness."[18]

Paul Meyer, who became a millionaire in his twenties because of his entrepreneurial skills, is someone else who discovered the power of forgiveness. Paul grew up in an interesting home. His father never forgave a soul. If he was ever crossed or offended, he carried the offense all his life and into the grave. He simply didn't forgive anyone—not even family members. His life was full of broken relationships.

But Paul said his mother, on the other hand, "forgave absolutely everyone." Paul said she based her forgiving spirit on God's Word, for she preferred to live with forgiveness than to live with unforgiveness. As a result, she had such peace and joy that it bubbled out of her life.

"There I was, stuck between polar opposites. I loved both my parents and am still indebted to them for what they taught me; but in this area, I knew I had to choose forgiveness or reject it. Which was the better offer? When I was about 16 years old, I made a conscious decision to start forgiving people and to live a life of forgiveness. I had watched my parents and knew which of the two had more peace and joy. The difference was not hard to see."[19]

It Takes Love

And that brings me to my final takeaway: living for Jesus in a world marked by cancel culture takes love.

Do you remember the passage in the Gospels where Jesus "canceled" a young woman? He had been teaching in the temple courts when a group of Pharisees forcibly dragged a girl in front of Him. They had caught her in the act of adultery. "Stone her!" Jesus declared. "That is the punishment proscribed by the law. She is guilty of sin, and she must be permanently removed. She is canceled."

Wait, you don't remember Jesus saying any such thing? Neither do I. Instead of canceling that young woman, Jesus told her accusers, "He who is without sin among you, let him throw a stone at her first" (John 8:7). Then, after everyone had left in shame, Jesus spoke tenderly to the girl, saying, "Neither do I condemn you; go and sin no more" (v. 11).

As we've seen, cancel culture is laser focused on judgment, accusation, and punishment. The goal of those who cancel others is to broadcast their sins from pillar to post and never allow them to be removed or forgotten. Christ's goal, on the other hand, is love, mercy, and grace. In the words of Scripture, "And above all things have fervent love for one another, for 'love will cover a multitude of sins'" (1 Peter 4:8).

Daylan McLee was not a fan of police officers. Who could blame him after being falsely accused of pointing a gun at an officer? McLee spent a full year in prison before he was finally acquitted. "Definitely a lot of animosity," McLee said when asked to describe how he felt about police. "As in, if I see them, I want to go the other way."

Then came the day when McLee rounded a street corner in his hometown of Uniontown, Pennsylvania, and heard a tremendous cacophony. It was a vehicle crash involving a police car. As McLee approached, he saw one officer frantically trying to open the passenger door. Another officer was trapped inside, and the gas tank had been breached. Flames were already approaching the cabin. Without a second thought, Daylan McLee ran forward to help. He helped rip open the door and pulled the officer to freedom before the car burst fully into flames.

"It's amazing when there's true love in people and they can get you out of something like that," said Jay Hanley, the officer who was rescued, "no matter who you are or where you come from." Then, speaking of McLee, he added, "There should be more people like that."[20]

Yes, there should be. Sometimes I'd like to cancel culture itself, wouldn't you? I'd like to cancel all the hatred and division, the crimes and lawlessness, the smugness and snobbery of the pundits and pencil pushers. I'd like to cancel the violence and the vitriol.

One day Jesus will do that.

But for now, there is one form of cancel culture I do embrace, and I want to recommend it to you. This is the canceling we need!

The Bible says, "When you were dead in your sins. . . . God made you alive with Christ. He forgave us all our sins, having canceled the charge of our legal indebtedness, which stood against us and condemned us; he has taken it away, nailing it to the cross" (Col. 2:13–14 NIV).

When we come to Jesus Christ, He cancels our sins and welcomes us into His family. Instead of disdain, deception, and disconnection, He gives us love, truth, and a place by His side. He fills us with wisdom, courage, and compassion. He commissions us to counter the cancel culture with the power of the cross—which can never be canceled, revoked, or annulled either in time or in all of eternity. We can go to bed tonight knowing with all our hearts that nothing or no one can ever cancel the One who cancels our sins.

The prophet Isaiah accurately described our generation when he wrote, "truth is fallen in the street" (Isa. 59:14). Almost everywhere you look, we are turning a deaf ear to truth as we desperately seek for meaning and fulfillment in all the wrong places. While searching for truth, we are actually running away from the truth.

Meanwhile, the truth goes from taught to tolerated in the public square and from believed to banned in our public schools. What was once the rule of faith and practice in our culture has been relegated to a negative icon used to illustrate the "narrow-mindedness" of our founding fathers. As we are running away from the truth, truth is running away from us.

We are in the midst of a famine. "Not a famine of bread, nor a thirst for water, but of hearing the words of the LORD" (Amos 8:11).

Chapter 8

A Spiritual Prophecy—
Spiritual Famine

*"Behold the days are coming," says the Lord God, "That
I will send a famine on the land."*

AMOS 8:11

When actor Benedict Cumberbatch took on the role of Greville Wynne in the movie *The Courier*, he faced some scenes that required him to endure severe weight loss. The movie was inspired by real events. Wynne was an English businessman recruited by MI-6 and the CIA to spy against Russia during the Cold War. When Wynne was captured by the Soviets, he spent a few years in lockup. His near-starvation diet reduced him to skin and bones.

For about four scenes in the movie, Cumberbatch had to replicate the look of a man nearly starved to death.

The movie's crew took a break from filming while Cumberbatch went on a harsh diet to make him look emaciated for this portion of the movie. It was a brutal experience. "You get very disoriented," Cumberbatch recalled. "You feel dehydrated, you feel hungry all the time. You feel emotionally and physically very vulnerable. . . . It's horrible. I felt . . . mental instability."[1]

Have you ever wondered why our world seems so hungry all the time? Why we are perpetually thirsty? Why so many people are emotionally and physically vulnerable, feel horrible, and seem mentally unstable?

The answer is that our generation is famished. We are starved for truth, hungry for hope, and thirsty for the God-given message of Scripture.

The Bible teaches there will be a famine of truth in the last days. The most vivid biblical prediction about this comes from the rugged prophet Amos, who wasn't a trained preacher or an educated theologian. He was a herdsman who spent most of his time keeping his sheep from straying off. He also picked fruit during harvest season.

Even so, Amos churned with courage and spoke with conviction. His homespun message was direct: "Prepare to meet your God, O Israel!" (Amos 4:12).

Whenever I read those words, I recall seeing them painted on rocks and signposts along highways when I was growing up. Now they've almost disappeared from our consciousness. People take offense at that message in the modern world.

They did in Amos's time too. The priests and politicians tried to drive him away. "Get out of here, you prophet!" they said. "Go on back to the land of Judah, and earn your living by prophesying there! Don't bother us with your prophecies here in Bethel. This is the king's sanctuary and the national place of worship!" (Amos 7:12–13 NLT).

They didn't know with whom they were dealing! This southern farmer wouldn't be cowed or intimidated. Instead, Amos met their threats with this piercing prediction:

> "Behold, the days are coming," says the Lord GOD,
> "That I will send a famine on the land,
> Not a famine of bread,
> Nor a thirst for water,

But of hearing the words of the LORD.
They shall wander from sea to sea,
And from north to east;
They shall run to and fro, seeking the word of the LORD,
But shall not find it."

8:11–12

Amos was describing a particularly deadly type of famine—a problem of the ears, not of the stomach. We may well be in the early stages of a "hearing famine" in our generation as another layer of biblical prophecy unfurls.

This isn't the only time we encounter such predictions in the pages of God's Word.

The prophet Ezekiel declared, "Disaster will come upon disaster, and rumor will be upon rumor. Then they will seek a vision from a prophet; but the law will perish from the priest, and counsel from the elders" (Ezek. 7:26).

The prophet Micah warned, "Therefore you shall have night without vision, and you shall have darkness without divination; the sun shall go down on the prophets, and the day shall be dark for them" (Micah 3:6).

In the New Testament, the apostle Paul said, "But know this, that in the last days perilous times will come: For men will be . . . always learning and never able to come to the knowledge of the truth" (2 Tim. 3:1–2, 7).

Doesn't it feel as if those days are upon us? Look around you. Everywhere you turn, there's widespread emotional famine, calamity upon calamity, rumor upon rumor, perilous times, and an acceleration of learning without the ability to absorb the truth. People are running to and fro, seeking significance and satisfaction. But they have lost their appetite for the objective, infallible truth of God's Word.

The psalmist lamented, "We are given no signs from God; no prophets are left, and none of us knows how long this will be" (Ps. 74:9 NIV).

It's not the absence of the Word of God that's troubling. There are Bibles aplenty in most of the world, and a virtual army of Bible translators are working night and day to get the Scripture into every tongue. We've made great strides. More than 1,500 languages now have access to the New Testament, and Bible translation work is currently being done on the rest. Missionary and translation societies are focusing now on the 1.5 billion people who do not have the entire Bible in their language, working feverishly to meet their need.[2]

That means about 6 billion of earth's 7.6 billion people now have access to the full Bible, both Old and New Testaments. God's Word has never been more accessible. In many places in the world, it's only a smartphone or laptop click away.

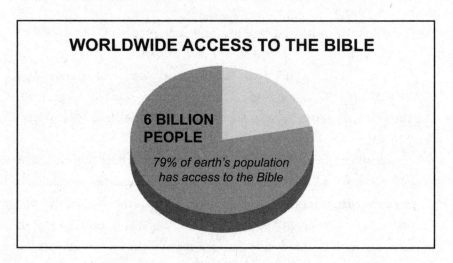

WORLDWIDE ACCESS TO THE BIBLE

6 BILLION PEOPLE

79% of earth's population has access to the Bible

What was Amos talking about, then? The prophet's warnings concerned a loss of *hunger* for God and His truth. This is a self-inflicted famine.

A. W. Tozer wrote, "The great people of the Bible and Christian history have had an insatiable hunger for God. He waits to be wanted. Too bad that with so many of us He waits so very long in vain."[3]

I remember as a young preacher receiving a copy of *Hudson Taylor's Spiritual Secret*. It is a book written by a man who was a great missionary, and it talks about the things in his life that set him apart from others. I will always remember copying out of that book this little statement and writing it into the Bible I was using at that time: "I saw Him and I sought Him, I had Him and I wanted Him."[4]

That's how he felt about God. No wonder he turned his world upside down for the Lord!

The Scriptures are filled with reminders to us of the importance of having a spiritual hunger for God:

- "One thing I have desired of the LORD, that will I seek: that I may dwell in the house of the LORD all the days of my life, to behold the beauty of the LORD, and to inquire in His temple" (Ps. 27:4)
- "As the deer pants for the water brooks, so pants my soul for You, O God. My soul thirsts for God, for the living God. When shall I come and appear before God?" (42:1–2)
- "O God, You are my God; early will I seek You; my soul thirsts for You; my flesh longs for You in a dry and thirsty land where there is no water. So I have looked for You in the sanctuary, to see Your power and Your glory" (63:1–2).

I'll never forget the impact another little book had on my life some years ago, this one written by Sherwood Eliot Wirt. *A Thirst for God* was basically a commentary on Psalm 142. Wirt said that one of the problems we have when we talk about spiritual hunger is that we think spiritual hunger and physical hunger are exactly alike. But they are as diverse from each other as they could be:

> Spiritual hunger . . . works just opposite from physical hunger. When we are physically hungry, we eat and satisfy our appetites and cease to be hungry. But when we are spiritually undernourished and are then given a feast of good spiritual food, it makes us hungrier than ever. Thus the more we learn about God's love, the more we want to know; we can't get enough.
>
> The reverse . . . is also true. When we are physically hungry and miss a meal, our appetite becomes ravenous. But if time passes and we

receive no spiritual food, we may lose our appetite for it. Malnutrition sets in and we cease to care.[5]

The reality is that our hearts are easily drawn away from God and His Word. Human beings have a terrible habit of losing their appetite for God's truth.

Dr. D. A. Carson wrote:

Apart from grace-driven effort, people do not gravitate toward godliness, prayer, obedience to Scripture, faith, and delight in the Lord. We drift toward compromise and call it tolerance; we drift toward disobedience and call it freedom; we drift toward superstition and call it faith. We cherish the indiscipline of lost self-control and call it relaxation; we slouch toward prayerlessness and delude ourselves into thinking we have escaped legalism; we slide toward godlessness and convince ourselves we have been liberated.[6]

What Does This Mean?

I know there may be some reading these pages who will wonder about the inclusion of a chapter on spiritual famine. After all, many of the other topics discussed in this book may seem more cataclysmic or apocalyptic in nature—the COVID-19 pandemic, the threat of socialism, the economic danger poised to crush all resistance during the tribulation, and more.

Yet what we see prophesied in the book of Amos and other passages of Scripture is nothing less than spiritual starvation. It's a crisis affecting not our bodies but our souls.

To appreciate the serious nature of this coming spiritual famine, we need to dig a little deeper into its implications. What does it mean for the last days? What does it mean for our lives right now?

Here are four ways our culture is currently under threat from spiritual malnourishment.

Our Heritage Is Being Lost

The psalmist said, "You have given me the heritage of those who fear Your name" (Ps. 61:5). It's not just our knowledge of the Bible that's being lost in today's culture. It's the entirety of our Christian history. Revisionist historians have removed every shred of wholesome biblical influence from the records of America and Europe and have instead filled our textbooks with the questionable contributions of everyone else.

How many school children know the first thing George Washington did after he took the oath of office as America's first president? He stooped over and kissed the Bible on which his hand had just rested.

How many school children know that the Liberty Bell is encircled by the words of Leviticus 25:10? That the first shots of the Revolutionary War were fired at a pastor and his church members in Lexington, Massachusetts? That the first American to be killed for the freedom of the press was a Christian abolitionist named Elijah Lovejoy? That the top of the Washington Monument is capped with an exclamation of praise to God?

But wait! It's not just the secular institutions of our society that are spiritually underfed.

How many children in Sunday school and church know anything about the two thousand years of Christian history? Where are the missionary stories? What's happened to the heroes and martyrs and stalwarts of the past, whose courage brought the gospel down the ranks to us? How many children grow up learning the Twenty-third Psalm and the Lord's Prayer? And what has happened to our classic hymns?

Our spiritual heritage is slipping away.

Our Theology Is Being Weakened

We must also guard our theology. It's easy for churches to become malnourished in times of spiritual famine. George Barna and his researchers issued a 2020 report warning, "American Christians are undergoing a 'post-Christian Reformation.'"

"The irony of the reshaping of the spiritual landscape in America is that it represents a post-Christian Reformation driven by people seeking to retain a Christian identity," said Barna. "The most startling realization . . . is how many people from evangelical churches are adopting unbiblical beliefs."

The report went on to say, "Evangelicals have traditionally emphasized the importance of seeing the Bible as the infallible, inerrant Word of God. Now, however, 52 percent do not believe in objective moral truth."[7]

The researchers concluded, "What used to be basic, universally-known truths about Christianity are now unknown mysteries to a large and growing share of Americans—especially young adults."[8]

SPIRITUAL FAMINE IN AMERICA

5 out of 10 Christians <u>do not believe</u> in objective moral truth

4 out of 10 Christians <u>do not read</u> the Bible

As a pastor, I'm deeply concerned about the wayward theological patterns trending in churches everywhere. It's not simply the liberal old Protestant mainstream denominations that are diminishing their doctrines. It's evangelical churches, who, in trying to reach a resistant audience, go too far in compromising biblical truth.

For centuries, God's Word has been at the center of Christian preaching. Today, questioning scriptural authority is in vogue, even in certain faith communities. Popular speakers advocate processing God's Word through cultural filters rather than the other way around.

Remember, we don't stand in judgment on the Bible. It stands in judgment on us. When we turn our backs on God and His Word, God may turn His back on us. The book of Romans speaks of God giving people over to their sinful wills (1:18–32). I fear many in our society will suffer from unintended consequences because of their desire to distance themselves from God's Word.

Our Bibles Are Being Overlooked

Mark Twain once defined a literary classic as, "A book which people praise and don't read." Unfortunately, that describes the way many people in modern society approach the Bible.

According to Dr. Jeremiah Johnston, the average American household owns between three and ten Bibles, but 42 percent of American Christians are too busy to read them. "As Christians we need to understand the reality of biblical illiteracy, first in our own lives and families but also in the church."[9]

It doesn't help that cultures around the world are trying to minimize Bible reading. China has just shut down Bible apps and Christian WeChat public accounts. Hard copy Bibles are no longer available for sale online in that country either.[10] And of course Islamic nations have restricted their citizens from exposure to the Scriptures for decades. Even centuries.

In America and the West, the Gideons are running into problems getting their Bibles into many hotel rooms. A recent survey showed the percentage of hotels willing to offer Bibles in their rooms has dropped from 95 percent to 48 percent. Hotels are finding younger travelers are "less devout than their parents or grandparents," and they don't want to offend atheists or those of other religious faiths.

One atheistic group created stickers for its members to attach to any Gideon Bible they did find in a hotel room. It said: "Warning: Literal belief in this book may endanger your health and life."[11]

I'd call that spiritual famine! People who disregard the Bible may someday get what they want—a society where the Bible is no longer read or proclaimed, and where they can freely sin without Scripture confronting their conscience. But they may get more than they bargained for—a society without the moral compass of Scripture will self-destruct from moral decay and decadence.

Our Appetite Is Being Ruined

That leads to my next thought. The reason we're facing a spiritual famine is because our appetite for God's truth is being ruined. A child that gorges on junk food and candy in the afternoon won't have much of an appetite for meat and potatoes at supper.

Tim Carman is a food writer and columnist for the *Washington Post*. His entire career and much of his life revolves around food. When COVID-19 came along, he read about people losing their sense of smell and taste. Carman went out of his way to protect himself, knowing some people have waited months for their olfactory senses and taste buds to return. If that happened to him, it would threaten his livelihood.

But Carman did get COVID. He never lost his sense of taste and smell, but something worse happened. He lost his appetite. "It's a cruel space to occupy as a food writer," he said. "You can smell the aromas of homemade tomato soup, chocolate chip cookies, Persian rice, fresh-brewed coffee, tonkotsu ramen, and none of them hold any appeal."[12]

In these last days, it seems as if Satan has unleashed an invisible spiritual virus that robs people of their appetite for God's Word. But it's worse than that, because it's not just a loss of appetite. It's a total distaste for the Bible. People grab a handful of Scripture, take a bite, find it distasteful, and spew it out like a child spitting out carrots. As likely as not, they'll dub it "hate speech" and attack anyone who offers a bite to others.

Often, God will respond to our lack of spiritual appetite with silence. He doesn't force His words in our ears, and He may withdraw for a time if we lose our appreciation for the privilege of His voice.

God's silence may be hardly noticeable at first. You may still remember times when God spoke to you, but you gradually realize you've not heard His voice for a long time. If you realize you are in a drought, immediately seek God and ask Him what adjustments your life requires so you can once again enjoy fellowship with Him.

It may be you've disobeyed His last instructions to you. Perhaps He's waiting on your obedience before giving you fresh direction. If there is unconfessed sin in your life or you have a damaged relationship, correct it at once.

By grace, we can stay healthy even during a large-scale spiritual famine. Paul told us to be "nourished in the words of faith and of . . . good doctrine" (1 Tim. 4:6). The psalmist described Scripture as sweeter than honey (Ps. 19:10). And the prophet Jeremiah said, "Your words were found, and I ate them, and Your word was to me the joy and rejoicing of my heart" (Jer. 15:16).

Everything about the Bible is special. It's God's gift to the human race—bread for the soul, honey for the heart, nourishment for the nerves, and wisdom for the mind. Every syllable represents God's own thoughts conveyed through inspired human writers who recorded the infallible message for the world. In this way, the Lord gave us a Book containing everything we really need for life and eternity. It makes us wise unto salvation through faith in Christ. It's portable; we can carry it anywhere.

It's simple; perfect for children. It's deep; engaging the lifetimes of earth's greatest scholars.

And it's yours! Jesus said, "People do not live by bread alone, but by every word that comes from the mouth of God" (Matt. 4:4 NLT).

Where Do We Go from Here?

What, then, should we do when our land is spiritually famished? Based on everything we've learned, where do we go from here? What's our call to action?

Near the end of the Bible, the apostle Peter wrote two letters to the churches of his day, penning the final one shortly before his gruesome death by upside-down crucifixion. As he wrote those last words, one thing was on his mind: making sure no one forgot the message of the gospel or the teachings of Scripture.

He said:

- "I will not be negligent to remind you always of these things, though you know and are established in the present truth" (2 Peter 1:12).
- "I will be careful to ensure that you always have a reminder of these things after my decease" (v. 15).
- "I now write to you this second epistle (in both of which I stir up your pure minds by way of reminder), that you may be mindful of the words which were spoken before by the holy prophets, and of the commandment of us, the apostles of the Lord and Savior, knowing this first: that scoffers will come in the last days" (3:1–3).

Peter was leaving the world, but he wanted his message to remain, to never be forgotten, and to be passed down through the generations until Jesus returns. He longed for the gospel to expand, to explode throughout the earth. He wanted to repel spiritual famine.

That same zeal must seize you and me. It must consume the church of today as we face the world of tomorrow. It must become not so much what we do as followers of Jesus, but who we are.

Based on Peter's words, let me give you four "Be's" to put into practice during times of spiritual famine.

Be Burdened

Peter spoke as a deeply burdened man who wanted to make sure his hearers were devouring the Word and sharing it with others. He was ready to make every effort as long as he lived.

The apostle Peter also gave us another example of what it's like to be burdened for a society facing spiritual famine. He described Lot, who lived in Sodom, as "a righteous man, who was distressed by the depraved conduct of the lawless (for that righteous man, living among them day after day, was tormented in his righteous soul by the lawless deeds he saw and heard)" (2 Peter 2:7–8 NIV).

In a similar way, the apostle Paul walked around Athens and "his spirit was provoked within him when he saw that the city was given over to idols" (Acts 17:16).

Jesus felt the same burden for His city, crying out, "Jerusalem, Jerusalem, the one who kills the prophets and stones those who are sent to her! How often I wanted to gather your children together, as a hen gathers her chicks under her wings, but you were not willing!" (Matt. 23:37).

We can't do much to alleviate the spiritual famine around us until we have a similar concern within us.

Bob Pierce was a Youth for Christ evangelist who started out for China in 1947, though he had only enough money for a ticket to Honolulu. When he did eventually make it to China, he saw thousands come to Christ. But he saw something else that haunted him for the rest of his life. He visited a cemetery where more than a hundred men, women, and children lived, struggling to survive. "They were starving, naked, and dying without any medical intervention. And most heartbreaking of all, their healthy babies died with them."

Afterward, Pierce was never the same man. He was overtaken with a burden for those in the world who were physically and spiritually starving. As a result, he nearly wrecked his own life trying to help others. But in the process he founded two great relief organizations: World Vision and Samaritan's Purse.[13]

We don't want to wreck our lives, but we need the compelling love of Christ burning like a fire in our hearts for a famished world. We need a fresh vision for the world. We need to be the Good Samaritan in someone's life.

Be Students

Second, Peter insists we become personal students of Scripture and devour its truth. He said, "As newborn babes, desire the pure milk of the word, that you may grow thereby, if indeed you have tasted that the Lord is gracious" (1 Peter 2:2–3).

Peter wanted us to know the nature of Scripture, which did not originate with human beings, "but holy men of God spoke as they were moved by the Holy Spirit" (2 Peter 1:21).

He even told us how to study the Bible. We're to search it "intently and with the greatest care," the way the prophets of old studied the Scriptures, earnestly looking for all they could find there about the Lord (1 Peter 1:10 NIV).

Do you study the Bible "intently and with the greatest care"? Fulfilling that command means not just reading Scripture but submitting to Scripture. It means we view God's Word not as something we are supposed to fit into our day when we have the time, but as the very foundation of our lives.

Peter also told us how studying God's Word would affect us. By poring over "exceedingly great and precious promises," we will "be partakers of the divine nature, having escaped the corruption that is in the world through lust" (2 Peter 1:4).

Charles Swindoll wrote,

Remember, famine does not mean an absence of something but a shortage of it. There can be a shortage of spiritual nourishment in our lives—in our marriages, our homes. A regular diet of the unadulterated truth of God is a rare experience. Sadly, our Christian culture provides the false sensation of being spiritually full with easy access to "fast food" spiritual snacks. Podcasts, snippets of truth offered in watered-down church services, radio sound bites, and self-help devotionals contribute to a culture of spiritual malnutrition. What's needed is a substantive intake of spiritual food. That only comes when we sit at the table—often—to receive the life-transforming and nutritious truths from the Word of God.[14]

Someone said the best way to teach children to eat well is for them to see their parents thoroughly enjoying a healthy meal. How can we expect the world to develop an appetite for Scripture when we ourselves never become diligent students of the Bible?

Bible teacher Warren Wiersbe was converted at a Youth for Christ rally in high school. Soon Wiersbe was devouring his Bible. "I think Bible study is one of the most exciting things I ever do," he said. "I've been living with the Bible ever since I got saved that night at a Youth for Christ rally. . . . As I study the Word, it always tells me something. I feel sorry for people who read it and put the Bible back on the shelf and forget about it."

He said, "In all of my conference ministry, I've tried to get people excited about the Bible. There's so much there that people ignore and they shouldn't do that. I find that when I trace the cross references, when I take time to pray and meditate, God says something to me. Then I can share that with others. So the joy of Bible study is not in learning something abstract. The joy of Bible study is seeing your life changed."[15]

I say, "Amen!"

Begin today! Learn to read the Bible systematically, study it diligently, apply it correctly, and share it boldly. Jesus said, "Blessed are those who hunger and thirst for righteousness, for they shall be filled" (Matt. 5:6).

Be Shepherds

Peter had a special word of instruction for pastors and Bible teachers: "Shepherd the flock of God which is among you, serving as overseers, not by compulsion but willingly" (1 Peter 5:2). In using the term *shepherd*, he was undoubtedly thinking of his own experience years before when Jesus walked with him along the shoreline of Galilee. The Lord asked him three times, "Do you love Me?"

"Yes, yes, and yes!" replied Peter.

Jesus said to him, "Feed My sheep" (John 21:15–17).

If I could do anything to influence today's evangelical churches around the world, it would be a clarion call to return solid biblical teaching to the pulpit—substantial sermons from biblical texts, correctly interpreted and wisely applied. Many sermons nowadays are little more than TED Talks. Too many pastors are delivering their own thoughts with a few verses thrown in to make the whole message sound more biblical than it really is.

I would remind us of the teachers of Ezra's day: "So they read distinctly from the book, in the Law of God; and they gave the sense, and helped them to understand the reading" (Neh. 8:8). Following that pattern would do much to alleviate today's spiritual famine.

And while I'm at it, let me remind us all that the greatest shepherds in the world today are Christian parents who must diligently feed the lambs entrusted to them with the Word of God.

The thought of spiritually malnourished children, especially in traditionally Christian families, troubles me deeply. While there are many family devotional resources available, nothing is richer than the frequent habit of sharing with your children what you've found yourself in His Word that day. The Bible tells us to share the Scripture with our children when we get up and when we go to bed, when we sit at home and when we travel down the road. We're even told to write it on placards and to post it on the walls of our homes (Deut. 6:9).

Matt Brown is an evangelist who credits his parents with instilling within him a love for God's Word. One Bible verse is especially memorable—Proverbs 22:29: "Do you see a man who excels in his work? He will stand before kings; he will not stand before unknown men."

"This verse is on the placard sitting on my dad's desk for the past few years," said Matt. "My mom made him this placard to remind him to excel in his work. Not that my dad needed any reminding—he is a very hard worker. In fact, my dad has worked hard all his life, raising four boys and putting himself through college while working a 60 hour a week job as a computer engineer and being actively involved in our church."

A few years ago, Matt's dad started a side business doing sound installations and event productions. Recently Matt received a call from his dad, who had just won a contract with the White House to help put on an event.

"My dad shared with me his experience of putting the curtain on the President's bullet proof shield that surrounds him while he speaks, and of sitting a few rows from where he spoke during the rally. Unbelievable to see this little verse lived out in real time in my dad's life!"[16]

I love that story, and also that last phrase. This devil-sent spiritual famine cannot exist among those in whom the Bible's little verses are lived out in real time in front of their children.

Oh, to have Peter's shepherding heart and to say, "I will always remind you of these things, even though you know them and are firmly established in the truth you now have. I think it is right to refresh your memory as long as I live" (2 Peter 1:12–13 NIV).

Be Evangelistic

Finally, to ease the spiritual famine in the world today, we have to aggressively give out the Bread of Life. Peter reminded us we have been "born again, not of corruptible seed but incorruptible, through the word of God which lives and abides forever. . . . Now this is the word which by the gospel was preached to you" (1 Peter 1:23, 25).

The best method of evangelism I've ever read was Peter's own strategy for winning the lost: "Sanctify the Lord God in your hearts, and always be ready to give a defense to everyone who asks you a reason for the hope that is in you" (3:15).

If you'd opened the Phoenix newspapers on June 11, 2015, you'd have seen the picture of a young, unsmiling Armenian immigrant named Vrouyr Manoukian, twenty-four years old, his eyes downcast. The headline said: "Phoenix man gets 4.5 years in burned-body case."[17]

Manoukian had let a classmate crash at his apartment, but the intoxicated friend grew violent. When he pulled out a knife, Manoukian whacked him over the head with a patio chair and killed him. Making a bad situation much worse, Manoukian and a friend took the body and the bloodied furniture into the desert and burned them. But they were seen by a passerby.

On his first night in jail, a sense of despair came over the young immigrant. But at that moment he remembered his grandmother's habit of reading the Bible. He fell to his knees, asking God for help.

Two days later, a fellow inmate gave Manoukian a copy of the Bible. Someone also gave him a tattered copy of a prison magazine featuring the salvation story of a fellow Armenian, Roger Munchian.

"I wrote Roger and was surprised when he came to visit me at my jail cell," Manoukian said. "He told me about Christ's unshakable love for me. God loved me so much, he said, that He wasn't going to let me walk this journey alone. . . . I soon asked Jesus Christ to be my Lord and Savior. The seeds that my grandmother had planted in my youth finally began to sprout. As I grew in my faith, God gave me love and compassion for those around me. I longed to reach at least one person for Christ."

Soon Manoukian was able to lead a fellow inmate, Joey, to faith in Christ. Today Manoukian is a mechanic with a Christian-owned shop. He has a beautiful wife and two "goofy dogs." He said, "I also spend time restoring cars. I love transforming crumpled, discarded Detroit steel into something beautiful in my shop, just like God transformed my crumpled life in His shop called prison."[18]

How interesting! A grandmother, a fellow inmate, and a writer of a magazine article—all these were used by God in bringing a prisoner to the Lord. And as soon as Manoukian came to Christ, he longed to reach "at least one person."

The way to banish spiritual famine in the world is one person at a time. We turn the tide as we share the gospel of Christ with boldness, ready to give an answer to anyone who asks for a reason for the hope within us.

This is the world's only hope in these last days—but it's the only hope we need. It is solid, biblical, true, and eternal hope. It's a certain hope in a risen Savior, who is Himself the "bread of life." God has warned us of coming days of spiritual famine, but He has given us living bread to share with the world.

I think it's best summed up in John 6:27, 32–35, where Jesus said:

"Do not labor for the food which perishes, but for the food which endures to everlasting life. . . . My Father gives you the true bread from heaven. For the bread of God is He who comes down from heaven and gives life to the world."

Then they said to Him, "Lord, give us this bread always."

And Jesus said to them, "I am the bread of life. He who comes to Me shall never hunger, and he who believes in Me shall never thirst."

May God whet our appetite for this Bread, and may He use us as relief workers in these days of spiritual drought and inward hunger!

Perhaps no piece of land on the planet has been as revered, disputed, or disrupted as Jerusalem. As the centerpiece of three of the world's major religions and the sticking point for international political maneuverings for generations, Jerusalem has been a place of pilgrimage and pillaging, miracles and mayhem. But it has also been, and continues to be, the most significant city on earth.

Jerusalem is mentioned in the Bible more than twice as many times as the next most-mentioned city, and the Lord Himself declared that Jerusalem was His own special city upon which He had placed His name.

So then, why is so much blood and ink spilled over this place? What is its significance in Scripture, in history, and in prophecy?

And why is it so important that we pray for the peace and prosperity of Jerusalem today?

Chapter 9

A Geographical Prophecy—Jerusalem

Thus says the Lord GOD: "This is Jerusalem; I have set her in the midst of the nations and the countries all around her."

EZEKIEL 5:5

History was humming in the air like electricity on May 14, 2018, as a blue-ribbon crowd assembled in front of the new American embassy in Jerusalem. The event coincided with the seventieth anniversary of the rebirth of the State of Israel. The weather was mild and sunny, and the gallery was filled with sunglasses and smiles.

After years of vacillation, the United States of America was officially moving its ambassador and diplomatic staff to the true capital of the Jewish State: Jerusalem.

The eight hundred guests in attendance that day included members of the United States Congress, the US Deputy Secretary of State, members of the Trump family, the US ambassador to Israel, the Middle East peace envoy, representatives of thirty-three other countries, pastors and rabbis, and, of course, Israel's president and its prime minister.

Standing in the sunshine before giant flags of the United States and Israel, an emotional Prime Minister Benjamin Netanyahu punched the podium with his finger and exclaimed, "What a glorious day! Remember this moment! This is history!"

He said, "In Jerusalem, Abraham passed the greatest test of faith and the right to be the father of our nation. In Jerusalem, King David established our capital three thousand years ago. In Jerusalem, King Solomon built our Temple, which stood for many centuries. . . . We are in Jerusalem and we are here to stay."

Then Netanyahu quoted a prophetic passage from the Old Testament, saying, "The prophet, Zechariah, declared over 2,500 years ago, 'So said the Lord, "I will return to Zion and I will dwell in the midst of Jerusalem. And Jerusalem shall be called the City of Truth."'"[1]

That can be said of no other city on earth! Jerusalem is interwoven like a golden thread into the tapestry of biblical history and future prophecy. Jerusalem is one of the oldest cities on earth, the place where Melchizedek met Abraham, where Abraham offered Isaac, and where Solomon met the Queen of Sheba. Its history lingers in the very air.

I've had the privilege of visiting that city many times, and each occasion has been memorable. As you drive in from the east, the sight takes your breath away. Emerging from a tunnel, your attention leaps to the left. There, shimmering in the sunshine, is the Temple Mount, the Wailing Wall, the glistening Dome of the Rock, the Al-Aqsa Mosque, the Mount of Olives, and the Church of the Holy Sepulchre. The walls around the Old City reflect a golden hue, and at night they're burnished with an eerie glow from great spotlights. The sight of them by day or night brings tears to many travelers.

By moving the US embassy to this hallowed city, the United States made a historic statement in support of Israel, illustrating a unique union between two of the greatest democracies on earth. Since then, other nations have moved their embassies to Jerusalem, though the decision to do so is controversial. In fact, many politicians and pundits proclaimed the move would lead to renewed conflict in the region. Even war.

Why? Why should there be such deep emotions about a piece of real estate? Why such love and hatred for a single city?

The Allure of the Holy City

One answer is that Jerusalem is bound up with prophecies from Almighty God! I can hardly believe the rebirth of the State of Israel occurred during my lifetime. And now I've had the privilege of watching another prophetic domino fall with yet another elevation of Jerusalem.

As one writer exclaimed:

> Just think about it: if you are convinced that the repatriation of the Jewish people to the state of Israel is something that must occur in the sequence of events leading up to the return of Christ, it is immensely exciting to think that the world's greatest superpower is acknowledging the absolute legitimacy of Israel's right to this hallowed ground.[2]

In the words of prophetic writer Randall Price, Jerusalem is now set to become "God's stage for the final drama."[3]

Jerusalem Is a Central City

The city of Jerusalem—sacred to Christianity, Judaism, and Islam—is arguably (and certainly prophetically) the world's most significant city. Jerusalem is mentioned in the Bible 811 times, with Babylon being the next most-mentioned city—287 times.

"Jerusalem . . . appears in about two-thirds of the books of the Old and almost one-half of the books of the New Testament."[4]

Jerusalem has been called by over seventy names throughout its history.[5] The most important of them are in the Bible:

- The City of David (2 Sam. 5:7, 9)
- Zion (Ps. 87:2)
- The City of Righteousness (Isa. 1:26)
- The City of the Great King (Ps. 48:2)
- The Holy City (Isa. 48:2; 52:1; Rev. 21:2)

Do you realize Jerusalem is so renowned that more than thirty other locations have adopted that name? Eleven places in the United States are named *Jerusalem*. For example, Jerusalem, New York, is a town of about four thousand people in the Finger Lakes district of that state.

The population of Jerusalem, the capital of Israel, is moving toward a million people. In our Lord's time, it was considerably smaller. Archaeologists vary widely in their estimates, from 20,000 to 200,000. It's likely the true population of Jerusalem was about 75,000 in the time of Christ, but the population swelled by hundreds of thousands for the Jewish feasts, such as Passover.[6]

Try to imagine the crowds—Jesus would have been among them—clogging the roads and climbing the hills up to Jerusalem. Hear them singing the ancient pilgrim psalms. One always "went up" to Jerusalem. Like Rome, Jerusalem is a city set on hills (elevation 2,575 feet). The psalmist wrote of Jerusalem, it is "beautiful in elevation, the joy of the whole earth" (Ps. 48:2).

According to the Bible, to be born in Jerusalem is a signature blessing from God: "And of Zion it will be said, 'This one and that one were born in her; and the Most High Himself shall establish her.' The LORD will record, when He registers the peoples" (87:5–6).

Though Jesus was born in nearby Bethlehem and raised in Nazareth, He visited Jerusalem many times. When our Lord was only a few days old, His parents brought Him to the temple and presented Him to the Lord (Luke 2:21–40). He tarried in Jerusalem at age twelve, spending three nights alone in its darkened streets and conversing by day with the teachers in the temple (vv. 41–50). After His baptism, Jesus was taken to Jerusalem by Satan, to the highest point of the temple (4:9–12).

John recorded four visits of Jesus to Jerusalem (John 2:13–3:21; 5:1–47; 7–10; 12–20), and the other Gospels add important details, particularly regarding the events of the Passion week. Jesus' death, resurrection, and ascension all took place in and around the city of Jerusalem.[7]

Jesus loved Jerusalem, and He mourned over her unbelief: "O Jerusalem, Jerusalem, the one who kills the prophets and stones those who are sent to her! How often I wanted to gather your children together, as a hen gathers her chicks under her wings, but you were not willing!" (Matt. 23:37).

Jerusalem is the center of Israel in the same way your heart is the center of your body. No city on earth has captured the world's attention through the centuries like Jerusalem. Ezekiel 5:5 says, "This is Jerusalem; I have set her in the midst of the nations and the countries all around her."

Randall Price wrote: "Jerusalem is the city at the center. It is the center of mankind's hopes and God's purposes. God loves it, Satan hates it, Jesus wept over it, the Holy Spirit descended in it, the nations are drawn to it, and Christ will return and reign in it. Indeed the destiny of the world is tied to the future of Jerusalem."[8]

Jerusalem Is a Chosen City

Jerusalem was chosen specifically by God for her role in the history of Israel, in the life of Jesus, and in the events of His return. According to 1 Kings 8:44, Jerusalem is "the city which [God has] chosen." This fulfills the five-fold prediction of Moses in Deuteronomy 12, that God will choose a city as the dwelling place for His great name after the children of Israel possessed their promised land (vv. 5, 11, 14, 18, 21).

Let me show you four other passages that uniquely link Jerusalem with Almighty God:

- "Since the day that I brought My people out of the land of Egypt, I have chosen no city from any tribe of Israel in which to build a house, that My name might be there, nor did I choose any man to

be a ruler over My people Israel. Yet I have chosen Jerusalem, that
My name may be there, and I have chosen David to be over My
people Israel" (2 Chron. 6:5–6).

- "For the LORD has chosen Zion; He has desired it for His dwelling
  place: This is My resting place forever; here I will dwell, for I have
  desired it" (Ps. 132:13–14).

- "The LORD loves the gates of Zion more than all the dwellings
  of Jacob. Glorious things are spoken of you, O city of God!"
  (87:2–3).

- "Moreover He rejected the tent of Joseph, and did not choose the
  tribe of Ephraim but chose the tribe of Judah, Mount Zion which
  He loved" (78:67–68).

These verses explain the feelings that come over me whenever I
visit Jerusalem. In those moments, it's like I'm setting one foot in the
past and the other in the future. The walls and buildings are made
of a kind of pale-golden limestone that has taken on the name of its
city—Jerusalem stone. There's always just a whiff of tension in this city
because everyone knows the ground beneath their feet is the powder
keg of the earth. Yet I don't feel unsafe there. Such a strange mixture
of feelings!

I'm stirred as I wander through the dusty streets . . . looking at the
old shops with their bins of spices and the hordes of humanity coming
and going . . . standing before the Wailing Wall and watching Israeli
soldiers praying for peace before going to war . . . hearing the haunting
church bells mingling with the mournful Islamic calls to prayer blaring
from the mosques . . . smelling the deep-fried chickpea falafels at the
corner stand . . . seeing the bearded Hasidic Jewish rabbis with side curls
in their hair . . . walking down the Via Dolorosa and its historic stations
of the cross. It's almost too much to take in.

There are places in Jerusalem where I literally walk where Jesus
walked. We know some of the locations where He performed His
miracles, debated His enemies, and faced His execution. Most of all, I

love going to the quiet beauty of the Garden Tomb and visualizing how it must have been on resurrection day.

Having spent my life studying and teaching the Bible, when I'm in Jerusalem it's as though I were jumping through its pages, transported to the very scenes of action. I hope I've given you a taste of the special feeling I get when visiting the Holy City.

But in researching this book, I've discovered something that goes far beyond emotions and enjoyment. As never before, I've realized Jerusalem belongs to God as no other city ever has or ever will. There's a biblical sense in which Jerusalem is eternal. It will never die! Jerusalem is God's own unique eternal city. That fact, more than any other, explains the wonder of the Holy City to me!

Jerusalem Is a Capital City

Jerusalem became the capital of Israel by decree of King David over 3,000 years ago. It has remained Israel's capital ever since. Though other nations conquered and settled in the land of Israel, none ever declared Jerusalem their capital. Over the past 2,000 years, even during times of occupation and persecution, a Jewish community has resided in Jerusalem and maintained it as their "eternal capital."

In 1948, when President Harry Truman led the United States in recognizing the reborn State of Israel, the new nation reaffirmed Jerusalem as its capital. This is where the prime minister lives, where government agencies are housed, where the Knesset (Israel's parliament) sits, and where the Supreme Court presides.

During the 1948 War of Independence, Jordanian forces conquered and occupied the eastern part of Jerusalem containing the historic Jewish Quarter, the Temple Mount and Western Wall, Hebrew University, and Hadassah Hospital. But in the Six-Day War of 1967, these areas were retaken by Israel, and Jerusalem was reunified. Every prime minister since has declared the city to be "the eternal and undivided capital of the Jewish State."

Winston Churchill was among the first to advocate for the recognition of Jerusalem as the modern Israeli capital. He remarked to British diplomat Evelyn Shuckburgh, "You ought to let the Jews have Jerusalem—it was they who made it famous."[9]

For many years, American public opinion spoke in favor of moving the United States embassy from Tel Aviv to Jerusalem, and politicians agreed. Presidential candidates promised to do it. In October 1995, the US Congress called for the move to occur by May 1999. But one after another, our American presidents deferred, citing national security considerations.

In June 2017, the US Senate unanimously passed a resolution (90–0) that reaffirmed the 1995 congressional decision and called on the president to implement it. Six months later, President Trump recognized Jerusalem as Israel's capital and moved the embassy away from Tel Aviv. Critics whined and complained, saying Trump should have used the issue to negotiate with the Palestinians. But in short order, the embassy was relocated to an area in Western Jerusalem in which Israel commands unquestioned sovereignty.[10]

And with that event, I believe another key has been turned in the grand lock of biblical prophecy.

What Does This Mean?

As we cast our vision forward, what are the implications for the ongoing place of Jerusalem and of Israel? Even as I'm writing these words, missiles are flying past each other between areas of Israel and targets in Gaza. How many of the world's headlines this very day contain the words "Middle East," "Israel," and "Jerusalem"?

Well, here is the truth in nine words: The second advent of Christ cannot happen without Jerusalem.

Almost all the Christ-centered events in the future will take place in Jerusalem. Without Jerusalem, these events would be impossible. Were I living in Jerusalem today, I'd take these prophecies with a sense of reassurance. They assume the continual existence of this mystical city, a fact that seems at odds with the threats she constantly faces.

In each of my visits to Jerusalem, I've had the opportunity to preach on the Southern Steps of the temple, a spot Jesus traversed long ago. To my right is the Mount of Olives, the hilltop where Jesus ascended into heaven at the close of His gospel ministry. To this very place He will come again.

In his book *The End*, Mark Hitchcock gave three passages of Scripture that place Jesus in Jerusalem at His second advent:

First, Zechariah 14:4 addresses the second coming of Christ: "In that day His feet will stand on the Mount of Olives, which is in front of Jerusalem on the east" . . .

Second, the Mount of Olives is where Jesus gave His great prophetic discourse, which included the signs of His coming (Matt. 24–25).

Third, when Jesus ascended to heaven from the Mount of Olives (Acts 1:9–11), the angels said that He would return just as He had left. Jesus will return to the Mount of Olives, where He will make a perfect two-point landing.[11]

Not only will Christ return to Jerusalem at His second advent, but as we learned in chapter 2, that city will be the seat from which He reigns on earth during the millennium—the thousand-year period of Christ's rule on earth.

The reference to a thousand-year reign of Christ occurs six times in Revelation 20. But the millennium itself is described extensively in the Bible, especially in the writings of the Old Testament prophets. According to Dr. J. Dwight Pentecost, "A larger body of prophetic Scripture is devoted to the subject of the millennium, developing its character and conditions, than any other one subject."[12]

Pentecost wrote, "The coming of the Millennium will not be a gradual and imperceptible process but rather, sudden, supernatural, and apparent to the whole world. It will be preceded by a series of worldwide catastrophic events—wars, plagues, famines, and cosmic disturbances. It will be ushered in by a special manifestation of God and His glory; 'all flesh shall see it together' (Isa. 40:5)."[13]

The Bible uses various terms to identify this thousand-year period. It is referred to as "the kingdom of heaven" (Matt. 3:2; 8:11), "the kingdom of God" (Mark 1:15), "times of refreshing" (Acts 3:19), "times of restoration" (v. 21), "the day of Jesus Christ" (Phil. 1:6), "the fullness of the times" (Eph 1:10), and "the world to come" (Heb. 2:5).

Psalm 2:6–8 places Jesus in Jerusalem (Zion) during the millennium: "I have set My King on My holy hill of Zion. I will declare the decree: The LORD has said to Me: 'You are My Son. Today I have begotten You. Ask of Me, and I will give you the nations for your inheritance, and the ends of the earth for Your possession.'"

The prophet Jeremiah added: "At that time Jerusalem shall be called The Throne of the LORD, and all the nations shall be gathered to it, to the name of the LORD, to Jerusalem" (Jer. 3:17).

The Gospel of Luke says of Jesus during this era: "He will be great, and will be called the Son of the Highest; and the Lord God will give Him the throne of His father David. And He will reign over the house of Jacob forever" (Luke 1:32–33).

Jerusalem will be the Messiah's millennial capital (Zech. 14:20–21) and the home of a temple in which the sacrifices will be memorial.

But that's only the beginning. The everlasting capital city of Jesus throughout eternity will be Jerusalem—what we often call "the New Jerusalem." Earthly Jerusalem, to which Jesus will return and from where He will reign a thousand years, is the prelude to another Jerusalem—a city with foundations whose builder and maker is God (Heb. 11:10). New Jerusalem is the Celestial City, currently existing in the highest heaven, that will descend to its rightful place on the new earth at the dawning of eternity.

Many theologians refer to the New Jerusalem as "the crown of the new creation." John, in a glorious vision of the eternal state, saw "the holy city, New Jerusalem, coming down out of heaven from God" (Rev. 21:2).

This is the city anticipated by Abraham (Heb. 11:16), promised by Christ (John 14:2–3), and awaited by the saints (Heb. 13:14). This is the "city of the living God, the heavenly Jerusalem" (12:22). This is the "Jerusalem above" (Gal. 4:26).

"As the final and eternal home of redeemed humanity, the New Jerusalem will shine with the glory of God. In contrast to man-made cities, which display only human achievements, this heavenly city, which will come to earth, will be ablaze with light, the light of the glory of God. At last Jerusalem will deservedly be called the Holy City."[14]

And this is a *real* city! The final two chapters of the Bible use the word *city* thirteen times to describe our eternal home. This isn't a figure of speech; it's an actual physical place. Since our resurrected bodies will be physical bodies, as real and tangible as Christ's, they will need a real place and an actual home. They will require a physical location.

Here in the book of Revelation we have our fullest glimpse of the details of this city, starting with this promise from the lips of the glorified Christ: "He who overcomes, I will make him a pillar in the temple of My God, and he shall go out no more. I will write on him the name of My God and the name of the city of My God, the New Jerusalem, which comes down out of heaven from My God. And I will write on him My new name" (Rev. 3:12).

Listen as John wrote in awe:

Now I saw a new heaven and a new earth, for the first heaven and the first earth had passed away. Also there was no more sea. Then I, John, saw the holy city, New Jerusalem, coming down out of heaven from God, prepared as a bride adorned for her husband. And I heard a loud voice from heaven saying, "Behold, the tabernacle of God is with men, and He will dwell with them, and they shall be His people. God Himself will be with them and be their God. And God will wipe away every tear from their eyes; there shall be no more death, nor sorrow, nor crying. There shall be no more pain, for the former things have passed away." Then He who sat on the throne said, "Behold, I make all things new." And He said to me, "Write, for these words are true and faithful." (21:1–5)

This description implies the Holy City was designed, built, and ready-made for the new earth. John didn't see the New Jerusalem created. As I said, it exists now! It's where my parents live! I have other loved ones there, as do you. It's the current and eternal home for all the redeemed of all the ages.

Anthony Hoekema wrote: "The New Jerusalem . . . does not remain in heaven far off in space, but it comes down to the renewed earth, there the redeemed will spend eternity in resurrection bodies. So, heaven and earth, now separated, will then be merged: the new earth will also be heaven, since God will dwell there with his people. Glorified believers, in other words, will continue to be in heaven while they are inhabiting the new earth."[15]

This city of New Jerusalem is the place Jesus is preparing for us (John 14:1–6), and the Bible draws to a close with a breathtaking description of its dimensions, its description, its streets, its vast river, its wonderous throne, its translucent gold, its glittering light.

Try this exercise. Think of the most beautiful spot you've ever seen on earth.

For me, it's an island in the Aegean Sea called Santorini. Several years ago, Donna and I visited Greece and Turkey. As we sailed toward this island, I remember telling Donna it looked like we were sailing toward heaven. Santorini is a volcanic island only thirty square miles in size. As we stood on the deck of the ship and looked at the blindingly white little town with its rounded roofs and quaint simplicity, elevated along the clifftops above the blue sea and jutting upward toward the blue sky, it almost appeared to be suspended in space.

But as breathtaking as it is, Santorini does not come close to the beauty of the New Jerusalem.

In earlier books, I've devoted entire chapters to the description of the New Jerusalem. I can't go into that kind of detail now, but let me give you three points to ponder.

You'll Be Overjoyed with Its Beauty

The Bible describes the New Jerusalem as a city built upon a foundation of precious stones. Entry into the city will be through gates of pearl, and the streets will be paved with gold. The light of the city will emanate from the Lamb of God.

Near the city center we'll find the Tree of Life, which has been missing to us since the garden of Eden. The inhabitants of the city will be able to eat the leaves of the tree, and those leaves will somehow provide a deeper sense of our well-being in heaven.

In the very heart of the city, the River of Life will pour forth from beneath the throne, flow through the landscape, and delight the whole earth (Rev. 22:1). I believe this is the same river mentioned by the psalmist: "There is a river whose streams shall make glad the city of God, the holy place of the tabernacle of the Most High" (Ps. 46:4).

The beauty of New Jerusalem will be amplified by its size. I grew up in a little village in Ohio, and until I enrolled in seminary in Dallas, I didn't know anything of city life. Over the years, Donna and I have been blessed to travel all over the world, visiting some of the most beautiful cities on earth. I love cities, and sometimes we discover fascinating facts along the way.

For example, do you know the name of the largest city in the United States, in terms of square miles? It's not New York or Los Angeles or Jacksonville, Florida. It's a place you may not even know about unless you've traveled with us on one of our Bible-teaching cruises to Alaska. Sitka, Alaska, with a population of less than 10,000 people, covers 4,815 square miles—an area larger than Rhode Island, Delaware, and the District of Columbia combined. And is it ever beautiful!

But Sitka can't compare in size with New Jerusalem. The boundaries of the Celestial City exceed anything ever envisioned by human engineers. Sometimes people ask me, "How can heaven be large enough to hold all the redeemed of all the ages?" Well, first of all we'll have an outsized new earth at our disposal. But consider the dimensions of the city itself. It's "a city four-square," 1,500 miles long, 1,500 miles wide, and 1,500 miles high. Steven Lawson helps us understand this:

> Picture an area in the western United States between the Pacific Coast and the Mississippi River, roughly the distance from Los Angeles to Saint Louis or New York to Denver. . . . That's 2,250,000 square miles on the ground. Then 1,500 miles up from there! Hang on! Are you ready for this? That's 3,375,000,000 cubic miles, enough room to comfortably accommodate 100,000 billion people!
>
> It has been estimated that approximately thirty billion people have lived in the long history of the world. Even if everyone who ever lived was saved—which is not the case—that would still allow each person

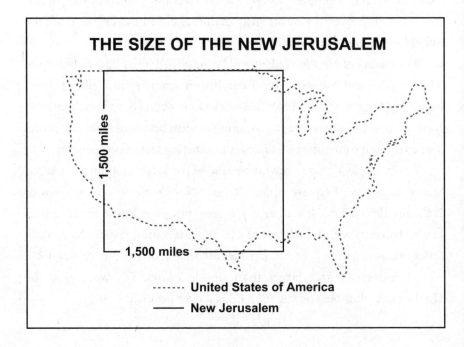

THE SIZE OF THE NEW JERUSALEM

1,500 miles

1,500 miles

------ **United States of America**

——— **New Jerusalem**

200 square miles on the ground alone. . . . There will be plenty of room for everyone who makes it to Heaven. And that's just in the city![16]

E. J. Fortman suggested that when the Holy City is permanently located, it would logically be centered in Jerusalem: "If the 'New Jerusalem' has more than symbolic reality, why should it not have it in the 'Holy Land'? Why should it not throughout eternity be where 'Old Jerusalem' was, where our Redeemer taught, suffered, died that we might live a life of glory and happiness throughout the endless reaches of eternity? . . . What better site could there be for this eternal cosmic religious center than *Old Jerusalem*?"[17]

You'll Be Overwhelmed with Its Holiness

Three times in Revelation 21 and 22, John called the New Jerusalem a "holy" city.

- "Then I, John, saw *the holy city*, New Jerusalem" (21:2).
- "And he carried me away in the Spirit to a great and high mountain, and showed me the great city, *the holy Jerusalem*, descending out of heaven from God" (v. 10).
- "And if anyone takes away from the words of the book of this prophecy, God shall take away his part from the Book of Life, from *the holy city*" (22:19).

As I said, Donna and I have visited some of the most beautiful cities in the world, but none of them have been holy. We live in San Diego, California, which is a beautiful city with an almost perfect climate, tucked like a gem between desolate mountains and the rugged Pacific. We love it here. But believe me, it is not a holy place. To my grief, it's a cesspool of crime and corruption. All the great cities of the world have an underside to their beauty. They are all polluted, corrupt, filled with vice, brimming with immorality, riddled with crime, plagued by death and disease, and struggling with every known sin.

Not so in the New Jerusalem! It is a holy city. The *Wycliffe Bible Commentary* says, "A holy city will be one in which no lie will be uttered in one hundred million years, no evil word will ever be spoken, no shady business deal will ever even be discussed, no unclean picture will ever be seen, no corruption of life will ever be manifest. It will be holy because everyone in it will be holy."[18]

Wow! I want a condo in that city! John described it like this: "But there shall by no means enter it anything that defiles, or causes an abomination or a lie, but only those who are written in the Lamb's Book of Life" (21:27).

John listed eight kinds of people who will never step foot inside the gates of the New Jerusalem: "But the cowardly, unbelieving, abominable, murderers, sexually immoral, sorcerers, idolaters, and all liars shall have their part in the lake which burns with fire and brimstone, which is the second death" (v. 8).

This is a critical warning to all of us. The one and only thing that can bar us from heaven is our failure to trust Christ as Savior and Lord.

The writer of Hebrews went out of his way to describe the city inhabitants: "But you have come to Mount Zion and to the city of the living God, the heavenly Jerusalem, to an innumerable company of angels, to the general assembly and church of the firstborn who are registered in heaven, to God the Judge of all, to the spirits of just men made perfect" (Heb. 12:22–23).

Dr. Pentecost wrote: "It would seem, then, that the writer to the Hebrews is giving us a picture of the heavenly city, in which place there will be gathered together with Christ, the unfallen angels, the resurrected and translated saints of the church age, and all resurrected Old Testament and tribulation saints."[19]

Frederick Buechner wrote: "Everything is gone that ever made Jerusalem, like all cities, torn apart, dangerous, heartbreaking, seamy. You walk the streets in peace now. Small children play unattended in the parks. No stranger goes by whom you cannot imagine as a fast friend."[20]

You'll Be Overcome with Its Savior

There's so much to anticipate about heaven, but there's one priority above all others—seeing the Lord Jesus Christ. That includes seeing His face, glimpsing His smile, enjoying His fellowship, and worshiping His glory. Revelation 22:4 says, "They shall see His face, and His name shall be on their foreheads."

The blind hymnist Fanny Crosby wrote poignantly about this. She was blinded as an infant by a doctor who gave her the wrong medicine for her eyes. In 1894, she wrote a hymn from the depths of her heart. She called it "My Savior First of All." She said that when her life's work was ended and she opened her eyes in heaven, "His smile will be the first to welcome me. I shall know Him! I shall know Him! And redeemed by His side I shall stand."

In this hymn, Miss Crosby wrote of the mansion prepared for her, of the loved ones she longed to see, of the beauteous gates and the sparkling river. "But," she said, "I long to meet my Savior first of all."

Me too! And I hope you do too!

Where Do We Go from Here?

What does all this have to do with us today? How do these prophecies about tomorrow explain the problems we have today? I want to answer that question with some chapter-ending calls to action.

Stay Fervent in Your Prayer for Israel

The psalmist wrote, "Pray for the peace of Jerusalem. 'May they prosper who love you. Peace be within your walls, prosperity within your palaces.' For the sake of my brethren and companions, I will now say, 'Peace be within you.' Because of the house of the LORD our God I will seek your good" (Ps. 122:6–9).

We must pray for the internal peace of Israel. One writer asked, "What do we do with a city that is called 'holy' by one billion Catholics, one billion Muslims, 400 million Orthodox Christians, 400 million

Protestants, and countless members of numerous sects? No city can be peacefully divided to satisfy once and for all the religious claims and demands of so many diverse and conflicting groups."[21]

If you visit Jerusalem and walk through the Old City from end to end, you'll encounter a labyrinth of languages, cultures, and passions. Only Jesus Christ can bring unity to such a tangle of tongues and tempers. We need to pray for the Jews, the Palestinians, the Christians, and all the others who make this land their home.

Secondly, stay fervent in your prayers for the international safety of Israel and Jerusalem. Modern Israel has been forced to maintain a continual state of warfare throughout its years. Someone described it as living in a very nice house in a very bad neighborhood. Israel is in a fight for its very survival, and not everyone is sympathetic.

The title of an article by *WORLD* Newsgroup editor-in-chief Marvin Olasky succinctly summarizes the nation's dilemma: "Slammed if you do, dead if you don't." When Israelis take the tough but necessary measures to defend themselves, they are slammed by world censure. If they fail to take those measures, they are left vulnerable to hostile neighbors.[22]

If you doubt the hostility of the world toward the Jewish nation, you'll be jolted by this statistic from the United Nations. Israel has been the single most discriminated-against state at the UN. "From 2012 through 2019, the UN General Assembly had adopted a total of 202 resolutions criticizing countries. Israel was the subject of 163 of those, accounting for 81% of all resolutions."[23]

Put a map of Israel in your prayer journal, or put a paper clip on the page in the back of your Bible with a map of Israel. Remember to pray for its place among the nations.

Stay Faithful in Your Service and Ministry

Christianity and Judaism both encourage us to anticipate the Messiah's coming by concentrating on being godly people and doing acts of kindness. In doing so, we will hasten the end and start our new beginning. As Peter instructed in the Bible, "Since everything will be destroyed in this way, what kind of people ought you to be? You ought to live holy and godly lives as you look forward to the day of God and speed its coming" (2 Peter 3:11–12 NIV).

I believe this is what Isaiah was thinking about when he wrote: "Is it not to share your bread with the hungry, and that you bring to your house the poor who are cast out; when you see the naked, that you cover him, and not hide yourself from your own flesh?" (Isa. 58:7).

I know Jerusalem is far away for many who will read this book. In some cases, it's literally the other side of the world. Many will not have the privilege of visiting that city on this side of eternity.

Yet as we've seen, all who trust in Christ as their Savior will encounter the New Jerusalem. Even now, you and I are moving toward that wondrous city. It's our eternal destiny. It's our home!

For these reasons and more, let us live right now as citizens of New Jerusalem. We aren't physically housed in that eternal city, but our faithful service will reflect its light and reveal its goodness even as we tarry here.

Stay Focused on Israel and Jerusalem

Today the largest country in the world by population is China with nearly 1.5 billion people. Of the 193 countries in the world, Israel ranks in the bottom half in terms of its citizenry, with a population of about nine million. That's less than 1 percent of China's teeming multitudes.

Yet Israel's international influence far outweighs the number of people living there. The *New York Times* reported that Israel is the seventh most mentioned country in their newspaper, just behind Russia, England, and Germany; and ahead of much larger countries like Japan, India, and Italy.[24]

As you witness the US embassy being moved to Jerusalem and marvel at the Abraham Accords—the new alliances Israel has created with the United Arab Emirates, Bahrain, Morocco, and the Sudan—you're witnessing a major shift in the geopolitical landscape of the Middle East.

Gradually over the past decade the faultlines have moved. Until recently, the Middle East has been "everybody against Israel." Israel was public enemy number one in the eyes of her neighbors. But as Iran has pounded its chest and rattled its sword, it's become obvious that the greatest threat to existence in the Middle East is no longer the little nation of Israel. It's the aggressive radical Islamic terrorist nation of Iran.

Iran doesn't just represent *radical* Islam. They represent *apocalyptic* Islam, and they envision end-of-the-world scenarios.

While the Palestinian controversy still exists, it's being put on the back burner as nations create coalitions with Israel in defense against Iran. According to *U.S. News and World Report*, Israel is the tenth most powerful nation in the world, and it is certainly the most powerful military force in the Middle East. But the leadership of Iran is plotting, and the neighborhood is nervous.

Paradoxically, I also want to tell you that recent reports thrill us with the numbers of Iranians coming to Christ. The Lord is at work there. But the nation's leadership remains aggressive. The other Arab nations could never survive a conflict with Iran, so, remarkably, they are looking to Israel. How fascinating! We couldn't have imagined that a few years ago.

So, keep your eyes on the chessboard of the Middle East. Follow news from there. Become an expert on the land God has marked as the flashpoint of prophecy.

Speaking of experts, many people around the world have enjoyed the wit and personality of Kathie Lee Gifford, who has been a TV host on *Regis & Kathie Lee* as well as The *TODAY* Show. What many people don't know is that Kathie Lee is a dedicated student of God's Word and a huge fan of Israel.

In her words:

My love affair with the land of Israel began the moment I took my very first step onto the Promised Land in June of 1971. I was seventeen years old, and my father's high school graduation gift was a trip for me and my mother to attend the first Jerusalem Conference on Biblical Prophecy. I missed my graduation ceremony, but I couldn't have cared less. I was where it all happened! All the stories I had heard, all the Scriptures I had studied since I was a young girl—*everything* I believed from the Word of God had taken place thousands of years before in this land I was experiencing for the very first time! That thought took my breath away all those years ago. It still does today.

Like me, Kathie Lee Gifford has been a frequent visitor to Israel. She even wrote a book called *The Rock, the Road, and the Rabbi: My Journey into the Heart of Scriptural Faith and the Land Where It All Began.*

One trip in particular was especially memorable. That was when Kathie Lee's husband, Frank Gifford, agreed to join her in Israel for the first time. Frank had grown up in poverty, but later became a famous football player and TV announcer. He also was a man of faith—or so he thought. According to Kathie Lee, "What Frank didn't realize until our trip to Israel is that he had a *religion* all his life, but he never had a *relationship* with the living God."

During that trip, the group visited the Valley of Elah, where David fought Goliath. The leader explained that the miracle of that story was not David's victory over the giant. After all, David had already defeated a lion and a bear. Instead, the miracle of that story was David's genuine, personal relationship with Almighty God.

The leader then instructed everyone in the group to go down to the same brook David had visited and pick up a stone. He asked, "What is *your* stone? Where are you going to throw it?" In Kathie Lee's words, "I will never forget the look in Frank's eyes as this man who was in six Halls of Fame obediently reached down to pick up his stone, just as a young shepherd boy had done three thousand years ago."

She continued:

This experience lit a fire in my belly, and it satisfied a deep longing in Frank's soul. Though the rest of the trip was profoundly moving and illuminating, it was this truth he learned in the Valley of Elah—that religion is nothing without relationship—that gave Frank a strong sense of peace and purpose until the day he died. Finally, at the age of eighty-two, he had found his stone.[25]

Jesus said, "This gospel of the kingdom will be preached in the whole world as a testimony to all nations, and then the end will come" (Matt. 24:14). This is the final prophecy—the triumph of the gospel.

We can have unwavering joy, even in these last days, because the gospel is triumphant, and Jesus is victorious. Nothing can stop Him, and no one can stall His work on earth. As the apostle Paul said, "Now thanks be to God who always leads us in triumph in Christ" (2 Cor. 2:14).

Where do we go from here? We go to the gospel of Jesus Christ! It is this message that will triumph over everything we are facing at this critical hour. Let us preach the gospel from our pulpits and share it with everyone we meet!

Chapter 10

The Final Prophecy— The Triumph of the Gospel

"This gospel of the kingdom will be preached in the whole world as a testimony to all nations, and then the end will come."

MATTHEW 24:14

Back in 2018, as the Easter season was approaching, the SiriusXM radio company came together with the Billy Graham organization to play Dr. Graham's messages 24/7 throughout the Easter season. This was advertised as a limited time agreement, and when the Easter season ended, the messages went away.

Well, the response to the great evangelist's preaching must have been very positive because he is back on SiriusXM. This time it is a full-time, every-day, 24-hours-per-day, permanent agreement. You can now hear Dr. Graham's messages on channel 460 around the clock.

And I have been listening.

Each message is introduced and located by the date on which it was preached. Some of the messages were recorded live from his huge stadium events, and some of them are the replay of his weekly thirty-minute radio program. All are worth your time.

For over seven decades, Billy Graham preached the gospel. He preached during times of war. He preached during times of peace. He preached during times of racial unrest. He preached when our nation was going through serious financial crises. He preached in the aftermath of the assassination of President Kennedy and when we landed our astronauts on the moon. He preached through the administrations of twelve US presidents (Truman, Eisenhower, Kennedy, Johnson, Nixon, Ford, Carter, Reagan, Bush 41, Clinton, Bush 43, and Obama). He preached during the terrible days that surrounded September 11. He preached when his children were growing up and when his wife died. No matter what was happening in our world or in his world, Billy Graham preached.

I am not telling you something you do not already know. You may have listened to him and perhaps even attended one of his many events. Instead, I am reminding you of the scope of Dr. Graham's preaching because I want to talk to you about the subject of his preaching.

I cannot begin to tell you how my heart has been stirred over these last several weeks as I have listened to his sermons. In spite of the myriad issues before him, he confronted them all with one thing: the gospel of Jesus Christ. He never wavered, he never changed, he never apologized, and he seemed to get stronger and better as he got older. As I have listened to him, I have found myself thinking of Paul's words: "I determined not to know anything among you except Jesus Christ and Him crucified" (1 Cor. 2:2).

As I listened, I became convinced of the answer to the question on the front cover of this book. Where do we go from here? We go to the gospel of Jesus Christ. I believe the gospel alone can triumph over the many challenges we are facing in our culture and our world at this hour.

That is what was confirmed to me as I listened to the great evangelist on the radio. He knew the gospel was the answer to any question, and he preached that gospel as if it were our only hope.

Because it is!

I have unwavering joy, even in these last days, because the gospel is triumphant, and Jesus is victorious. Nothing can stop Him, and no one can stall His work on earth.

In the early days of the church, the Jewish high officials in Jerusalem couldn't figure out what to do with the apostles. During a gathering to discuss the issue, Israel's most respected rabbi, Gamaliel, rose to speak. He told the officials: "Leave these men alone! Let them go! For if their purpose or activity is of human origin, it will fail. But if it is from God, you will not be able to stop these men; you will only find yourselves fighting against God" (Acts 5:38–39 NIV).

As far as we know, Rabbi Gamaliel was not himself a Christian. But on this occasion, he spoke true wisdom, and his words have rung true for two thousand years. They are true for you. Your influence, your work, and your service for the Master cannot be stopped.

Living in Triumph

In *Where Do We Go from Here?* we've learned about some of the key issues currently confronting our culture, all of them anticipated by biblical prophecy. We've literally gone from A to Z, from apostasy to Zion, analyzing the turmoil around us. We've sensed that spiritual warfare is real, and it's growing more intense as time grows shorter.

But with every peck at my keyboard, I've felt a sense of anticipation, for Christ is enthroned at God's right hand. He is there at this very moment, ruling and overruling. We cannot be discouraged, not a bit! There's no room in these days for defeated Christians. The Bible says, "Now thanks be to God who always leads us in *triumph* in Christ, and through us diffuses the fragrance of His knowledge in every place" (2 Cor. 2:14, emphasis added).

Don't you like that word *triumph?* Try saying it aloud. It's a powerful, biblical word.

Moses wrote, "I will sing to the LORD, for He has *triumphed* gloriously" (Ex. 15:1).

The psalmist told us, "Shout to God with the voice of *triumph!*" (Ps. 47:1).

According to the book of Revelation, this is the ultimate consummation of biblical prophecy: "See, the Lion of the tribe of Judah, the Root of David, has *triumphed*" (5:5 NIV).

As usual, the apostle Paul stated it brilliantly: "Having disarmed principalities and powers, [Jesus] made a public spectacle of them, *triumphing* over them" (Col. 2:15).

I saved that reference for last because I want to focus on Colossians in this chapter. I think the people of Colossae would be somewhat at home in our world. They were facing what we are facing. While surrounded by a vile and pagan culture, they were also endangered from within by false teachers and weakened doctrine. As I pointed out in the *Jeremiah Study Bible*, the apostle Paul probably never set foot in the town of Colossae, which was nestled in the Lycus Valley some one hundred miles east of Ephesus. A man named Epaphras, a native Colossian who had been converted under Paul's ministry, started a church in this small town.

Things went well at first, but then false teachers showed up. All around them was a pagan Roman culture, and now false teachers threatened to erode their internal foundation of faith. Epaphras was so alarmed that he sought out Paul, who was imprisoned in Rome, asking him to write to this little congregation. The great apostle did so—four glorious chapters about the transcendence of Christ and the triumph of the gospel.

Paul wasn't just writing to Colossae, but to us, as he exhorted us to never allow ourselves to be "moved away from the hope of the gospel" (Col. 1:23).

He went on to warn: "Beware lest anyone cheat you through philosophy and empty deceit, according to the tradition of men, according to the basic principles of the world, and not according to Christ. For in Him dwells all the fullness of the Godhead bodily; and you are complete in Him, who is the head of all principality and power" (2:8–10).

Who are the principalities and powers over whom Jesus triumphed?

They are fallen supernatural beings—principalities, powers, rulers of the darkness in this age, spiritual hosts of wickedness in the heavenly places (Eph. 6:12). They are malevolent forces in the unseen realm, associates of Satan. The devil has a dark and demonic network of evil—an invisible grid that encircles our world.

There is no way to explain the acceleration of evil in our day apart from principalities, powers, rulers of darkness, and the spiritual hosts of wickedness. They are firing at us like enemy combatants, and their intent is to kill. But Jesus Christ is victor over every shadowy figure in the universe.

That's the triumph of the gospel. Our Lord Jesus Christ has triumphed over every power, every principality, every ruler of darkness, every spiritual force of evil in the unseen realm. He has triumphed over the world, the flesh, and the devil. He conquered sin, death, and hell. He broke the power of him who holds the power of death—that is, the devil, and freed those who were held in slavery by their fear of death (Heb. 2:14–15).

In days to come, during the final moments of earth's history, the Antichrist and his cohorts will make one last stand. "They will wage war against the Lamb, but the Lamb will *triumph* over them because he is Lord of lords and King of kings—and with him will be his called, chosen and faithful followers" (Rev. 17:14 NIV).

Biblical prophecy never leads us down dark pathways of chaos and cataclysm. It leads us past chaos and cataclysm to Christ Himself, who is victorious over all.

Consider this. Every year on Palm Sunday we sing and preach about the triumphal entry of Jesus as He entered Jerusalem at the beginning of Passion Week. We see Him riding a donkey while multitudes cheer Him with cries of "Hosanna! 'Blessed is He who comes in the name of the LORD!'" (Mark 11:9). By the end of the week, Jesus had been crucified.

If we call our Lord's first coming "triumphal," what can we say of His return?

It will be triumphal times a trillion! That's why the signs of the times bring us songs, not sighs or sobs. When we see all that's happening around us, we lift up our eyes because our redemption—our Redeemer—is drawing near.

What Does This Mean?

Whenever we read the letters of Paul, we find him articulating the message of the gospel from different viewpoints. In Colossians, he put it like this: "He has delivered us from the power of darkness and conveyed us into the kingdom of the Son of His love, in whom we have redemption through His blood, the forgiveness of sins" (Col. 1:13–14).

Without Christ, we're in Satan's grip. But because of His great love for us, Jesus shed His blood and died to redeem us from our sins, giving us full forgiveness. He rose from the dead, ascended to heaven, and resumed His position of supreme authority. When we believe and receive His good news, He instantly conveys us into His family and into His kingdom. That is the triumph of the gospel—the victory of Jesus on our behalf.

The Message of the Gospel Is Transforming

This message is life-altering. It instantly changed the lives of a handful of people in the town of Colossae, snatching them from the power of darkness and conveying them into the kingdom of light. Two thousand years later, the same gospel is transforming hearts today.

It's not often I quote a press release from an atheist society, but just as the pandemic began to fade from the headlines, another news item caught my eye. A group called the "Atheists in Kenya Society" in Nairobi issued a press release dated May 30, 2021: "This evening, regretfully, the Secretary of the Atheists in Kenya Society Mr. Seth Mahiga, informed

[us] that he has made the decision to resign from his position as Secretary of the society. Seth's reason for resigning is that he has found Jesus Christ and is no longer interested in promoting atheism in Kenya. We wish Seth all the best in his newfound relationship with Jesus Christ. . . . The position of Secretary of the Society has been rendered vacant."[1]

We cannot imagine how many people like Seth are saved by the blood of Christ every single day in this world. Only heaven knows that statistic, but each life is radically transformed.

Paul told the Colossians, "We heard of your faith in Christ Jesus and of your love for all the saints; because of the hope which is laid up for you in heaven, of which you heard before in the word of the truth of the gospel, which has come to you" (1:4–6).

The Work of the Gospel Is Expanding

Furthermore, the work of the gospel is expanding. Paul went on to say, "[The gospel] has come to you, as it has also in all the world, and is bringing forth fruit" (v. 6). Even in Paul's day, he saw the gospel spreading and expanding like concentric circles throughout the entire known world.

Jesus said, "And this gospel of the kingdom will be preached in all the world as a witness to all the nations, and then the end will come" (Matt. 24:14).

From my own experience, I can tell you I've never seen a moment in my lifetime of ministry in which followers of Jesus are reaching more people, witnessing more conversions, and touching more nations than now. It's hard to be discouraged with the headlines when a bigger story is unfolding. We can't fully document it, but the gospel is yielding unprecedented fruit around the globe.

Yes, I know we've talked about apostasy and the perceived decline of Christianity in the West. But that's not the whole story. The triumphant gospel is penetrating new areas, and truly amazing things are happening.

Perhaps you've heard rumors of the growth of Christianity within the borders of Iran. Those rumors are true! One report said the gospel is spreading through that nation at a "sizzling pace." Another report said the Holy Spirit is "on fire" in Iran.[2]

As you know, the leaders of Iran adhere to an apocalyptic form of Islam, and they're doing everything possible to discourage this revival. Anyone suspected of being a Christian is arrested or oppressed. But do you know what's happening? Plans are unfolding for Billy Graham to preach in Iran! Yes, Dr. Graham's sermons are being dubbed into Farsi and broadcast into the country. It's believed his sermons will reach over twenty million Iranians in the safety of their own homes.[3] That's only one tidbit about the spiritual awakening currently taking place in this country which, as I've indicated, will play a role in the unfolding of the tribulation.

In another case, there's an evangelist named Dr. Hormoz Shariat. In 1979, Dr. Shariat was on the streets of Iran shouting, "Death to America!" He was a fanatical Muslim, but something happened to him when he started reading the Bible and comparing it to the Quran. "I realized Jesus is the way," he said. "And when my life was changed so dramatically, I knew I mustn't keep it to myself."[4] He uses satellite TV to reach millions of Iranians, and his messages are penetrating homes twenty-four hours a day.[5]

As followers of Christ, we read the news differently than other people. When you hear reports of the Iranian nuclear deal or the ayatollah's apocalyptic threats, remember there's more going on than meets the eye. The Lord is at work behind the headlines, and the gospel is spreading into every corner of the earth with its message of triumph.

The Followers of the Gospel Are Maturing

Furthermore, the followers of the gospel are maturing. The apostle Paul told the Colossians he was praying "that you may be filled with the knowledge of His will in all wisdom and spiritual understanding; that you may walk worthy of the Lord, fully pleasing Him, being fruitful in every good work." He asked God to strengthen them with all might and to give them power, patience, and endurance (Col. 1:9–11).

How we need that, and how God is doing that! While the world is worsening, the Lord's servants are increasing and His churches are advancing. When I look at the students and young adults in my own church and in the schools we support, I'm encouraged. We have a young generation whose growth in zeal and godliness will be tested, but which will triumph in the years ahead.

Perhaps you know about the worldwide ministry of AWANA Clubs International. Recently their leadership team met to share childhood stories with one another. This was a bonding exercise, but it quickly became very personal and even painful. One member after another told about the anguish they faced when they were younger. One remembered the night his father went on a violent rampage. Another told how his mother had beaten him every morning for wetting his bed. As the painful truths unfolded, the group grieved together over the deep childhood hurts they had sustained.

But a phrase kept recurring. One person after another said, "But there was a church . . . ."

- "I was my mother's whipping boy, but there was a church who loved me."
- "No one knew how dysfunctional we were and how abused and humiliated I was at home, but there was a church where people fathered and mothered me."
- "My dad abandoned my mother and me . . . but there was a church who took my mom and me to its heart."[6]

Jesus said, "I will build My church, and the gates of Hades shall not prevail against it" (Matt. 16:18). Despite all the anguish and abuse of our age, the gospel will triumph through the church as we mature in Christ and bear fruit in every good work. Never underestimate the power of your local church, for Jesus died to plant it in this world. He rose again to empower it to reach every new generation with His glorious gospel.

The Author of the Gospel Is Preeminent

The Author of the gospel—our Lord Jesus Christ—"is the image of the invisible God, the firstborn over all creation. For by Him all things were created. . . . And He is before all things, and in Him all things consist. And He is the head of the body, the church, who is the beginning, the firstborn from the dead, that in all things He may have the preeminence" (Col. 1:15–18).

Richard Chin, national director of the Australian Fellowship of Evangelical Students, has a profound ministry with young people on multiple continents. But it wasn't always that way. Back in July 1983, Chin was himself a student whose Christian experience was nominal. One day while attending a conference he heard the speaker ask one question: "Is Jesus number one in your life?"

"I knew he was a good number two or three," Chin recalled. "But he was not number one. Sometime that week, I joyfully received Jesus as my Lord." As Chin began studying his Bible, he was drawn to the book of Colossians, which he memorized, and he was amazed at the triumphant picture of Christ found in its pages.

As we see Jesus more clearly, the gospel gets bigger and bigger in our hearts. His death becomes more wonderful. His resurrection becomes more astonishing. Sin becomes more disgusting and the devil seems more evil. The restoring work of the Spirit gets mightier. The global extent of the gospel becomes more important. The connections between everything within the Bible become clearer. Our yearning for eternity becomes greater. And the love of God becomes more delightful.

"Jesus is preeminent in everything," wrote Chin. "He rules everything in this creation, and He rules everything in the age to come."[7]

The question that changed Richard Chin's life is profoundly important now. Is Jesus truly preeminent in your life? Is He number one? If He's "a good two or three," there will be nothing victorious about your experience. In this careening culture and in these perilous days, we must say as never before: "All to Jesus I surrender, all to Him I freely give."

As someone said long ago, "Only in the Christian life does surrender bring victory."

The Theme of the Gospel Is Energizing

Another triumphal note in Colossians sounds like the blast of a trumpet: "Christ in you, the hope of glory" (1:27). What a slogan and what a motto! But it's so much more. When Charles Spurgeon preached from this verse, he used a very simple outline, which I can't beat:

- The essence of the gospel is: Christ
- The sweetness of the gospel is: Christ in you.
- The outlook of the gospel is: Christ in you, the hope of glory.

Taken together, this is the triumph of the gospel, and you can make it your own: "Christ in me, the hope of glory!" The moment we proclaim Christ as our Savior, He comes, through His Spirit, to live and reign within us. One day we'll see Him face-to-face. One day soon we'll literally walk and talk with Him as the disciples did long ago. We will share His glory and have a part in His inheritance, reigning with Him over the new heaven and the new earth.

This hope is the theme of the gospel, and it's just as certain as the death of Christ. Just as sure as His resurrection. Just as exciting as His return. And just as real as His indwelling Spirit. The New Living Translation says, "And this is the secret: Christ lives in you. This gives you assurance of sharing his glory."

Where Do We Go from Here?

Whenever I write, I pray for God's power on every word. But when I quote the Word of God, I know there is limitless power in every syllable. So I would like to highlight five passages, directly from the book of Colossians, that will tell you where to go from here.

Because Jesus is preeminent and His gospel is triumphant, you can live and labor in victory in several critical areas.

Preach the Gospel with Your Lips

As followers of Jesus, we must keep preaching Christ and holding up the cross. Colossians 1:28 says: "Him we preach." We must keep doing that till the end.

Naomi Reed interviewed an Asian Christian named Resham, who told her his story.

> I have Parkinson's Disease now. I can't walk anymore and I'm mostly in my bed. I can't leave this room, or go to church, or visit people. It's a change for me. I spent my whole adult life sharing the Gospel. Back then, I walked through 72 districts in Nepal, preaching the Gospel . . . and we started a Bible correspondence course. In total, we've had 700,000 students.
>
> I was put in jail three times for my faith, and I was tortured. But I can't walk anymore, or get out of bed. The challenge for me, today, is in reading Colossians 1:28–29. The apostle Paul said, "Christ is the one we proclaim, admonishing and teaching everyone with all wisdom, so that we may present everyone fully mature in Christ. To this end I strenuously contend with all the energy Christ so powerfully works in me." . . .
>
> I want to be like Paul. I know that he used all his energy to share the Gospel, right to the end. And I want to do that too. I don't have any energy in my body, anymore, but I still have energy in my heart and my mind. Even now, people can ring me on my phone . . . and they ask me about Jesus and I still tell them. I'm still taking calls from our Bible correspondence students. I'm still using all my energy, even while I'm lying on my bed—all the energy that Christ has given me![8]

To the very end of life, to the very end of time, and to the very ends of the earth, let's use all our strength to preach Him and His triumphant gospel. The Lord has blessed us with the opportunity of reaching, I believe, one of the last generations prior to His return for us.

Picture the Gospel with Your Life

When twin brothers Brett and Alex Harris were teenagers, they wrote a book titled *Do Hard Things*. They suggested readers get up early, do more than required, find a cause, and be better than our culture. They wrote as Christians. Both boys finished high school at age sixteen, clerked with the Alabama Supreme Court, and organized political campaigns. Both boys enrolled at Patrick Henry College, took first place in the Moot Court nationals, wrote another book, and spoke at conferences. Then they both got married. Alex and his wife moved to Massachusetts, where Alex enrolled in Harvard.

After Harvard, Alex clerked for Judge Neil Gorsuch and Justice Anthony Kennedy. He was named one of *Forbes* magazine's 30 Under 30 for Law and Policy. His legal career soared, but Alex also faced hardship. His mother's death was devastating to him. His brother's wife developed a debilitating disease, and Brett became a caregiver.

"We ultimately do hard things and we have the power to do hard things," Alex said in an interview, "because Jesus Christ has done the ultimate hard thing. . . . he died on the cross beating sin and death forever for our sakes. And because of that, we have this incredible hope, we have this incredible security, we have this incredible understanding that failure is not the end and our own failures do not negate his faithfulness. As Christians, the person and work and salvation of Christ is what ultimately grounds us in the ability to do maybe some of the hardest things . . . the ability to faithfully walk through suffering that is hard even to wrap your mind around the way that Christians throughout history have done because, again, of that hope you have in Christ."[9]

What young Alex Harris said is that each of us can use our lives to paint a picture of the gospel—to illustrate what Jesus accomplished on the cross.

Charles Spurgeon called this "adorning the gospel."

What is appropriate to the gospel? Well, *holiness* suits the gospel. Adorn it with a holy life. How pure, how clean, how sweet, how heavenly, the gospel is! Hang, then, the jewels of holiness about its neck, and place them as rings on its hands.

The gospel is also to be adorned with *mercifulness*. It is all mercy, it is all love, there is no love like it: "God so loved the world." Well, then, adorn the gospel with the suitable jewels of mercifulness and kindness. . . .

The gospel also is the gospel of *happiness*; it is called, "the glorious gospel of the blessed God." A more correct translation would be, "the happy God." Well, then, adorn the gospel by being happy. . . .

Adorn the gospel, next, by your *unselfishness*. . . . If you would adorn the gospel, you must love others, love them intensely, and make it one object of your lives to make other people happy, for so you will then be acting according to the spirit and genius of the gospel.[10]

All that is summed up in Colossians 2:6: "As you therefore have received Christ Jesus as Lord, so walk in Him."

"Walk" is a term that is used often to describe the Christian life. In Colossians 2:6, the word is in the present tense, indicating an ongoing process. Walking implies a steady, step-by-step effort and progress toward a goal. In other words, our actions are to consistently align with our words and beliefs. We preach the gospel with our lips, and we picture the gospel with our lives.

Our gospel message must be reinforced by a growing, dynamic gospel experience.

Ponder the Gospel with Your Mind

The gospel of Jesus Christ informs not only our actions but also our thoughts.

Colossians 3 begins with some of the most positive words ever written: "Since you have been raised to new life with Christ, set your sights on the realities of heaven, where Christ sits in the place of honor at God's right hand. Think about the things of heaven, not the things of earth" (vv. 1–2 NLT).

When you think of Jesus, don't limit your thoughts to a cross and an empty tomb, as wondrous as those moments are. Think of our Lord's present glory, seated at the right hand of God. John saw the glorified Lord Jesus in the first chapter of Revelation, and he wrote about it with astonishment and awe: "He had in His right hand seven stars, out of His mouth went a sharp two-edged sword, and His countenance was like the sun shining in its strength. And when I saw Him, I fell at His feet as dead. But He laid His right hand on me, saying to me, 'Do not be afraid; I am the First and the Last. I am He who lives, and was dead, and behold, I am alive forevermore. Amen'" (vv. 16–18).

Set your heart on this! Let your mind focus on the dazzling glory of our triumphant Christ. Think of it often. Meditate on it constantly. The world with all its troubles is a fleeting spectacle, but Jesus is the same yesterday, today, and forever.

Henry Ward Beecher once said, "The soul without imagination is what an observatory would be without a telescope." Moses and the seventy elders saw the foundation of the Lord's throne. Ezekiel and Isaiah saw the throne of God. Stephen saw Jesus standing at the right side of the throne. John saw it in the book of Revelation. All these writers described what they saw, and that allows us to use our God-given imaginations to see, as best we can by faith, the same throne of grace, victory, and eternal rule.

Meditate frequently on the throne of Christ, and you'll sleep better by night and feel more enthusiasm by day. My friend, set your heart on things above, where Christ is seated at the right hand of God.

Practice the Gospel with Your Love

Oklahoma governor Kevin Stitt issued a remarkable statement to commemorate the 100th anniversary of the Tulsa Race Massacre. For eighteen hours between May 31 and June 1, 1921, a white mob attacked a predominately Black neighborhood in Tulsa, killing hundreds of people and leaving thousands homeless. The story is soul-wrenching to study, but for decades few people knew about it. News outlets didn't report it in those days.

Listen to what Governor Stitt said: "Oklahoma's history, like every other state in the nation, has moments that we are not proud of. One hundred years ago, heinous acts of racism and hatred left a deep wound on our fellow Oklahomans in Greenwood. The pain is still felt by many of our neighbors today. . . . It is our responsibility that peace and love are taught in our homes, schools, workplaces and churches. God commands this of us in Colossians 3:14–15: 'Above all, clothe yourself with love, which binds us together in perfect harmony. And let the peace that comes from Christ rule in your hearts. For as members of one body you are called to live in peace.'"[11]

As followers of Christ, we must never forget that His gospel isn't something we simply believe—it's something we do. Something we must practice by choosing to love others.

Jesus said, "A new commandment I give to you, that you love one another; as I have loved you, that you also love one another. By this all will know that you are My disciples, if you have love for one another" (John 13:34–35).

In his book *The Mark of a Christian*, the late Francis Schaeffer pointed out that Jesus gave the world the right to judge believers by their love for one another:

> Jesus says, "By this shall all men know that you are my disciples, if you have love one to another." In the midst of the world, in the midst of our present dying culture, Jesus is giving a right to the world. Upon his authority he gives the world the right to judge whether you and I are born-again Christians on the basis of our observable love toward all Christians.
>
> That's pretty frightening. Jesus turns to the world and says, "I've something to say to you. On the basis of my authority, I give you a right: you may judge whether or not an individual is a Christian on the basis of the love he shows to all Christians."

In other words, if people come up to us and cast in our teeth the judgment that we are not Christians because we have not shown love toward other Christians, we must understand that they are only exercising a prerogative which Jesus gave them.

And we must not get angry. If people say, "You don't love other Christians," we must go home, get down on our knees and ask God whether or not they are right. And if they are, then they have a right to have said what they said.[12]

The gospel teaches us to clothe ourselves with love, for only the love of the gospel can overcome the venom of sin in our world. We have a triumphant gospel, but those who share it must be clothed in love and carry in their hearts a genuine burden for our neighbors and for our enemies.

Finish Strong

There are many other instructions for us in the book of Colossians, exhortations for these last days we should take to heart. But I want to end with a strange little verse at the very end of the book. It's a personal message, addressed to one individual—to you.

Well, actually, it's to a man named Archippus, but you can put your name in that spot. It says: "Take heed to the ministry which you have received in the Lord, that you may fulfill it" (4:17). In other words, finish the work. Complete the task. Make sure by the end of your life you have also come to the end of your assigned earthly work.

We believe Archippus was the son of Philemon. In Philemon 1:2, Paul called him "our fellow soldier." He had a personal ministry assigned to him, perhaps at the direction of Paul. Since Philemon and his family lived in Colossae, Paul added a postscript to his letter to the Colossians, telling Archippus to make sure he finished his assigned work.

Yes, let's all put our own name in Colossians 4:17. We're likely living in the final eras before the return of Christ, and God has assigned certain tasks to us all. Our Lord's first recorded words as a youngster were, "I must be about My Father's business" (Luke 2:49). And at the end of His natural life, He said, "I have glorified You on the earth. I have finished the work which You have given Me to do" (John 17:4).

God has given you certain gifts for His glory and certain tasks for His kingdom. Make sure you complete them. We don't have to get out of this world alive, but we do have to complete the work God has assigned us.

The apostle Paul said, "My life is worth nothing to me unless I use it for finishing the work assigned me by the Lord Jesus—the work of telling others the Good News about the wonderful grace of God" (Acts 20:24 NLT).

I can think of no one who sought to fulfill this verse more than someone I mentioned earlier in this chapter—Billy Graham. As I continue listening to Dr. Graham's sermons afresh, I confess I'm as moved as ever by his ringing proclamation of the triumph of the gospel. Even now, his iconic voice touches my heart and inspires me to be a better preacher.

On January 9, 1955, Billy said on his *Hour of Decision* radio program: "If I didn't believe that the Bible and the Gospel of Jesus Christ held the answer to this world's baffling problems, I would go back to the farm and the rural life that I love and spend my days in peaceful solitude."[13]

On April 3, 1966, Billy said, "We are looking for a universal solution to our problems, but the cross presents itself in the midst of our dilemma as our only hope."[14]

In a press conference in Poland on October 16, 1978, he said, "I have read the last page of the Bible. It is all going to turn out all right."[15]

Billy held more than four hundred crusades in his life, in more than 185 countries. His final crusade was in New York City in 2005, where he said, "I have one message: that Jesus Christ came, He died on a cross, He rose again, and He asked us to repent of our sins and receive Him by faith as Lord and Savior, and if we do, we have forgiveness of all our sins."[16]

I could give you quote after quote. I had the privilege of knowing Dr. Graham, and I heard him preach many times. He delivered his final sermon in a television broadcast on this ninety-fifth birthday, saying: "Our country is in a great need of a spiritual awakening. There have been times that I've wept as I've gone from city to city and I've seen how far people have wandered from God. Of all the things that I've seen and heard, there is only one message that can change people's lives and hearts. I want to tell people about the meaning of the cross. . . . The real cross of Christ. . . . He loves you, willing to forgive you of all your sins."[17]

Throughout my ministry, I've met people who told me they were saved at a Billy Graham Crusade or by listening to him on television or radio. Billy's entire personality was touched by God with an unusual power.

None of us are Billy Graham. He was unique. But we all have the same gospel. It didn't belong to Billy Graham. It is God's gift to all of us. It is the good news of Jesus Christ for you as much as for anyone in all the world, and it trumps all the headlines of history. The gospel is the only beam of light shining on this dark world, but its megawatts are unlimited. It can brighten any life and dispel every shadow.

We are not beaten down people. We're not on the ropes. We are not an endangered species. Despite the title of this book, we are not a people worried about where we go from here. We know where we're going, and we know Him who has prepared the way. We are more than conquerors through our Lord Jesus Christ.

That's the triumph of the gospel, and I hope you've discovered it for yourself. Whatever you're facing, Christ is your victory. Wherever you're going, He is your guide. However you're feeling, He is your sole and solid hope. Whenever you're worried by the falling fragments of our collapsing planet, you can look up to heaven and see Him who came down to earth for you—and who is soon coming again!

We're soldiers in the battle now, but one day we will be heirs in the kingdom. The world may wage war against the Lamb, but the Lamb will triumph over them because He is Lord of lords and King of kings, and He will bring His called, chosen, and faithful followers with Him. Oh, may we all be there! May He be your Lamb and your Lord as we triumphantly but humbly tell Him:

> Just as I am, without one plea
> But that Thy blood was shed for me
> And that Thou bid'st me come to Thee
> O Lamb of God, I come! I come![18]

Acknowledgments

Every day of my life I have the privilege of devoting my time and energy to the only two things in the whole world that are eternal: the Word of God and people. I am so blessed to be surrounded by a team that is deeply committed to these two priorities.

At the center of that team is my wife, Donna, who has endured the crazy pressure that accompanies every book I write. Together we have dreamed and planned and worked toward the goal of influencing our world for Christ. More than ever before in our fifty-seven years together, we have been seeing our dreams come true.

My oldest son, David Michael, is now the president of Turning Point Ministries. His role continues to expand each year, and it is because he has taken so much off of my administrative plate that I am able to produce books like the one you have just read.

Dianne Sutherland is my administrative assistant at our media center, and she coordinates my schedule, my travel, and basically my life! As my life has gotten more complicated, so has hers. We are both thankful that He brought Beth Anne Hewett to us to help us maintain some sanity in the whirlwind that is our office.

Beau Sager is the coordinator of research and editing. He provides considerable research himself and also works with our team to assure that our information is timely and accurate. During the six months that these books are created, Beau and I talk every day and sometimes many times each day. We think alike and have learned to work together at the speed of trust. Beau, I do not want to even imagine doing this without you. Thank you for taking this journey with me!

Thank you also to Sam O'Neal, whose editorial eye and insights helped make this a better book.

There are thirteen visual illustrations in this book, and the creator of those illustrations is a young artist at Turning Point named Martin Zambrano.

For many years, Rob Morgan has worked with us at Turning Point. He is a pastor and one of my best friends. I don't know anyone who knows as much about everything as Rob Morgan. He preaches for me when I have to be absent from my church, and it is our joy to feature many of his books through the ministry of Turning Point. He adds so much to each writing project that we do. Thank you, Rob Morgan, for your sacrificial partnership.

All of the people I have just mentioned were totally involved in the creation of *Where Do We Go from Here?* But there is so much more to a book than its mere release. The promotion, marketing, and circulation efforts of both the author and his team and the publisher and its team determine the fate of the book.

Our creative department, led by Paul Joiner, is second to none in the development and deployment of the finest and most up-to-date marketing and promotional strategies being utilized today. Everyone who has seen Paul's work agrees with my assessment. Paul Joiner is one of God's best gifts to Turning Point.

And this year we have once again had the privilege of teaming up with Mark Schoenwald and Thomas Nelson. Damon Reiss is our editor and go-to guy at Thomas Nelson, and we have become good friends over the last few books we have done together. Thank you, Damon, for always being there to answer my questions and listen to my ideas. It is a joy to work with you to make sure our message is reaching as many readers as possible.

As with all my other writing projects, I am represented by Sealy Yates of Yates & Yates. We consider Sealy, his whole family, and his business associates members of our Turning Point team. We have watched as God has honored this relationship now for almost thirty years.

None of us deserves to have our names on the same page with the name of our Lord and Savior, Jesus Christ. This is really His project. Most of all, I want to express my hope that God will be glorified as we tell the story of His plans for our future!

David Jeremiah
San Diego, California
July 2021

Notes

Introduction

1. Aleksandr Solzhenitsyn, *The Gulag Archipelago* (New York, NY: Harper & Row, 1974), 178.

Chapter 1: A Cultural Prophecy: Socialism

1. Joshua Goodman, "AP Exclusive: Imprisoned Supercop's Escape from Venezuela," *Associated Press*, June 25, 2019, https://apnews.com/article /c45c3d6225a7423fad2b44478452b9d5.

2. Brinley Hineman, "Fact Check: Socialist Policies Alone Did Not Destroy Venezuela's Economy in Last Decade," *USA Today*, August 8, 2020, https:// www.usatoday.com/story/news/factcheck/2020/08/08/fact-check -socialism-alone-did-not-destroy-venezuelas-economy/3323566001/.

3. Maxim Lott, "How Socialism Turned Venezuela from the Wealthiest Country in South America into an Economic Basket Case," *Fox News*, January 26, 2019, https://www.foxnews.com/world/how-socialism -turned-venezuela-from-the-wealthiest-country-in-south-america-into -an-economic-basket-case.

4. "U.S. Attitudes Toward Socialism, Communism, and Collectivism," Victims of Communism Memorial Foundation, October, 2020, https:// victimsofcommunism.org/wp-content/uploads/2020/10/10.19.20-VOC -YouGov-Survey-on-U.S.-Attitudes-Toward-Socialism-Communism-and -Collectivism.pdf.

5. Felix Salmon, "Gen Z Prefers 'Socialism' to 'Capitalism,'" *AXIOS*, January 27, 2019, https://www.axios.com/

socialism-capitalism-poll-generation-z-preference-1ffb8800-0ce5-4368
-8a6f-de3b82662347.html.

6. Emma Green, "Bernie Sanders's Religious Test for Christians in Public Office," *The Atlantic*, June 8, 2017, https://www.theatlantic.com/politics /archive/2017/06/bernie-sanders-chris-van-hollen-russell-vought/529614/.

7. Paul Kengor, *The Devil and Karl Marx: Communism's Long March of Death, Deception, and Infiltration* (Gastonia, NC: TAN Books, 2020), 150.

8. Daily Wire News, "Survivor of Mao's China: Critical Race Theory 'Is Racist,' China Used 'Wokeness' to Install Communism," *The Daily Wire*, June 11, 2021, https://www.dailywire.com/news/survivor-of-maos -china-critical-race-theory-is-racist-china-used-wokeness-to-install -communism.

9. Erwin Lutzer, *We Will Not Be Silenced: Responding Courageously to Our Culture's Assault on Christianity* (Eugene, OR: Harvest House, 2020), 21.

10. Robert Payne, *Marx: A Biography* (New York, NY: Simon & Schuster, 1968), 315.

11. Richard Wurmbrand, *Marx & Satan* (Wheaton, IL: Crossway Books, 1986), 47.

12. Franz Mehring, *Karl Marx: The Story of His Life* (New York, NY: Routledge, 1936), 92.

13. Karl Marx, "The Pale Maiden," *Early Works of Karl Marx: Book of Verse*, accessed July 12, 2021, https://www.marxists.org/archive/marx /works/1837-pre/verse/verse24.htm.

14. Karl Marx, "The Player," 1841.

15. Kengor, *The Devil and Karl Marx*, 72.

16. Karl Marx, letter of May 20, 1882, to Friedrich Engels, MEW, XXXV, 65.

17. Kengor, *The Devil and Karl Marx*, 123.

18. Kengor, 127.

19. Alexander Yakovlev, *A Century of Violence in Soviet Russia* (New Haven, CT: Yale University Press, 2002), 155, 163.

20. Anne Applebaum, *Iron Curtain: The Crushing of Eastern Europe, 1944–1956* (New York, NY: Knopf Doubleday Publishing Group, 2012), Kindle edition.

21. Rod Dreher, *Live Not by Lies: A Manuel for Christian Dissidents* (New York, NY: Sentinel, 2020), 8.

22. Kengor, *The Devil and Karl Marx*, xix.

23. Aleksandr Solzhenitsyn, "A World Split Apart," *American Rhetoric*, June 8, 1978, https://www.americanrhetoric.com/speeches /alexandersolzhenitsynharvard.htm.
24. Milan Kundera, *The Book of Laughter and Forgetting*, trans. Michael H. Heim (Harmondsworth, England: Penguin, 1983), 157.
25. Dreher, *Live Not by Lies*, 8–9.
26. Lutzer, *We Will Not Be Silenced*, 22–23.
27. Iain Murray in "The Temptations of Socialism: A Conversation with Economist Iain," *Thinking in Public*, February 1, 2021, https:// albertmohler.com/2021/02/01/iain-murray.
28. Patrick J. Buchanan, *Suicide of a Superpower* (New York, NY: Thomas Dunne Books, 2011), 207.
29. Stephanie Pagones, "Police Defunded: Major Cities Feeling the Loss of Police Funding as Murders, Other Crimes Soar," *Fox News*, April 1, 2021, https://www.foxnews.com/us/police-defunded-cities-murders -crime-budget.
30. Albert Mohler, "The Coming Socialist Storm," *Decision Magazine*, January 1, 2021, https://decisionmagazine.com/albert-mohler -the-coming-socialist-storm/.
31. Aleksandr Solzhenitsyn, "Live Not by Lies," accessed July 8, 2021, https:// journals.sagepub.com/doi/pdf/10.1080/03064220408537357.
32. Dreher, *Live Not by Lies*, 17.
33. Søren Kierkegaard, *Provocations: Spiritual Writings of Kierkegaard* (Farmington, PA: Plough Publishing, 1999), 88.
34. Dreher, *Live Not by Lies*, 174.
35. "Hillsdale High School Principal Tells Valedictorian Enough of the Religious Speech," WBCK 95.3, June 1, 2021, https://wbckfm.com /hillsdale-high-school-principal-valedictorian-religious-speech/.
36. Stefano Pozzebon, "Venezuela Is Quietly Quitting Socialism," *CNN*, December 18, 2020, https://www.cnn.com/2020/12/18/americas /venezuela-death-of-socialism-intl/index.html.
37. "Venezuela," *Human Rights Watch* (World Report, 2021), https://www .hrw.org/world-report/2021/country-chapters/venezuela.

Chapter 2: An International Prophecy: Globalism

1. Jeffrey D. Sachs, *The Ages of Globalization* (New York, NY: Columbia University Press, 2020), v-xiii.

2. Larry Elliott, "Gordon Brown Calls for Global Government to Tackle Coronavirus," *The Guardian*, March 26, 2020, https://www .theguardian.com/politics/2020/mar/26/gordon-brown-calls-for -global-government-to-tackle-coronavirus.

3. Arvind Ashta, "It Is Time to Seriously Consider the Advantages of a World Federal Government," March 18, 2021, https://blogs.lse.ac.uk /europpblog/2021/03/18/it-is-time-to-seriously-consider-the-advantages -of-a-world-federal-government/.

4. Albert Mohler, "Globalization and the Christian Mission," *Tabletalk*, November 2017, https://tabletalkmagazine.com/article/2017/11 /globalization-christian-mission/.

5. Jason Fernando, "Globalization," *Investopedia*, December 12, 2020, https://www.investopedia.com/terms/g/globalization.asp.

6. David Jeremiah, *The Coming Economic Armageddon* (New York, NY: FaithWords, 2010), xvii–xviii.

7. Alexis Wichowski, *The Information Trade* (New York, NY: HarperOne, 2020), 10.

8. Amy Webb, *The Big Nine: How the Tech Titans and Their Thinking Machines Could Warp Humanity* (New York, NY: Hachette, 2019), 10.

9. Leigh Phillips, "We Need a World Government—But It Has to Be Democratic," *Jacobin*, July 14, 2020, https://jacobinmag.com/2020/07 /one-world-government-democracy-covid-19.

10. Michael S. Heiser, *The Unseen Realm: Recovering the Supernatural Worldview of the Bible* (Bellingham, WA: Lexham Press, 2015), 111.

11. Heiser, *The Unseen Realm*, 111.

12. Will Durant, *Our Oriental Heritage* (New York, NY: Simon and Schuster, 1954), 224.

13. Durant, *Our Oriental Heritage*, 224.

14. Philip Renner, *Worship Without Limits* (Shippensburg, PA: Destiny Image Publishers, Inc., 2019), chapter 1.

15. Mohler, "Globalization and the Christian Mission."

16. Leah MarieAnn Klett, "Former Drug Addict Baptized at Church He Vandalized 6 Months Earlier: 'God Is Real,'" *The Christian Post*, October 10, 2019, https://www.christianpost.com/news/former-drug-addict-baptized-at -church-he-vandalized-6-months-earlier-god-is-real.html.

17. "A Prisoner Relentlessly Pursued by God," *The Voice of the Martyrs*, accessed May 5, 2021, https://www.persecution.com/2021-02-min-ji /?_source_code=EM21B1.

18. John Baillie, *Memoir of the Rev. W. H. Hewitson: Late Minister of the Free Church of Scotland, at Dirleton* (New York, NY: Robert Carter & Brothers, 1851), 89–90.
19. Edith Bolling Galt Wilson, *My Memoir* (New York, NY: Putnam, 1939), 225.

Chapter 3: A Biological Prophecy: Pandemic

1. Clem Boyd, "Cedarville Stories Podcast: Trusting God's Sovereignty During COVID-19," *Cedarville University*, July 10, 2020, https://www.cedarville.edu/news/2020/cedarville-stories-podcast-trusting-god's-sovereignty-during-covid-19.
2. "WHO Director-General's Opening Remarks at the Media Briefing on COVID-19—11 March 2020," *World Health Organization*, March 11, 2020, https://www.who.int/director-general/speeches/detail/who-director-general-s-opening-remarks-at-the-media-briefing-on-covid-19-11-march-2020.
3. "WHO Coronavirus (COVID-19) Dashboard," *World Health Organization*, accessed July 5, 2021, https://covid19.who.int.
4. "WHO Coronavirus (COVID-19) Dashboard."
5. Emily Zanotti, "India's Health Care System in 'Total Collapse' as COVID Surge 'Ravages' Country," *The Daily Wire*, April 25, 2021, https://www.dailywire.com/news/indias-health-care-system-in-total-collapse-as-covid-surge-ravages-country; Jessie Yeung, "India Is Spiraling Deeper into Covid-19 Crisis. Here's What You Need to Know," *CNN*, May 11, 2021, https://www.cnn.com/2021/04/26/india/india-covid-second-wave-explainer-intl-hnk-dst/index.html.
6. Adapted from Joel C. Rosenberg, "What Does the Bible Teach About Pestilence, Plagues and Global Pandemics?" *The Joshua Fund*, accessed July 9, 2021, https://www.joshuafund.com/images/blog_uploads/FACTSHEET-BibleAndPandemics_BRANDED_v2.pdf.
7. David Jeremiah, *The Book of Signs* (Nashville, TN: W Publishing, 2019), 241–42.
8. Mark Hitchcock, *The End* (Carol Stream, IL: Tyndale House Publishers, Inc., 2012), 109
9. John MacArthur, *The Second Coming: Signs of Christ's Return and the End of the Age* (Wheaton, IL: Crossway Books, 1999), 89.
10. John C. Lennox, *Where Is God in a Coronavirus World?* (UK: The Good Book Company, 2020), 8.

11. Nicole Acevedo, "Tom Hanks and Rita Wilson Return to U.S. After Recovering from Coronavirus," *NBC News*, March 28, 2020, https://www .nbcnews.com/pop-culture/celebrity/tom-hanks-rita-wilson-return-u-s -after-recovering-coronavirus-n1171236.

12. Jason Seville, "King Jehoshaphat and the Coronavirus," *The Gospel Coalition*, February 6, 2020, https://www.thegospelcoalition.org/article /jehoshaphat-and-coronavirus/.

13. David Williams, "Woman Gets Part-Time Job at Nursing Home so She Can Visit Her Dad During Pandemic," *CNN*, March 4, 2021, https://www .cnn.com/2021/03/04/us/daughter-nursing-home-dad-trnd/index.html.

14. Martin Luther, "Martin Luther: Whether One May Flee from a Deadly Plague," *Christianity Today*, May 19, 2020, https://www.christianitytoday .com/ct/2020/may-web-only/martin-luther-plague-pandemic-coronavirus -covid-flee-letter.html.

15. Michael P. Green, ed., *Illustrations for Biblical Preaching* (Grand Rapids, MI: Baker Book House, 1989), 376–77; adapted from Corrie Ten Boom, *The Hiding Place* (Grand Rapids, MI: Baker Publishing Book, 1984).

16. Isobel Kuhn, *In the Arena* (Singapore: OMF Books, 1960), 225–32.

17. David Jeremiah, *What Are You Afraid Of?: Facing Down Your Fears with Faith* (Carol Stream, IL: Tyndale House Publishers, Inc., 2013), 49.

18. J. R. Miller, "Do the *Next* Thing," *Grace Gems*, accessed May 12, 2021, https://www.gracegems.org/Miller/do_the_next_thing.htm.

19. Emily P. Freeman, *The Next Right Thing* (Grand Rapids, MI: Revell, 2019), 14–15.

20. Quoted by Justin Taylor, "Do the Next Thing," *The Gospel Coalition*, October 25, 2017, https://www.thegospelcoalition.org/blogs/justin-taylor /do-the-next-thing/.

Chapter 4: A Financial Prophecy: Economic Chaos

1. Stacey Naggiar, "People Are Getting Microchipped in Sweden, and It's Pretty Normal," *Vice*, May 3, 2020, https://www.vice.com/en/article /y3madg/people-are-getting-microchipped-in-sweden-and-its-pretty -normal.

2. Board of Governors of the Federal Reserve System, "The 2019 Federal Reserve Payments Study," *FederalReserve.gov,* accessed May 6, 2021, https://www.federalreserve.gov/paymentsystems/2019-December-The -Federal-Reserve-Payments-Study.htm.

3. Liz Frazier, "Already Leaning Towards Digital Money, Covid-19 Pushes More People Towards Contactless Payments," *Forbes*, August 21, 2020, https://www.forbes.com/sites/lizfrazierpeck/2020/08/21/already-leaning -towards-digital-money-covid-19-pushes-more-people-towards -contactless-payments/?sh=316cd5703012.

4. James Royal and Kevin Voigt, "What Is Cryptocurrency? Here's What You Should Know," *Nerd Wallet*, July 9, 2021, https://www.nerdwallet .com/article/investing/cryptocurrency-7-things-to-know.

5. Dondi Black, "Digital Currencies Skyrocket During Pandemic," *FIS*, January 11, 2021, https://www.fisglobal.com/en/insights/what-we-think /2021/january/digital-currencies-skyrocket-during-pandemic.

6. Sam Polk, "For the Love of Money," *New York Times*, January 18, 2014, https://www.nytimes.com/2014/01/19/opinion/sunday/for-the-love-of -money.html.

7. John Piper, "What It Means to Love Money," *Desiring God*, accessed May 24, 2021, https://www.desiringgod.org/articles/what-it-means-to-love-money.

8. "Global Inequality," *Inequality.org*, accessed May 6, 2021, https:// inequality.org/facts/global-inequality/.

9. Jeff Cox, "CEOs See Pay Grow 1,000% in the Last 40 Years, Now Make 278 Times the Average Worker," *CNBC*, August 16, 2019, https://www .cnbc.com/2019/08/16/ceos-see-pay-grow-1000percent-and-now-make -278-times-the-average-worker.html.

10. Chase Peterson-Withorn, "How Much Money America's Billionaires Have Made During the Covid-19 Pandemic," *Forbes*, April 30, 2021, https:// www.forbes.com/sites/chasewithorn/2021/04/30/american-billionaires -have-gotten-12-trillion-richer-during-the-pandemic/?sh=4474dbf9f557.

11. Scott Simon, "Understanding NXIVM, Group Critics Call a 'Cult'," *NPR*, August 4, 2018, https://www.npr.org/2018/08/04/635583140 /understanding-nxivm-group-critics-call-a-cult.

12. Frederick A. Tatford, *Prophecy's Last Word: An Exposition of the Revelation* (Glasgow, Scotland: Pickering & Inglis, 1947), 154.

13. Owen Ullmann, "'Free Solo' Alex Honnold: How I Achieved the Impossible—Scaling El Capitan," *USA Today*, January 31, 2019, https:// www.usatoday.com/story/news/2019/01/31/free-solo-alex-honnold-how -did-impossible-scaling-el-capitan/2732945002/.

14. Stew Friedman, "Walking Away from Wall Street," *Wharton Work/Life Integration Project*, accessed May 7, 2021, http://worklife.wharton.upenn .edu/2014/08/walking-away-wall-street-sam-polk/.

Chapter 5: A Theological Prophecy: The Falling Away

1. Joshua Harris, *I Kissed Dating Goodbye* (Colorado Springs, CO: Multnomah Books, 2003), 67.
2. Caleb Parke, "Well-Known Christian Author, Purity Advocate, Renounces His Faith: 'I Hope You Can Forgive Me,'" *Fox News*, July 29, 2019, https://www.foxnews.com/faith-values/christian-author-joshua-harris-kissed-dating-goodbye-faith.
3. Ethan Renoe, "Everyone Is Leaving Christianity. Few Know Where They're Going," *Faith It*, April 13, 2021, https://faithit.com/everyone-is-leaving-christianity-few-know-where-theyre-going-ethan-renoe/.
4. Richard Fry, "Millennials Overtake Baby Boomers as America's Largest Generation," *Pew Research Center*, April 28, 2020, https://www.pewresearch.org/fact-tank/2020/04/28/millennials-overtake-baby-boomers-as-americas-largest-generation/.
5. Kelsey Dallas, "Want Some Good News About the Future of Faith? Look to Generation Z," *Deseret News*, March 1, 2020, https://www.deseret.com/indepth/2020/3/1/21156465/millennial-faith-religion-generation-z-research-trends-nones-church-attendance.
6. Jeffrey M. Jones, "U.S. Church Membership Down Sharply in Past Two Decades," *Gallup*, April 18, 2019, https://news.gallup.com/poll/248837/church-membership-down-sharply-past-two-decades.aspx; Jeffrey M. Jones, "U.S. Church Membership Falls Below Majority for First Time," *Gallup*, March 29, 2021, https://news.gallup.com/poll/341963/church-membership-falls-below-majority-first-time.aspx.
7. Ryan J. Bell, "A Year Without God: A Former Pastor's Journey into Atheism," *Huffington Post*, March 2, 2014, https://www.huffpost.com/entry/a-year-without-god_b_4512842.
8. NPR Staff, "After Year of Atheism, Former Pastor: 'I Don't Think God Exists,'" *NPR*, December 27, 2014, https://www.npr.org/2014/12/27/373298310/after-year-of-atheism-former-pastor-i-dont-think-god-exists.
9. John F. Walvoord in *The Theological Wordbook: The 200 Most Important Theological Terms and Their Relevance for Today* (Nashville, TN: Word Publishing, 2000), 19.
10. Michael Finnegan, "Hollywood Actor Indicted for Fake HBO and Netflix Deals," *Los Angeles Times*, May 4, 2021, https://www.latimes.com/california/story/2021-05-04/actor-zachary-horwitz-indicted-ponzi-scheme.

11. Quoted by Zach Bollman in "Nominal Christianity," Fellowship in Christ Christian Church, January 20, 2021, https://www.fellowshipinchrist.org /nominal-christianity/.

12. "I Thought I Was a Christian," *Navigators*, August 29, 2012, https://www .navigators.org/i-thought-i-was-a-christian/.

13. Shannon Williams, *Autism: A Journey of Faith and Hope* (Bloomington, IN: AuthorHouse, 2013), 10.

14. Nancy DeMoss Wolgemuth, "Up Close and Personal: An Interview with Nancy DeMoss Wolgemuth in 2011," Revive Our Hearts, accessed June 30, 2021, https://www.reviveourhearts.com/articles/close-and -personal/.

15. Scott Davis, "LeBron James Reportedly Spends $1.5 Million Per Year to Take Care of His Body—Here's Where It Goes," *Business Insider*, July 29, 2018, https://www.businessinsider.com/how-lebron-james-spends-money -body-care-2018-7#lebron-james-reportedly-spends-seven-figures-a -year-on-his-body-malcolm-gladwell-once-told-bill-simmons-that-in-a -conversation-with-james-business-partner-maverick-carter-carter-said -that-cost-was-15-million-1.

16. Andrew Murray, *The Holiest of All*, accessed June 27, 2021, https://www .biblestudytools.com/classics/murray-holiest-of-all/the-third-warning. html.

17. AnneClaire Stapleton, "Girl, 12, Accidentally Runs Half Marathon," *CNN Health*, April 27, 2016, https://www.cnn.com/2016/04/27/health/12-year -old-accidentally-runs-half-marathon/index.html.

Chapter 6: A Biographical Prophecy: End Times People

1. Shon Hopwood, "God's Hot Pursuit of an Armed Bank Robber," *Christianity Today*, April 23, 2014, https://www.christianitytoday.com /ct/2014/april/gods-hot-pursuit-of-armed-bank-robber.html. See also Shon Hopwood, *Law Man: Memoir of a Jailhouse Lawyer* (Washington, DC: Prison Professors, 2017), chapters 1–2.

2. Adapted from Kevin DeYoung, "The Villain with a Thousand Faces," *The Gospel Coalition*, October 7, 2011, https://www.thegospelcoalition.org /blogs/kevin-deyoung/the-villain-with-a-thousand-faces/.

3. Theodore Dalrymple, "The Frivolity of Evil," *City Journal*, Autumn 2004, https://www.city-journal.org/html/frivolity-evil-12835.html.

4. Kevin DeYoung, "The Villain with a Thousand Faces," *The Gospel Coalition*, October 7, 2011, https://www.thegospelcoalition.org/blogs /kevin-deyoung/the-villain-with-a-thousand-faces/.

5. Bill Chappell, "Asian Grandmother Who Smacked Her Attacker with A Board Donates Nearly $1 Million," *NPR*, March 24, 2021, https://www .npr.org/2021/03/24/980760622/asian-grandmother-who-smacked-her -attacker-with-a-board-donates-nearly-1-million.

6. John Calvin, *The Second Epistle of Paul the Apostle to the Corinthians and the Epistles to Timothy, Titus and Philemon* (Grand Rapids, MI: W. B. Eerdmans Publishing Company, 1996), 322.

7. John Taylor, "The Descent to the Bottom Line," *New York Times*, July 8, 1990, https://www.nytimes.com/1990/07/08/books/the-descent-to-the -bottom-line.html.

8. Tony Evans, "Why Men Matter," *Tony Evans The Urban Alternative*, April 1, 2021, https://tonyevans.org/podcast/why-men-matter-part -1/; https://tonyevans.org/podcast/why-men-matter-part-2/.

9. "Assistant Pastor Cameron Cole," Packsaddle Fellowship, accessed June 16, 2021, https://www.packsaddle.us/?page_id=96.

10. "The Teddy Bear Ministry," *The Christian Heart*, June 15, 2021, https:// thechristianheart.com/the-teddy-bear-ministry/.

11. R. C. Sproul, *The Holiness of God, Chosen by God, Pleasing to God* (Carol Stream, IL.: Tynedale House, 1985), 3, 5.

12. Anna Kelsey-Sugg and Ann Arnold, "Doubts Cast over Mountaineers' Record Claims, with Calls for More Honesty at High Altitude," *ABC News*, June 4, 20021, https://www.abc.net.au/news/2021–06–05 /mountain-climbers-fourteen-highest-peaks-claims-in-doubt /100187534.

13. "Meet a Christian: Amanda," *Castlefields Church*, accessed July 4, 2020, https://castlefieldschurch.org.uk/meet-a-christian-amanda/.

14. Hopwood, "God's Hot Pursuit of an Armed Bank Robber."

Chapter 7: A Political Prophecy: Cancel Culture

1. Anna Beahm, "Birmingham Housing Authority Ends Work with Church of the Highlands," *AL.com*, June 8, 2020, https://www.al.com/news/2020 /06/birmingham-housing-authority-ends-work-with-church-of-the -highlands.html.

2. Greg Garrison, "Birmingham Schools, Housing Authority Cut Ties with Church of the Highlands," *AL.com*, June 9, 2020, https://www.al.com /news/2020/06/birmingham-schools-may-ban-church-of-the-highlands -pastor-clinic-respond-as-housing-authority-turns-away-free-covid-testing .html. See also Greg Garrison, "Pastor Chris Hodges Responds to Social Media Controversy," *AL.com*, June 14, 2020, https://www.al.com/news/2020/05 /pastor-chris-hodges-responds-to-social-media-controversy.html.

3. Ed Stetzer, "Unliked Likes: Cancelling Pastor Chris Hodges and Church of the Highlands," *Christianity Today*, June 11, 2020, https://www .christianitytoday.com/edstetzer/2020/june/chris-hodges-trump-kirk -cancel-culture.html.

4. Evan Gerstmann, "Cancel Culture Is Only Getting Worse," *Forbes*, September 13, 2020, https://www.forbes.com/sites/evangerstmann /2020/09/13/cancel-culture-is-only-getting-worse/.

5. Lesley Hauler, "I Was 'Canceled' and It Nearly Destroyed My Life," *Good Morning America*, January 17, 2020, https://www.goodmorningamerica .com/living/story/canceled-destroyed-life-68311913.

6. Lizzie Troughton, "Cancelling Christians," *The Critic*, June 14, 2021, https://thecritic.co.uk/cancelling-christianity/.

7. *CyberCivics*, https://www.cybercivics.com/cyber-civics-team, accessed July 6, 2021.

8. Luke Barr, "Senior Citizens Lost Almost $1 Billion in Scams Last Year: FBI," *ABC News*, June 18, 2021, https://abcnews.go.com/Politics /senior-citizens-lost-billion-scams-year-fbi/story?id=78356859.

9. Susie Coen, "The Secret Cyber Vigilante Snaring Scammers: Susie Coen Reveals How One Crusader Has Saved People Losing £4million by Turning the Tables in Spectacular Fashion," *Daily Mail*, June 18, 2021, https://www.dailymail.co.uk/news/article-9702275/SUSIE-COEN-Secret -cyber-vigilante-saves-scam-victims-turning-tables-fraudsters.html.

10. Abdu Murray, "Canceled: How the Eastern Honor-Shame Mentality Traveled West," *The Gospel Coalition*, May 28, 2020, https://www .thegospelcoalition.org/article/canceled-understanding-eastern -honor-shame/.

11. Cathy Cassata, "Yes, You're Probably Experiencing Social Pain Right Now: How to Cope," *Healthline*, January 25, 2021, https://www.healthline .com/health-news/yes-youre-probably-experiencing-social-pain-right -now-how-to-cope#1.

12. Lee Mannion, "Britain Appoints Minister for Loneliness Amid Growing Isolation," *Reuters*, January 17, 2018, https://www.reuters.com/article /us-britain-politics-health/britain-appoints-minister-for-loneliness-amid -growing-isolation-idUSKBN1F61I6.

13. Rachel Martin, "In 'Together,' Former Surgeon General Writes About Importance of Human Connection," *NPR*, May 11, 2020, https://www .npr.org/sections/health-shots/2020/05/11/853308193/in-together-former -surgeon-general-writes-about-importance-of-human-connection.

14. Barry Corey, "The Radical Call of Kindness," *Biola Magazine*, June 1, 2016, https://www.biola.edu/blogs/biola-magazine/2016/the-radical -call-of-kindness.

15. John Piper, "Christian Courage," *Desiring God*, May 11, 1999, https:// www.desiringgod.org/articles/christian-courage.

16. Todd Nettleton, *When Faith Is Forbidden* (Chicago, IL: Moody Publishers, 2021), 61–62.

17. Mike Nappa, *The Courage to Be Christian* (West Monroe, LA: Howard Publishing, 2001), 3.

18. Ryann Blackshere, "Widower Forges Friendship with Man in Crash That Killed Wife, Unborn Baby," *Today*, February 3, 2014, https://www.today .com/news/man-crash-killed-woman-forges-friendship-her-widower -2D12044681.

19. Paul J. Meyer, *Forgiveness . . . the Ultimate Miracle* (Orlando, FL: Bridge-Logos, 2006), xiii-xv.

20. Steve Hartman, "Man Saves Police Officer from Burning Vehicle Despite His History with Police," *CBS News*, July 10, 2020, https://www.cbsnews. com/news/pennsylvania-man-saves-cop-despite-history-with-police/.

Chapter 8: A Spiritual Prophecy: Spiritual Famine

1. Neeraj Chand, "Benedict Cumberbatch Recalls the Horrible Experience of Losing Weight for *The Courier*," *Movieweb*, March 26, 2021, https:// movieweb.com/the-courier-benedict-cumberbatch -weight-loss/; Jessica Napoli, "'Courier' Star Benedict Cumberbatch Talks His Dramatic Weight Loss for the Film," *Fox News*, March 27, 2021, https://www.foxnews.com/entertainment/benedict-cumberbatch -the-courier-weight-loss-transformation.

2. "Why Bible Translation?" *Wycliffe Bible Translators*, accessed May 18, 2021, https://www.wycliffe.org/about/why.

3. A. W. Tozer, *The Pursuit of God* (Harrisburg, PA: Christian Publications, Inc., 1948), 17.

4. Howard Taylor, *Hudson Taylor's Spiritual Secret* (Chicago, IL: Moody Publishers, 1979), 22.

5. Sherwood Eliot Wirt, *A Thirst for God* (Minneapolis, MN: World Wide Publications, 1989), 29.

6. D. A. Carson, *For the Love of God, Vol. 2* (Wheaton, IL: Crossway Books, 2006), devotion for January 23.

7. Jessica Lea, "Barna: We're Experiencing Another Reformation, and Not in a Good Way," *Church Leaders*, October 8, 2020, https://churchleaders.com/news/383605-george-barna-another-reformation.html.

8. "Six Megathemes Emerge from Barna Group Research in 2010," *Barna*, December 13, 2010, https://www.barna.com/research/six-megathemes-emerge-from-barna-group-research-in-2010/.

9. Jeremiah J. Johnston, *Unanswered* (New Kensington, PA: Whitaker House, 2015), 143, 147, 153.

10. Anugrah Kumar, "China Shuts Down Bible App, Christian WeChat as New Crackdown Policies Go into Effect," *The Christian Post*, May 2, 2021, https://www.christianpost.com/news/china-shuts-down-bible-app-christian-wechat-accounts.html.

11. Hugo Martín, "More Hotels Are Checking Out of the Bible Business," *Los Angeles Times*, December 4, 2016, https://www.latimes.com/business/la-fi-hotel-bibles-20161204-story.html.

12. Tim Carman, "As a Food Writer with Covid, I Worried I'd Lose My Sense of Taste. It Turned Out to Be Much Worse," *The Washington Post*, November 29, 2020, https://www.washingtonpost.com/food/2020/11/29/food-writer-covid/.

13. Marilee Pierce Dunker, "Women Who Inspired World Vision's Founding Father," *World Vision*, February 28, 2013, https://www.worldvision.org/christian-faith-news-stories/women-inspired-bob-pierce.

14. Charles R. Swindoll, *Good Morning, Lord . . . Can We Talk?* (Carol Stream, IL: Tyndale House, 2018), 13.

15. Jonathan Petersen, "The Joy of Bible Study Is Seeing Your Life Changed: An Interview with Warren Wiersbe," *BibleGateway Blog*, March 26, 2019, https://www.biblegateway.com/blog/2019/03/the-joy-of-bible-study-is-seeing-your-life-changed-warren-wiersbe/.

16. Matt Brown, "The Skilled Man Will Serve Before Kings," *Think Eternity* (blog), accessed May 19, 2021, https://thinke.org/blog/2011/2/24/he-will-serve-before-kings.html.

17. Sarah Jarvis, "Phoenix Man Gets 4.5 Years in Burned-Body Case," *AZ Central*, June 11, 2015, https://www.azcentral.com/story/news/local/phoenix/2015/06/11/phoenix-man-burn-body-dump-abrk/71073988/.

18. H. Joseph Gammage, "Transformed by God in Prison," *Victorious Living*, accessed May 19, 2021, https://victoriouslivingmagazine.com/2021/05/transformed-by-god-in-prison/.

Chapter 9: A Geographical Prophecy: Jerusalem

1. "PM Netanyahu's Remarks at the Opening of the US Embassy in Jerusalem," May 14, 2018, *Israel Ministry of Foreign Affairs*, https://mfa.gov.il/MFA/PressRoom/2018/Pages/PM-Netanyahu-s-remarks-at-the-opening-of-the-US-embassy-in-Jerusalem-14-May-2018.aspx.

2. Will Maule, "Here Are the Biblical Prophecies Connected to the US Embassy Opening in Jerusalem," *CBN News*, May 19, 2018, https://www1.cbn.com/cbnnews/israel/2018/may/here-are-the-biblical-prophecies-connected-to-the-us-embassy-opening-in-jerusalem.

3. Randall Price, *Jerusalem in Prophecy: God's Stage for the Final Drama* (Eugene, OR: Harvest House, 1991), front cover.

4. Harold D. Foos, "Jerusalem in Biblical Prophecy," *Dictionary of Premillennial Theology*; ed. Mal Couch (Grand Rapids, MI: Kregel Publications, 1996), 207.

5. "Jerusalem," *Agencia Judaica*, accessed May 21, 2021, http://www.eitan.com.br/Nomes%20de%20Jerusalem.pdf.

6. Hershel Shanks, "Ancient Jerusalem: The Village, the Town, the City," *Biblical Archaeology Review* (May/June, 2006), https://www.biblicalarchaeology.org/daily/biblical-sites-places/jerusalem/ancient-jerusalem/. Also see "Jerusalem at Passover," *Bible History*, accessed May 22, 2021, https://www.bible-history.com/backd2/jerusalem.html.

7. Adapted from Charles Swindoll, ed., *The Theological Workbook* (Nashville, TN: Word Publishing, 2000), 196.

8. Price, *Jerusalem in Prophecy*, 74.

9. Simon Sebag Montefiore, *Jerusalem: The Biography* (New York, NY: Knopf Doubleday Publishing Group, 2011), 507.

10. Eytan Gilboa, "Trump: The Most Pro-Israel President in American History," *Clingendael Spectator*, July 8, 2020, https://spectator.clingendael.org/en/publication/trump-most-pro-israel-president-american-history.

11. Mark Hitchcock, *The End* (Carol Stream, IL: Tyndale House Publishers, 2012), 385.

12. J. Dwight Pentecost, *Things to Come: A Study in Biblical Eschatology* (Grand Rapids, MI: Zondervan, 1958), 476.

13. Adapted from unpublished notes by Alva J. McClain, Grace Theological Seminary, Winona Lake, Indiana.

14. Swindoll, ed., *The Theological Workbook*, 197.

15. Anthony Hoekema, "Heaven: Not Just an Eternal Day Off," *Christianity Today*, June 1, 2003, https://www.christianitytoday.com/ct/2003/juneweb-only/6-2-54.0.html.

16. Steven J. Lawson, *Heaven Help Us!* (Colorado Springs, CO: Nav Press, 1995), 131–32.

17. E. J. Fortman, *Everlasting Life After Death* (New York, NY: Alba House, 1976), 318.

18. Charles F. Pfeiffer and Everett F. Harrison, eds, *The Wycliffe Bible Commentary: A Phrase by Phrase Commentary of the Bible* (Chicago, IL: Moody Publishers, 1962), 1522.

19. Pentecost, *Things to Come*, 541.

20. Frederick Buechner, quoted in *A Little Bit of Heaven* (Tulsa, OK: Honor Books, 1995), 118.

21. Price, *Jerusalem in Prophecy*, 94.

22. Marvin Olasky, "Israel at Age 67: Slammed If You Do, Dead If You Don't," *World*, April 21, 2015, https://wng.org/articles/israel-at-age-67-slammed-if-you-do-dead-if-you-dont-1617287541.

23. Gilboa, "Trump: The Most Pro-Israel President in American History."

24. Chris Weller, "The 12 Most Important Countries of the Year, According to the *New York Times*," *Business Insider*, December 23, 2015, https://www.businessinsider.com/the-most-important-countries-of-the-year-2015-12.

25. Kathie Lee Gifford, *The Rock, the Road, and the Rabbi* (Nashville, TN: HarperCollins Christian Publishing, 2018), preface and chapter 1.

Chapter 10: The Final Prophecy:
The Triumph of the Gospel

1. Harrison Mumia, "Press Statement—Secretary Seth Mahiga Resigns," *Atheists in Kenya*, May 30, 2021, https://atheistsinkenya.org/2021/05/30 /press-statement-secretary-seth-mahiga-resigns/.

2. Leah Nablo Yecla, "Gospel Making Inroads in Iran Despite Strong Persecution," *Christianity Daily*, November 16, 2020, http://www .christianitydaily.com/articles/10094/20201116/gospel-making-inroads -in-iran-despite-strong-persecution.htm.

3. "Bring the Life-Changing Gospel to Iran Through Billy Graham's Sermons," *Iran Alive Ministries*, accessed June 10, 2021, https://iranalive .org/billy-graham.

4. Charles Gardner, "Iranian Awakening," *Israel Today*, February 27, 2021, https://www.israeltoday.co.il/read/iranian-awakening/.

5. Bruce Davis, "Iran's Great Awakening with Dr. Hormoz Shariat," *In Awe by Bruce Podcast*, November 11, 2020, https://www.inawebybruce.com /podcast/2020/11/11/irans-great-awakening-with-dr-hormoz-shariat.

6. Valerie Bell et al., *Resilient: Child Discipleship and the Fearless Future of the Church* (Steamwood, IL: Awana Clubs International, 2020), 62.

7. Richard Chin, *Captivated by Christ* (Youngstown, OH: Matthias Media, 2019), 16, 26.

8. Naomi Reed, "I Was Put in Jail Three Times for My Faith, and I Was Tortured," *Eternity*, July 30, 2020, https://www.eternitynews.com.au/faith -stories/i-was-put-in-jail-three-times-for-my-faith-and-i-was-tortured/.

9. Sarah Eekhoff Zylstra and Alex Harris, "Alex Harris: How to Do Hard Things" (podcast), *The Gospel Coalition*, May 6, 2021, https://www .thegospelcoalition.org/podcasts/tgc-podcast/alex-harris-do-hard-things/.

10. Charles Spurgeon, "Adorning the Gospel," *The Spurgeon Center*, May 26, 1887, https://www.spurgeon.org/resource-library/sermons/adorning -the-gospel/#flipbook/.

11. Cassidy Mudd, "Governor Stitt Commemorates 1921 Tulsa Race Massacre," *Channel 8 News*, May 28, 2021, https://ktul.com/news/local /governor-stitt-commemorates-1921-tulsa-race-massacre.

12. Francis A. Schaeffer, *The Mark of the Christian* (Downer's Grove, IL.: InterVarsity Press, 1970), 22–23.

13. Billy Graham, "100 Quotes from Billy Graham," *Billy Graham Evangelistic Association of Canada*, accessed June 10, 2021, https://www.billygraham .ca/100-quotes-from-billy-graham/.

14. Billy Graham, "100 Quotes from Billy Graham."

15. Billy Graham, "100 Quotes from Billy Graham."

16. "Billy Graham 1918–2018 Official Obituary," February 21, 2018, https:// memorial.billygraham.org/official-obituary/.

17. Radstyles007, "Billy Graham's Last Sermon at Age 95, God, Jesus Christ, Bible, Christianity & Truth," *YouTube*, February 24, 2018, https://www .youtube.com/watch?v=wPkNtG5IVcA.

18. Charlotte Elliott, "Just As I Am, Without One Plea," 1755, public domain.

About the Author

Dr. David Jeremiah serves as senior pastor of Shadow Mountain Community Church in El Cajon, California. He is the founder and host of Turning Point, a ministry committed to providing Christians with sound Bible teaching relevant to today's changing times through radio and television, the Internet, live events, and resource materials and books. A bestselling author, Dr. Jeremiah has written more than fifty books, including *Agents of Babylon, Agents of the Apocalypse, Captured by Grace, Living with Confidence in a Chaotic World, What in the World Is Going On?, The Coming Economic Armageddon, God Loves You: He Always Has—He Always Will*, and *What Are You Afraid Of?* A dedicated family man, Dr. Jeremiah and his wife, Donna, have four grown children and twelve grandchildren. Connect with Dr. Jeremiah on Facebook (@drdavidjeremiah), Twitter (@davidjeremiah), and on his website (davidjeremiah.org).

stay connected to the teaching of

DR. DAVID JEREMIAH

• • • • • • • •

Publishing | Radio | Television | Online

FURTHER YOUR STUDY OF THIS BOOK

· · · · · · · ·

Where Do We Go From Here? Resource Materials

To enhance your study on this important topic, we recommend the correlating audio message album, study guide, and DVD messages from the *Where Do We Go From Here?* series.

Audio Message Album

The material found in this book originated from messages presented by Dr. Jeremiah at Shadow Mountain Community Church where he serves as senior pastor. These ten messages are conveniently packaged in an accessible audio album.

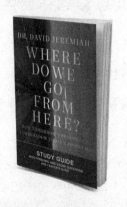

Study Guide

This 144-page study guide correlates with the messages from the *Where Do We Go From Here?* series by Dr. Jeremiah. Each lesson provides an outline, an overview, and group and personal application questions for each topic.

DVD Message Presentations

Watch Dr. Jeremiah deliver the *Where Do We Go From Here?* original messages in this special DVD collection.

To order these products, call us at 1-800-947-1993
or visit us online at www.DavidJeremiah.org.

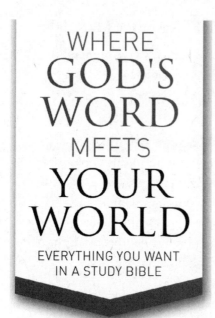
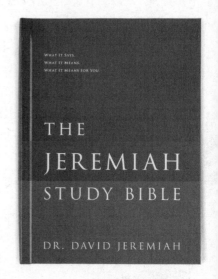